How to use the CD-ROM

This CD-ROM has been created in HTML and should be used on a Windows 95 or Windows NT system, or a Macintosh using a 68030 (or greater) or Power PC microprocessor running System 7.5, with a browser capable of viewing Java applets.

At the time this CD was produced the only browser capable of reading Java applets was Netscape Navigator (2.0 or greater) for the PC. No final Macintosh version was available.

However, the Java Development Kit (JDK) by Sun Microsystems included on this CD-ROM does have the ability to read Java applets from HTML documents. System requirements for the JDK are the same as above.

NOTE: This CD will *not* run on Windows 3.*x* systems.

To run the CD with Windows 95/NT

1. Place the CD-ROM in your CD-ROM drive.
2. Launch your Java-enabled Web browser.
3. From your Web browser, select Open File from the File menu. Select your CD-ROM drive (usually D), then select the file called welcome.htm.

NOTE: We have found some incompatibilities with NT systems while testing this CD. Should you have any problems running this CD on your NT system, please contact Technical Support at (317) 581-3833.

To run the CD on a Macintosh

1. Place the CD-ROM in your CD-ROM drive.
2. Launch your Java-enabled Web browser.
3. From your Web browser, select Open File from the File menu. Choose your CD-ROM drive and open welcome.htm.

NOTE: At the time this CD was created, only beta versions of Java-enabled browsers were available for the Macintosh platform. During testing we found that some functions of these browsers were unstable.

INSTANT JAVA APPLETS

INSTANT JAVA APPLETS

Owen Davis, Tom McGinn, and Amit Bhatiani

Ziff-Davis Press
An imprint of Macmillan Computer Publishing USA
Emeryville, California

Acquisitions Editor	Suzanne Anthony
Development Editor	Kelly Green
Copy Editor	Margo Hill
Technical Reviewer	Tim Arnold
Project Coordinator	Ami Knox
Cover Illustration and Design	Megan Gandt
Book Design	Gary Suen
Cd-ROM Illustrator	Dave Feasey
Word Processing	Howard Blechman
Page Layout	Janet Piercy and Bruce Lundquist
Indexer	Valerie Robbins

Ziff-Davis Press imprint books are produced on a Macintosh computer system with the following applications: FrameMaker®, Microsoft® Word, QuarkXPress®, Adobe Illustrator®, Adobe Photoshop®, Adobe Streamline™, MacLink®*Plus*, Aldus® FreeHand™, Collage Plus™.

Ziff-Davis Press, an imprint of
Macmillan Computer Publishing USA
5903 Christie Avenue
Emeryville, CA 94608
510-601-2000

ISBN 1-56276-386-5

Manufactured in the United States of America
10 9 8 7 6 5 4 3 2 1

Owen Davis—To my family

Tom McGinn—For Patrick

Amit Bhatiani—For my wife and parents

TABLE OF CONTENTS

Acknowledgments

The authors would like to thank the great editors at Ziff-Davis: Suzanne Anthony, Kelly Green, Steven DeLacy, Ami Knox, Juliet Langley, and everyone else who contributed to completing this book.

Amit Bhatiani would also like to thank Dr. Claude Anderson, one of the best teachers he has known.

Tom McGinn would also like to thank Marybeth for her continued support.

Introduction

The network is inevitable.

In the last two years, as cyberspace has grown from the realm of geeks and transformed itself into the future thoroughfare of all communications, it's become clear that one day, far sooner than many thought, we all will be networked. Our homes will be networked to our cars, which will be networked to our workplaces, and so on.

With the adoption of the Internet by the public as a viable communications highway, the Network has exploded the limits of a proprietary network, such as corporate LANs and WANs. As you travel along the Internet and visit its sites, you begin to understand the irrelevance of geography in the networked model. Enormous value is offered by the immediate flow of information—whether video, audio or text—beyond geographical boundaries.

With this great unification has also come a Tower of Babel phenomenon. The Network needs its own Esperanto, a universal trans-operating system programming language that could scale the heights of multilingual communications. Java is that language.

Java is in many ways similar to Spanish or Greek or German. It has a syntax and a structure. Just as you put together a grammatically correct sentence, so you write a "grammatically correct" applet or application. And just as with any language, there are certain "vocabulary" words to memorize and certain sentence structures to remember. If you follow the rules of any language, the result is a clear, integrated work, each part dependent on its predecessor and leading toward the next. In terms of applet development, the end result in following Java's rules is that your applet runs successfully.

Java accomplishes unique things. Common programs of the past did not give priority to communicating with other programs across the network, getting information from them and bringing it back. Java was built for that purpose and implemented in a way that improves on some of the most complained-about features of common programming languages in use today.

Java is also platform independent. There are differences in developing programs for a Mac as opposed to a PC as opposed to a UNIX machine. In an effort to be truly universal, Java executes a program in something of a cocoon (called a *virtual machine*). So no matter what operating system a Java program is running on, Java can run within its own cocoon.

One day there may be a PC-based command center in your home that will allow you to control your home network. On that network may be your coffee maker and alarm clock. These appliances may have a Java-based microchip (a product recently announced by Sun) or may have their own operating systems. If you would like your alarm clock, when it sounds, to send a message to your coffee maker to begin brewing, Java may be a great way to get that done.

Right now, Web animation and multimedia capabilities have heightened Java's reputation as a way to move the multimedia capabilities of the Web forward. But Java is a serious programming language, capable of much more than a ticker or a tumbling animation. It can and will be used to integrate disparate information sources across the network and will move past the "applet" phase into the "application" phase.

As computer programming becomes the *lingua franca* of our times, it becomes more and more essential to understand "computer speak" in order to be well informed about the world. With this book we have attempted to demystify Java, so that you can use Java for yourself and further your understanding of how things work in the "cryptic" world of The Network.

If you would like to contact us, you may reach us at

Owen Davis
Owend@dotcomdev.com

Tom McGinn
tom.mcginn@east.sun.com

Amit Bhatiani
bhatiani_amit@ny.psca.com

Introduction to Java

The history of Java

How Java works

Why is Java important?

What you need to make Java work

Using HTML tags with Java

Chapter 1

Java is a programming language.

Fortunately, there's a lot more to it than that! Java is the first multi-platform programming language that makes it possible to write programs that run from the World Wide Web. Up until now, the Web has been a wonderful presentation environment, allowing information to be collected and distributed by anyone interested on a wide range of subjects, but the information is static. Like a book, once read, pages don't provide any additional information, nor do they interact with the user. With some exceptions, such as the frog dissection program some innovative people created using CGI scripts (Figure 1.1), the Web has been dominated mostly by text links.

It is possible to embed forms and use CGI scripts running back on the server to provide some interactivity, but let's compare that to the kind of interactivity you can have with Java. How about 3-D wire-frame models (Figure 1.2) or a human dissection program navigatible with the mouse (Figure 1.3)? Java is where it is at!

Java makes it possible to create educational programs, games, animated advertising, online purchasing, live-feed information applications like ticker-tape style stock programs, and a host of other applications directly from your machine connected to the Web. What were once static pages of information can now become places to learn by doing, places to purchase products, or places to test skills. There is no limit to what can be done.

Pin the Frog
To secure the frog for the dissection, pin each of his four limbs to the pan.

Figure 1.1: The frog dissection program at http://curry.edschool.virginia.edu/go/frog

THE HISTORY OF JAVA

Most of the reasons Java is well designed for the Internet can be found in the history of how Java was created. You may have already heard this, so here is the "*Reader's Digest*" version.

Java was created as a platform-independent language designed to support a wide range of hardware architectures for a consumer-based product. Sun spun off a small group of engineers headed by James Gosling to create a hand-held interactive video selection device. The Green Project began with the development of a operating system designed for a hand-held video selection terminal. The device was to be used across a network, so that new functionality could be programmed in on-the-fly. Gosling knew that the operating system needed to be robust, since customers would not put up with operating system failures with a consumer electronics device. (When was the last time your TV crashed?) He also knew that it had to be secure because of its buy-on-demand feature. Furthermore, Gosling did not want to be tied to a single CPU and operating system, so he needed a way to write code that could be moved quickly from one platform to another. However, his team was frustrated by C++ and resolved to create a new language that would eliminate problems porting code.

Gosling began by stripping functionality from C++, and adding features he liked from other languages. As time went by, the team realized they had created

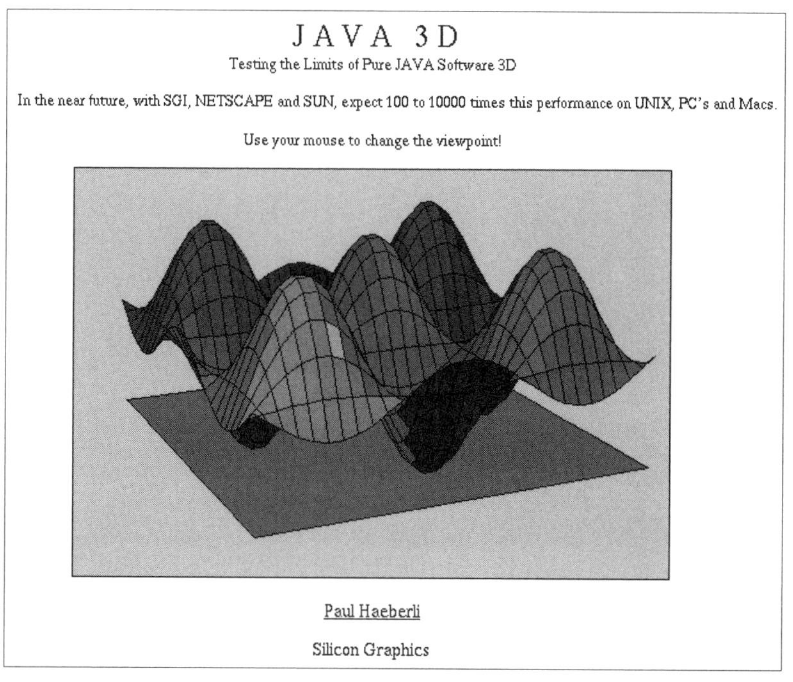

JAVA 3D
Testing the Limits of Pure JAVA Software 3D
In the near future, with SGI, NETSCAPE and SUN, expect 100 to 10000 times this performance on UNIX, PC's and Macs.
Use your mouse to change the viewpoint!
Paul Haeberli
Silicon Graphics

Figure 1.2: D wire-frame model created with Java at http://reality.sgi.com/grafica/java3d/

a whole new language, which Gosling named "Oak" for the tree that stood outside his office. Programs written in this new language could be interpreted by another program on a different platform.

The interactive device was ultimately a bust for Sun. Despite being recognized as having the best implementation technically, Sun was not selected as the company to lead a series of trials for the video-on-demand business. The hand-held device was scrapped, and the team was left with Oak. Fortunately, the Internet and the World Wide Web exploded shortly thereafter, and Oak was used to create a portable language for the Internet. Initial exploration of a browser that included Oak code "blew the socks off" of Scott McNealy, Sun's CEO. The language was saved and work began on making it a product. The name *Oak* was dropped after a patent search, and on a whim the name *Java* was selected and stuck. Despite many potential setbacks, the spirit of the Green Project is now embodied in the Java language, designed to be written once and run anywhere. The consumer electronics business was a bust for Sun, but the Java language created to support it has been reshaped into the de facto programming language of the Internet.

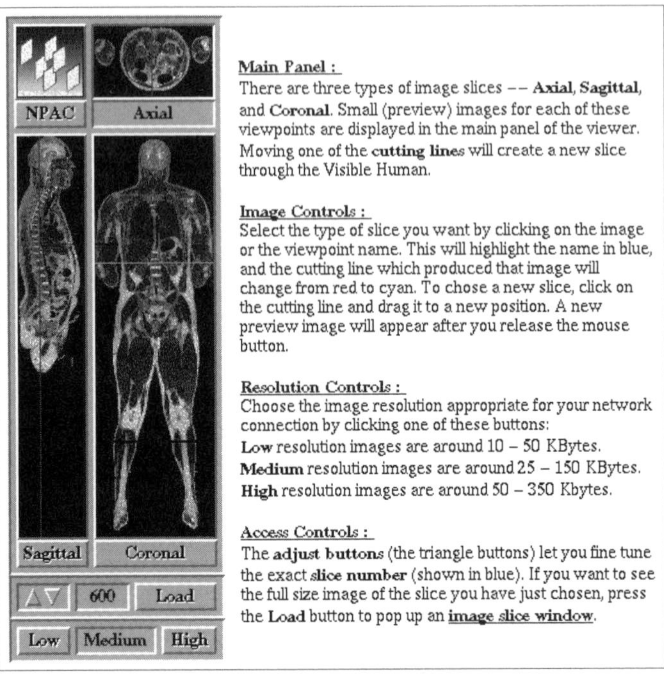

NPAC
Axial
Sagittal
Coronal
600
Load
Low
Medium
High
Main Panel :
There are three types of image slices -- Axial, Sagittal, and Coronal. Small (preview) images for each of these viewpoints are displayed in the main panel of the viewer. Moving one of the cutting lines will create a new slice through the Visible Human.
Image Controls :
Select the type of slice you want by clicking on the image or the viewpoint name. This will highlight the name in blue, and the cutting line which produced that image will change from red to cyan. To chose a new slice, click on the cutting line and drag it to a new position. A new preview image will appear after you release the mouse button.
Resolution Controls :
Choose the image resolution appropriate for your network connection by clicking one of these buttons:
Low resolution images are around 10 - 50 KBytes.
Medium resolution images are around 25 - 150 KBytes.
High resolution images are around 50 - 350 Kbytes.
Access Controls :
The adjust buttons (the triangle buttons) let you fine tune the exact slice number (shown in blue). If you want to see the full size image of the slice you have just chosen, press the Load button to pop up an image slice window.

Figure 1.3: A human dissection program created with Java at http://www.npca.syr.edu/projects/vishuman/VisibleHuman.html

How Java works

How does it all happen? Java programs are written as source files on any one of four platforms (Sun Solaris, Windows 95, Windows NT, and now Macintosh—more on this later). The program is precompiled then embedded in an HTML page using a special APPLET tag. A Java-powered browser like Netscape or HotJava that can read and execute Java code reads the APPLET tag, which is much like an anchor tag, and starts running the Java program, called an applet.

JAVA APPLETS

The term *applet* describes these miniature programs created to run on HTML pages. An applet is part of your HTML page in much the same way as an HREF tag is a link to an audio or graphic file. In most cases, though, the browser will load and start running the applet without a mouse click on a link. Java applets are designed to make use of resources provided by the browser.

To create an applet, you would first write a description of your applet using the Java language. The description is stored in a file with a .java extension; this is called the source file. The source file is then compiled using one of the tools provided in the Java Developer's Kit (JDK). Unlike computer programs like C or C++, the Java source file is not immediately executable, but instead compiles to a series of commands and codes specified by "bytes." These commands and codes are designed to run on a generic "virtual" computer, one that is the least common denominator of serveral computer architectures. Each Java browser provides an interpreter or runtime system that is capable of reading and executing these byte codes. The interpreter converts the generic virtual computer byte codes to more specific machine language that is understood by your computer.

In addition to creating applets, which require the support of a Java-powered browser, Java can also be used to create fully interactive applications. The primary difference between an application and an applet is that applets rely on a browser to function. Applications, on the other hand, are designed as stand-alone programs. Applications may be executed without the resources provided by a browser, even though they still need to be run by an interpreter that emulates the virtual computer. In general, an applet does not have a main() method and cannot run as a stand-alone program. An applet assumes that the main() method, the window frame and border, and a graphics context will be provided by the browser application for the applet to use.

One of the really wonderful things about Java applets is that by not having to worry about coding a frame and window manager, applet code can be very compact. Applets are small enough to download very quickly, minimizing waiting time by not relying on some server across the country to run a script on its behalf.

This is how the process works: A browser such as Netscape Navigator 2.0 is running on your local machine. As you browse a Web page through an http link, the browser loads the page and begins to decipher the HTML tags. When the browser encounters an APPLET tag, it loads the Java class file identified in the CODE tag, and creates a panel area and graphics context for the applet. It then calls several functions through the loaded applet class file. These functions are identified by the browser, and are called at specific times.

A little later we will take a look at each of these functions (called *methods* in Java) and determine how to make use of them.

APPLETS RUNNING ON MY MACHINE! OH, MY!

One obvious concern is, "Hey, there's a program running on my machine! How soon before it erases my hard disk or passes sensitive information about me to the whole world?" Well, the designers of the Java language had security foremost in their minds when they put Java together. Security is implemented two ways in Java.

First, before the code is run at all, the runtime system built into the browser tests the incoming code in a class code verifier. The verifier is responsible for feeding code to the Java interpreter, so the class code verifier makes sure that the incoming applet code is clean and safe.

The verifier tests the incoming code for format, making sure that the code does not violate Java rules:

- There are no attempts to access memory through a stack overflow/ underflow.
- There are no illegal access and stores to registers.
- All parameters for method calls are legal.
- There are no attempts to illegally convert values into pointers.

These are common tricks that hackers play to create a situation where your machine's memory is made available to the program. Once memory is available, a great deal of the machine's internal resources (like disk driver code and file allocation tables) are accessible to a geek with the know-how.

The class verifier is very picky and always errs on the side of conservatism. The verifier is independent of the compiler, and can verify byte-codes generated by other Java compilers, or other compilers that generate the byte-code format. If the verifier "blesses" the byte-codes passed, the code will run without fault on the virtual machine.

Verification happens before the code is actually run, so in the next step the code runs through the class loader, which determines where to get Java executable objects from (either locally or over the network). The class loader is carefully controlled by another part of the Java runtime process called Java's applet security manager. A browser implements security features by preventing the class loader from loading certain types of classes or class methods. The browser can decide what applets can do and how, regardless of whether or not they are written correctly. In general, applets may not

- Access files, either for reading or writing
- Make network connections to any host other than the originating server (the http machine)

- Load libraries in order to run native methods (more on this later)
- Execute scripts or any other program on the client

IT MAY BE SECURE, BUT IS IT USEFUL?

Java is useful because the design of the language provides several features for the Web programmer:

Simplicity—Java's constructs are C++ based, but the language is easy to learn because of its object-oriented nature.

Portability—Java code compiled on any Java platform runs on any Java platform.

Robustness—The design of the language makes it easy to create good code.

Richness—Java is a real computer language, and supports multithreading, genuine objects, and a full set of "libraries" called packages that include lots of useful prewritten code.

Availability!—Java itself is free, and in just a short time the amount of Java code available has grown enormously. What's more, a lot of these new applets are also free!

These features make it possible for a Webmaster to create HTML pages that feature some very cool programs that can run from any user's machine. The beauty of the Web is that information is available regardless of whether or not you are running a Sun, Windows, or Macintosh machine. All you need is a browser that runs on your platform, and there you also have a choice.

SIMPLICITY

Java is designed to be object-oriented from the ground up. This sounds like Java might be the opposite of simple, but in reality, most people think in terms of objects. For example, in your daily life you may commute to work in a car object, and you pass commands to the car object through another object, like the gas pedal object to make the car move forward and the brake object to stop.

Additionally, the car has state information that you use while you drive the car. The fuel gauge and speedometer provide state information that can be used to control the operation of the car object. Finally, both the operations and data of the object are part of the object itself, so it is easy to use the information in the car object context.

Java is a programming language you use to describe the operations and data of an object. In Java, every object is defined by creating a definition of what an instance of the object might look like. This definition of an instance is called a class. A *class* provides a template that defines what an object will look like and what operations it can perform.

In the next chapter we'll take a look at the syntax of the language and the way in which you write classes in order to define the operations and attributes of an object.

PORTABILITY

For the Webmaster, this feature of Java is undoubtedly the most exciting. "Write once, read anywhere" means just that: You write your Java applet once, compile it, and then it runs anywhere that Java runs. With the Netscape Navigator 2.0 browser, this includes Sun's Solaris, Sun's SunOS, SGI IRIX, OSF/1, HP-UX, Windows NT, Windows 95, and Macintosh. You can't get this list of client operating systems with any other programming language!

Java's architecture-neutral virtual machine makes it very easy to create Java runtimes and compilers. There are a number of porting efforts underway, by large systems like DEC machines as well as Apple Amiga and SEGA. The concept of making the network the computer itself looks more like reality than fantasy, and this is a boon for anyone writing applications for a wide distribution to a heterogeneous network environment.

ROBUSTNESS

Java is designed to create reliable code. The language removes a number of dubious features from C++ and C. For example, some 50 percent of program errors come from programs that run amok when memory is accessed incorrectly through pointers, so Java removes the ability to explicitly create pointers and use pointer arithmetic. Instead, Java uses true arrays and objects, which eliminate the need to allocate sized blocks of memory. Additionally, Java runtimes provide a *garbage collector.* This background monitor keeps track of objects as they are allocated and frees the memory they use when they are no longer needed.

Finally, exceptions are part of the Java language. This feature creates a mechanism for code to signal that a problem has occurred; for example, if a bad URL was encountered or there was a math error. The Java programmer can create code that anticipates problems and corrects them during runtime without crashing the system.

RICHNESS

Even though Java is easy to get started with, the language is designed for more than just pretty pictures. Java supports complex applications by providing multithreading, a full implementation of TCP/IP sockets, dynamic class linking at runtime, and a number of prebuilt building blocks that can be used to develop some very nice applications.

Multithreading makes it possible for Java applets to create nearly concurrent activities. For example, the applet might be able to read an image file while loading and playing an audio clip, update a graphics context while responding to a button click, run multiple animations on a single page, and so on.

A complete TCP/IP socket implementation makes it possible for Java applets to actually communicate over the Internet; and, depending upon the browser, applets may be able to communicate with each other. So information on HTML pages can be live and dynamic. Sports pages, live news feeds, and stock information all coming over the Internet can be displayed on the applet page. Check out http://www.sportsnetwork.com/ for an example of a live sports feed or http://www.nando.net/nt/nando.cgi?java for a Java-based newspaper.

The Java Developer's Kit (JDK) has a very comprehensive set of libraries that contain class files and methods that form the building blocks for both applets and applications. In the next chapter you will get a chance to see these in greater detail, but here is a quick synopsis of the libraries (called packages) that Java provides:

java.lang—A complete thread class, exceptions class, wrappers for data types

java.io—Methods and classes for accessing files, either as read-once and write-once streams or as random access

java.util—A set of utility classes for general purpose use, including date and time, dictionaries, hash tables, and encode/decode

java.net—A set of generic classes for accessing TCP/IP sockets and URLs

java.awt—The abstract windowing toolkit, providing classes and methods for building user interfaces including buttons, sliders, and lists

java.applet—Classes and methods specific to the development of applets, including loading images and audio

AVAILABILITY

The spirit of Java is to remain true to the global nature of the Web—information is available regardless of machine architecture. And of course, it's all for free! The Java Developer's Kit contains all the tools you'll need to create, compile, and test your applets and applications. You still need a browser to view HTML pages and applets, and you will hear about two Java-enabled browsers a little later; but to get started all you need is the Java Developer's Kit, which we have provided for you on the CD-ROM.

WHY IS JAVA IMPORTANT?

What makes Java important is that it enables the browser to become more than just a static delivery mechanism. Before Java, browsers were essentially page reading applications, albeit ones with an expansive reference and index section. Combined with Java, browsers are now capable of supporting a framework of applications. Imagine the browser of the future—a browser that you use to read the newspaper, get the latest sports scores, check traffic conditions for your local commute, and order take-out Chinese food for the evening meal. The browser is now the purveyor of information and allows you, the reader, to use it for commerce or entertainment, or even to control your environment.

On February 2, 1996, Sun Microsystems announced that it was producing three new Java-optimized microprocessors. These devices can be used in a variety of consumer and business applications. Everything from the toaster to the security system in the home could become a Java device, controlled through your browser.

Java-based systems also mean that the operating system-centered model may become the mainframe system of the future. Since Java makes it possible to create applications that run on multiple platforms, a Java-enhanced CPU might also forge a path for a Java-centric operating system. This would greatly reduce the overall cost of system administration by eliminating the need to upgrade software per individual customer machine. A Java-based computer need only have a network connection and a small amount of memory in order to run applications and store and retrieve information.

WHAT YOU NEED TO MAKE JAVA WORK

This next section will identify what you need to get started working with Java. First of all you will need to identify which operating system your computer uses and then download the appropriate Java Developer's Kit, version 1.0, from the CD-ROM. There are currently three JDKs available from Sun Microsystems and other mirror sites. Sun Microsystems JDK 1.0 implementations are for

- Sun Solaris 2.3 and higher
- Intel-based Windows 95 and Windows NT
- Macintosh 68030 or higher or PowerPC systems running Macintosh System 7.5 (Beta 1 release—February 15, 1996)

The JDK releases above are also available from Sun's Java Web page and from FTP servers and mirrors listed here:

- http://www.javasoft.com/JDK-1.0/index.html
- ftp://ftp.javasoft.com/pub/
- ftp://www.blackdown.org/pub/Java/pub/

See the release notes (http://www.javasoft.com/JDK-1.0/installation.html) for information about unpacking the release specific to your machine.

THE JDK 1.0

The JDK will enable you to compile and test applets and applications without the need for a browser—the JDK includes a small browserlike application (written in Java) called the AppletViewer, which provides the minimum functionality of a browser. This application will simulate the method calls and security checks that a full-blown browser like Netscape or HotJava will do. To use the AppletViewer, create an HTML file with an APPLET tag that contains the name of the compiled Java applet class. The HTML file is then passed to the AppletViewer either directly or through a URL that contains the path to an HTML file (*appletviewer HelloWorld.html* or *appletviewer http://server:80/HelloWorld.html*).

The AppletViewer does not, however, display any HTML tags, and it will generate a separate window and frame for each APPLET tag it encounters. There must be at least one APPLET tag in the HTML file.

The Java compiler, also written in Java, creates applet and application class files. These class files contain the byte-code information that is architecture neutral and secure. It does not matter which implementation of the JDK you choose to create, compile, and test Java applets and applications on; they will run on any machine that has the JDK or through any Java-powered browser. Figure 1.4 illustrates how the Java source file is compiled using the command *javac*, and how it creates a Java class file.

The compiler and AppletViewer provided with the JDK 1.0 create Java class files that conform to the current Java application programmers interface (API), which is also available on line at http://www.javasoft.com/JDK1.0/api/packages.html. The API describes each Java class package, which includes the classes, methods, and variables available. The API will be covered in more detail in the next chapter.

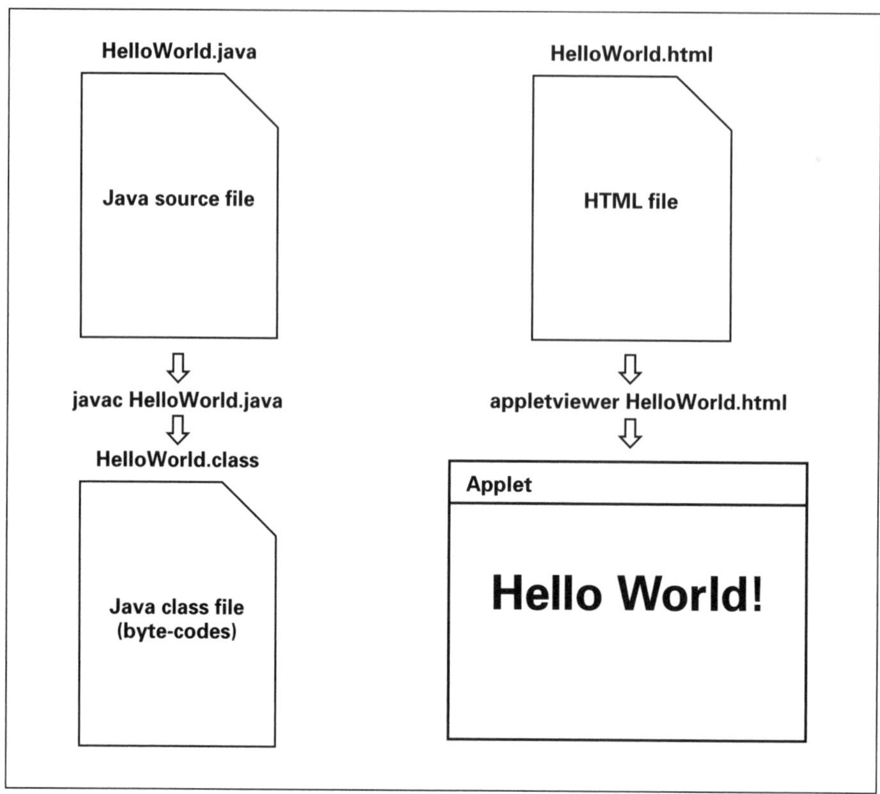

Figure 1.4: How Java and the AppletViewer work together

SHOULD I USE NETSCAPE OR HOTJAVA?

In order to browse other Java-powered Web pages and to fully test your own, you will need to use a Java-enabled browser such as HotJava or Netscape. The Java language was first released with its own HTML browser, one capable of reading Java applet tags. The browser was aptly named HotJava and conformed to the HTML 3.0 tag standard, with the addition of a single tag, the <APP> tag. Unfortunately, as of this writing HotJava has not been ported to the current Java API specification, JDK version 1.0. You cannot run Java applets created with the current versions of the JDK on HotJava. Sun has promised that there will be a HotJava browser capable of supporting the new API sometime soon, so keep checking.

The good news is that version 2.0 of Netscape's successful browser, Netscape Navigator, does support JDK 1.0 applets. This browser is also a full-service browser capable of reading e-mail and newsgroups as well as loading HTML pages with Java applets. Netscape Navigator 2.0 can be downloaded for a 90-day evaluation from http://www.netscape.com; or from one of their FTP sites, ftp://ftp<n>.netscape.com, where <n> can be replaced by the number 2 through 12 and 20. Netscape 2.0 also features the ability to run Java applets on machines that currently do not support a Java Developer's Kit, like Sun's SunOS 4.1.x, SGI IRIX, OSF/1, and HP-UX. This flexibility highlights how hard the Netscape engineers are working and how easy it is to port Java to many platforms!

JAVA ON DIFFERENT PLATFORMS

The Java Developer's Kit makes it possible for you to create Java applets on the four platforms that Sun supports, as well as other platforms as they become available. For each specific platform there are slight operational differences that you may need to be aware of. For example, on the Macintosh version of the JDK, you run the AppletViewer by dragging and dropping an HTML file (containing the APPLET tag) onto the AppletViewer icon instead of using a command line. For the specific information regarding your platform, consult the README file that is included with the JDK release.

Using HTML tags with Java

Once you have created your applet and are ready to test it under Netscape, you need to create an HTML file (or modify an existing one) to include the APPLET tag:

```
<HTML>
...
<APPLET CODE=HelloWorld.class>
</APPLET>
...
</HTML>
```

Required tags include the APPLET , CODE , WIDTH, and HEIGHT tags. The CODE tag specifies the name of the Java applet class file. WIDTH and HEIGHT tags specify the initial size of the Java applet in pixels:

```
<APPLET CODE=HelloWorld.class WIDTH=200 HEIGHT=200>
</APPLET>
```

Applets can also be passed parameters from the HTML page, allowing them to be customized by the user before they run. The PARAM tag is used to identify parameters to be passed:

```
<APPLET CODE=HelloWorld.class WIDTH=200 HEIGHT=200>
<PARAM NAME=images" VALUE="Duke1.gif|Duke2.gif|Duke3.gif">
<PARAM NAME=speed VALUE=10>
</APPLET>
```

Parameters are always read into Java applets as strings of characters. Even the characters *1* and *0* are read as a string and need to be converted to numbers within the Java program.

One more important tag is the CODEBASE tag. This tag allows you to keep your Java applets separate from the HTML file. CODEBASE identifies the location of the URL that contains the class file. If not specified, the browser will assume that the class file is in the same URL as the HTML file.

```
<APPLET CODE=HelloWorld.class CODEBASE="http://Javahost:80/~tom" WIDTH=200
HEIGHT=200>
</APPLET>
```

The complete specification of APPLET tag syntax can be found in the README file of your JDK.

Basic Java Programming Concepts

Classes and objects

Java syntax overview

Networking—connecting applets via sockets

Multithreading

JavaScript

Chapter 2

To say that Java is an object-oriented programming language implies a lot of knowledge about what is and is not object programming. One might ask, "What other languages are object-oriented?" or, "I thought C++ was object-oriented but Java is not exactly like C++, so what makes it object-oriented?" This section will answer these questions, focusing on the aspects of Java that make it an object language and, in fact, an object programming environment.

OBJECT TECHNOLOGY

The primary task of any programmer is to solve a particular problem through the software he or she writes. Programmers realize that the best way to solve programming problems is to break them down into smaller parts, then write code to solve each part. If all goes well, the aggregate of the solutions also solves the overall problem. Of course, programmers rarely work alone; rather, they are typically part of a larger development group. In order to ensure that each member of the development group is writing the same kind of code, the team chooses a single programming language and technique. Each software development technique tends to reflect the constraints of the language used.

Using functional languages like C and Pascal, the general approach of a programmer is to write small pieces of code that each perform a single task. Each task is performed in a block of code called a *function.* The sum of all the functions is a program. In order to control the activity of the functions, a single main function is created to manage the calls to each separate function. This approach has several disadvantages, including the problem of redundant functions and code that tends to be difficult to follow. Without careful management, the functions written can become *tightly coupled*; that is, one function calls another, and that one calls another, and so on. Tightly coupled functions can create a cascade effect on the program; for example, a function that is changed to solve a problem in one part of the system may have a dramatic and often undesirable effect on other functions that also rely on it.

Consider the following example: A car is being modeled with a functional language, and the programmer has created a stop function. Although this function was originally designed to apply the brakes for the car, let's say another programmer on the team has decided that the stop method should actually stop the engine. So when the user of this program steps on the brake, the engine will die! It may sound far-fetched, but this simple example illustrates what sometimes happens in large programming efforts with functional languages.

In an attempt to solve the problem of tightly coupled code, programmers have gravitated toward languages that allow them to design components that interact. Each component, or object, models a specific part of the overall problem. Objects include not only the functions required for the component, but also any data associated with the component. Object functions provide the interface that is used to access data within the object. The result is that objects are developed to present functions used to operate on the data they contain. Within an object, the code is tightly coupled, but the objects themselves are easily changed without effect on the system as a whole. Objects can be either abstract or concrete. For example, abstract objects could include an accounts payable object or employee object. Concrete objects could include a car object or motor object.

Languages that support an object-oriented approach include C++, Smalltalk, Objective-C, and of course, Java. The advantage of an object-oriented approach is that the overall implementation of the design is far easier to break up among multiple team members. Additionally, object languages make it possible to reuse code by supporting the ability to create new objects from old ones, a process called *inheritance*. Objects can build upon one another for greater flexibility during development with less code rewriting.

CHARACTERISTICS OF JAVA

Java is object-oriented, and supports four key features:

- *Encapsulation*—A single object in Java contains all of the functions (called *methods* in Java) and variables particular to that object.
- *Inheritance*—New object definitions may be created from existing ones, and may change parts of the definition.

- *Polymorphism*—In Java it is possible to create methods that will produce the same semantic result when applied to two different objects.
- *Dynamic loading*—Java objects can come from anywhere. Objects can be loaded from any machine that supports Java, even over the network.

In Java, the object template, or *class*, contains all of the methods and data variables that are required by the object. This is referred to as the *encapsulation* of methods and instance variables. In Java, there are no "external" functions or global variables. Everything is in an object class definition.

Inheritance in Java is not only supported, but strictly enforced. Java is a single inheritance language, and every object in Java has at most one parent. Single inheritance makes code easier to maintain. It is always possible to find the topmost parent of a variable or method.

Polymorphism in Java is supported through a special class type called an *interface.* An interface represents Java's technique for supporting multiple-inheritance. Java allows the programmer to define methods that are implemented by another class at any inheritance level.

Finally, Java is a network-centric language. By design, it can load objects from across the network, including servers that are not of the same architecture as the client or target machine.

CLASSES AND OBJECTS

Probably the most confusing terms involved with programming in an object-oriented language are *object* and *class.* Many people use these terms rather synonymously, but in fact they are distinct and it is important to understand the difference.

CLASSES

A class is a template that defines what a particular object might look like. An object created from a class is called an *instance* of the class. The process of creating a description of an object through a class template is called *modeling* the object.

Consider how you might model a typical object, like an airplane (Figure 2.1). First you need to decide what the state and functions of the typical object are. Airplanes have altitude, air speed, and a fuel level. These are called state variables.

Airplane functions are modeled like the state variables, by determining what an example airplane should do. Airplanes can take off and land (and, we hope, a few other things). These functions are part of the definition of the airplane. In Java, functions are referred to as *methods*, because they apply only to the class template in which they are defined. The benefit of keeping methods as

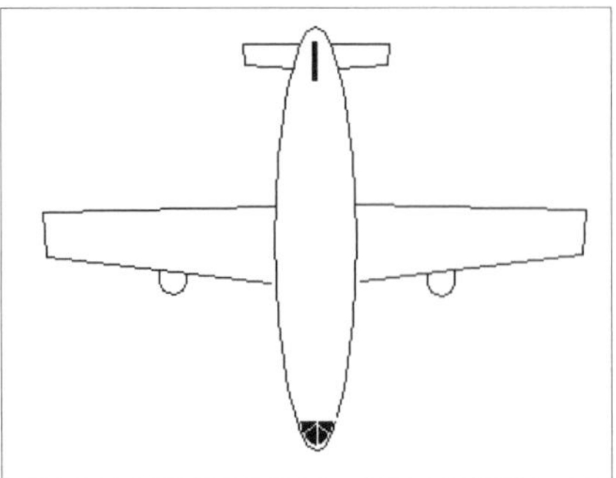

Figure 2.1: An Airplane class template

part of the definition of the airplane is that you can control access to the state variables through the takeoff and landing methods. In other words, only takeoff and landing should be able to affect the state of altitude, speed, and fuel level. It might be disastrous if some other function could set the fuel level to zero while the airplane's altitude was at 30,000 feet!

The Airplane Class After designing how the representative airplane object might operate and what state variables it might contain, you can begin to define the object's template class. For now, don't worry about defining what each method actually does, or about the specific syntax of Java. Here is the class definition for an airplane:

```
class Airplane {
    // state variables
    private int speed;
    private int altitude;
    private int fuel;
    // Class constructor - creates an instance of Airplane
    public Airplane () {
        speed = 0;
        altitude = 0;
        fuel = 12000;
    }
    // Class methods (operations)
    // takeoff method
    public void takeOff () {
        // change altitude and speed
        speed = 500;
        altitude = 30000;
    }
    // landing method
```

```
    public void land () {
        speed = 0;
        altitude = 0;
    }
}
```

Note: The double slash marks (//) represent comments, which we'll discuss later in the chapter.

This definition contains three state variables, speed, altitude, and fuel, which are private. The keyword *private* indicates that these variables may only be changed by methods within the class. Private variables are like thoughts that you have—only you can change them. Within a class, private variables and methods can only be accessed within the class.

The class also defines three methods that are declared as public. The keyword *public* allows any instance of this class to access these methods. The first method,

```
public Airplane() {
```

is a special kind of method called a constructor. In Java, constructors are methods with the same name as the class (including upper- and lowercase, since Java is case-sensitive). Also note that in Java, all methods specify a *return type*—the type of data you can expect to receive as the result of the method. The return type specifies the kind of data you want the method to give you as a status. For example, if you created a method to read the altitude, the return type should reflect the way the altitude data would return:

```
    public int read Altitude () {
        return altitude;
    }
```

Altitude is represented as an int data type, so the return type for the read Altittude () method is int. Constructors are the one exception to this rule and have no return type. During the creation of an instance of the Airplane class, the constructor is called to initialize the state variables of the new instance.

The other two methods in this class define takeoff and landing operations. Both methods affect the state of the altitude and speed variables. Obviously this is a simplified airplane; the class can define a great deal more detail, including the position of flaps, the consumption of fuel, engine settings, and so on.

The Airplane class illustrates how object-oriented programming languages encapsulate state variables and methods in a single template. The variables and methods that are particular to any instance of an airplane are part of the definition of the class, and are therefore encapsulated in the definition of the object. The Airplane class also illustrates how objects can hide implementation details. The altitude, speed, and fuel state variables are private, and how they are stored and whether they are integers, floating point numbers, or strings are hidden from the user. This makes it possible for the programmer to change the way a state variable is stored without affecting the methods. For example, suppose that you changed the speed state variable to a floating point number. The takeoff() method would still be called by the class user the same way:

```
public void takeoff () {
    speed = 500.0f;
    altitude = 30000;
}
```

OBJECTS

With this template for an airplane, it is now possible to create an instance of this class, or an Airplane object (Figure 2.2). In Java, the keyword *new* is always used to allocate memory space and call the constructor for the class. For example, to create an instance of the Airplane class, you first need to identify an object reference variable of the Airplane type:

```
Airplane boeing757;
```

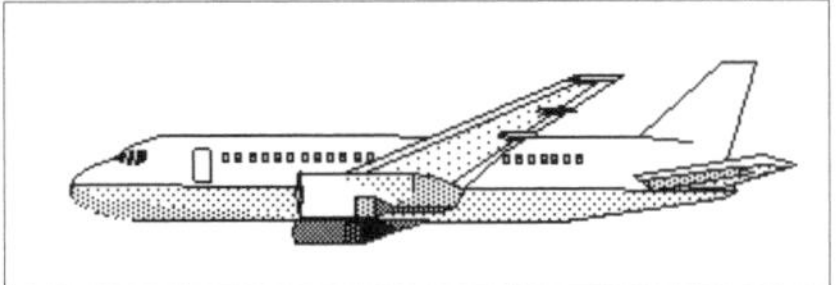

Figure 2.2: An instance of the Airplane class

At this point, no memory has been allocated—you have merely defined the variable *boeing757* as an object reference variable of the Airplane class. The initial value of the object is null. To allocate memory and create an instance of the Airplane class, you need to use the new keyword to allocate memory space, and the constructor for the class to initialize the memory space:

```
Airplane boeing757;
boeing757 = new Airplane ();
```

Once the second line is executed, there is memory storage allocated for an instance of the Airplane object, named boeing757, with an initial speed value of 0, an initial altitude value of 0, and an initial fuel value of 12,000.

Using the Object Once the object is created, methods are called through the object reference variable:

```
boeing757.takeoff ();
boeing757.land ();
```

These methods are public and thus are accessible through the instance of the class. The private variables—altitude, fuel, and speed—are not accessible except through the class. The following are illegal:

```
boeing757.altitude = -10;
boeing757.speed = 100;
```

Methods may also be private, whichmakes it possible to hide the details of your implementation of the method. A private method is something that only the class can execute. This is like a special skill that only you know you possess. A good case for a private method might be the declaration of methods to handle the brakes on the airplane:

```
class Airplane {
    ...
    // applyBrakes is private to hide detail
    private void applyBrakes () {
        // increase pressure on the wheel hydraulics
        ...
    }
    // stop method is used to stop the plane
    public void stop () {
        // use the current brake mechanism
        applyBrakes ();
    }
}
```

The stop() method is the public interface to the object and calls the appropriate method or methods to bring the plane to a stop. Hiding the implementation details promotes reuse and provides a consistent interface to a particular action. The pilot of the plane does not need to know that the plane has hydraulic or mechanical brakes; he or she needs to know that by applying the stop() method, the plane will come to a halt. You could change the implementation details of the brakes for the Airplane class without affecting the pilot in any way.

OBJECT INTERACTIONS

Creating a single class to handle all of the implementation of an airplane would be very difficult, and would not be object-oriented. Instead, you can break down a complex object into smaller, simpler objects that interact with each other. This provides two benefits:

- The code created is easier to maintain when the object component pieces are smaller.
- The objects are reusable and can be applied in other ways.

In the airplane example, you could model the engine as a single object, and then specify the interaction between the new object and the Airplane class:

```
class JetEngine {
    private int RPM;  // revolutions per minute
    private boolean started;  // true or false
    private int engineTemp;  // running temperature
    // JetEngine constructor
    public JetEngine () {
        RPM = 0; started = false;
    }
    // engine start method
    public boolean startEngine () {
        // attempt to start the engine
        fuelPump (on);
        // if fuel pressure is too low, can't start
        if (fuelPressure > 100) {
            startTurbine ();
        } else {
            return false;
        }
        return true;
    }
    ...
}
```

The JetEngine class defines the variables and methods that are particular to a jet engine. As you can probably guess, by separating the engine from the plane, you could also create a PropEngine class for a propeller-based engine, or a RocketEngine class for the space shuttle version (Figure 2.3) of an airplane.

Objects communicate in Java by calling each other's methods. For example, the Airplane class communicates to its related engine objects by calling the methods declared in the engine class:

```
class Airplane {
    // state variables
    private int speed;
    private int altitude;
    private int fuel;
```

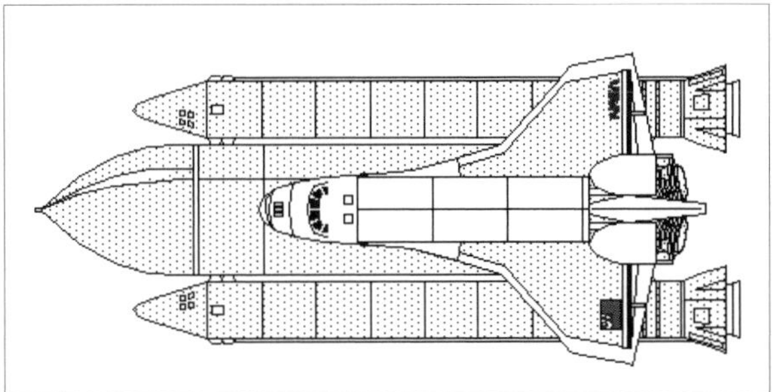

Figure 2.3: A Space Shuttle object

```
    // Object reference variables
    JetEngine engine[4];
     // Class constructor - creates an instance of Airplane
    public Airplane () {
        speed = 0;
        altitude = 0;
        fuel = 12000;
        // Create four jet engines
        engine = new JetEngine[4];
        for (int i = 0; i < engine.length; i++) {
            engine[i] = new JetEngine ();
        }
    }
    // method prepareTakeoff - starts the engines
    public boolean prepareTakeoff () {
        for (int i = 0; i < engine.length; i++) {
            if (engine[i].startEngine == false) {
                return false;
            }
        }
        return true;
    }
    ...
} // end Airplane class
```

Here the airplane's prepareTakeoff method calls the startEngine method of each of its four engine objects, and each object in turn returns its status (true or false) to indicate if it could successfully start the engine or not.

OBJECT CLASSIFICATION

An object class like Airplane is used to create a grouping of objects that share airplanelike behavior and state. You could instantiate almost any type of airplane object from the Airplane class—AirBus, Boeing757, LearJet, and so on. However, classification of these objects is limited to the current implementation of the Airplane class. According to the current definition, the Airplane class defines a fairly narrow group of object types. Suppose that you wanted to create a more generic template, say, a template of all flying object types. In object-oriented languages like Java, this is very easy. Here is an example of a generalization of the Airplane class to create a template for any type of flying object:

```
class FlyingObject {
    public boolean hasWings;
    public boolean hasEngines;
    private int speed;
    private int altitude;
    public FlyingObject () {
        speed = 0; altitude = 0;
    }
    // methods
    public void takeOff (int TOspeed, int TOalt) {
        // method to move flying object into the air
        speed = TOspeed;
        altitude = TOalt;
    }
    public void land () {
        // method to return flying object to ground level
       speed = 0;
       altitude = 0;
    }
    public void stop () {
        applyWheelBrakes ();
    }
    ...
}
```

In this class, we define three methods: takeOff(), land(), and stop(). These are methods that can be applied to any type of flying object—airplanes, helicopters, space shuttles, gliders, and even UFOs! For example:

```
FlyingObject helicopter;
helicopter = new FlyingObject();
helicopter.hasWings = false;
helicopter.hasEngines = true;
```

Generalization is not an object-oriented mechanism per se, but the example above illustrates how to take a specific class like Airplane to a more general definition. When the the class is generalized this way, each and every instance of the class must then identify what separates it from other general objects. This may not seem like a real benefit to generalization, and in fact, there is a better way.

INHERITANCE

Rather than creating general objects and specializing them through every instance, a better technique is to create a new class template from the general class through inheritance. In object-oriented languages, you can create a new class definition by causing it to inherit, or *subclass*, an existing class. A subclass will inherit all of the variables and methods of the parent, or superclass. The benefit to subclassing is that you can reuse all of the parent class code, yet add specific implementation details. For example, you could create a class for helicopters by subclassing FlyingObject and adding a new method specific to helicopters. In Java, the keyword to do this is *extends*:

```
class Helicopter extends FlyingObject {
    public Helicopter () {
        hasWings = false; hasEngine = true;
    }
    // Add the hover method - helicopters can operate
    // at an altitude w/o a change in forward speed
    // or direction
    public void hover (int hoverAlt) {
        altitude = hoverAlt;
    }
}
```

Now when we instantiate an instance of Helicopter, we will automatically get a FlyingObject that can hover, has no wings, and has an engine.

Another benefit to subclassing is that it is possible to change the operation of the parent object's methods without changing the interface. This feature is called *method overriding*. A method in Java will override another when the name of the method, the return type, the argument count, and the argument type match the inherited method. For example:

```
class Helicopter extends FlyingObject {
    public Helicopter () {
        hasWings = false; hasEngine = true;
    }
    // override stop method from FlyingObject
    public void stop () {
        // helicopters stop by landing with no forward speed
        altitude = 0;
        speed = 0;
        stopEngine ();
```

```
    }
    ...
}
```

Here the stop() method is overridden because the helicopters do not have wheels!

METHOD OVERLOADING

Object-oriented languages also provide a way for you to specify a single method name but vary the number and type of the arguments. With overloading, the method name stays the same but the user is provided with more ways to call the same method. For example, suppose that we would like our helicopter to be able to take off vertically, with no forward speed, but also be able to take off with a forward speed:

```
class Helicopter extends FlyingObject {
    public Helicopter () {
        hasWings = false; hasEngine = true;
    }
    // takeoff method with just altitude
    public void takeOff (int TOalt) {
        // altitude can increase w/o speed
        altitude = TOalt;
    }
    public void takeOff (int TOspeed, int TOalt) {
        speed = TOspeed;
        altitude = TOalt;
    }
    ...
}
```

Now our helicopter class has two methods for takeoff: one that takes a single altitude argument for vertical takeoff and another that takes both altitude and speed.

Any method may be overloaded in Java, including constructor methods. Providing multiple overloaded constructors allows the user of your class to choose which kind of instance to create.

ABSTRACT CLASSES IN JAVA

If you have already started programming with Java applets, you may have noticed that some of the classes defined by the Java Application Programmer's Interface (API) are defined as abstract. The Graphics class, for example, is defined as abstract, and yet in applets this is the primary class for drawing methods. How does this work?

An *abstract class* is an incomplete description of an object template. Previously the Airplane class defined necessary instance variables and methods needed for an airplane object. When the class was generalized to create the FlyingObject class, it was still necessary to define the specific implementation of each subclass, and overload the methods defined in FlyingObject in order to get the appropriate behavior for the new class.

Another way to create a generalized class is to create an abstract class. In Java, an abstract class must be subclassed and cannot be instantiated. Creating an abstract class for FlyingObject is a good idea, considering that an instance of a FlyingObject by itself doesn't really make any sense.

As an abstract class, FlyingObject can declare methods as abstract and still retain the advantages of a generic class:

```
abstract class FlyingObject {
    // abstract methods
    // Take off at speed and altitude
    public abstract void takeOff (int speed, int alt);
    // land
    public abstract void land ();
    // Hover at specified altitude
    public abstract void hover (int alt);
    // Take off vertically - no forward speed
    public void takeOffVertical (int alt) {
        takeOff (0, alt);
    }
    ...
}
```

The takeOff(), land(), and hover() methods are declared public and abstract. In this class, the interface is defined, but the methods don't have any code bodies. It is up to the programmers who subclass the FlyingObject class to create bodies for the methods they choose to use. Further, it is possible to have a method in an abstract class that is not declared abstract—the takeOffVertical() method is an example of a method that is not abstract. Of course, for this method to be useful, the abstract method takeOff() must be given a code body.

To illustrate how an abstract class is used, here is the rewritten version of a Helicopter class and Airplane class:

```
class Helicopter extends FlyingObject {
    private int altitude, speed;
    public Helicopter () {
        altitude = 0; speed = 0
    }
```

```
    // implement the abstract takeOff method
    public void takeOff (int TOspeed, int TOalt) {
        speed = TOspeed;
        altitude = TOalt;
    }
    // hover method - helicopters can operate
    // at an altitude w/o a change in forward speed
    // or direction
    public void hover (int hoverAlt) {
        speed = 0;
        altitude = hoverAlt;
    }
    // Land method
    public void land () {
        speed = 0;
        altitude = 0;
    }
    ...
}
class Airplane extends FlyingObject{
    // state variables
    private int altitude, speed, fuel;
    // Class constructor - creates an instance of Airplane
    public Airplane () {
        speed = 0;
        altitude = 0;
        fuel = 12000;
    }
    // takeoff method
    public void takeOff (int TOspeed, int TOalt) {
        // change altitude and speed
        speed = TOspeed;
        altitude = TOalt;
    }
    // landing method - pass landing altitude
    public void land () {
        speed = 0;
        altitude = 0;
    }
    ...
}
```

Note that the Helicopter class and Airplane class contain code bodies for take-Off() and land(), but hover() is not implemented for an airplane.

An instance of this new class Helicopter can now make use of all of the methods defined in the Helicopter class and the method inherited from the FlyingObject class:

```
Helicopter BellRanger;
BellRanger = new Helicopter();
BellRanger.takeOffVertical ();
BellRanger.hover();
BellRanger.land();
```

JAVA SYNTAX OVERVIEW

This section doesn't pretend to be your sole source of information on Java syntax, but to help you through the next few sections, here is a quick overview of how Java programs are put together. For a more complete look at the Java syntax, take a look at the Java home page: http://www.javasoft.com.

JAVA PROGRAM OUTLINE

A simple Java applet is shown below:

```
import java.awt.*;
import java.applet.Applet;
// A simple Java applet to write a series of 5 Hello World!
public class HelloWorld extends Applet {
    String s;
    int i;
    // init method is called first
    // initialize the String object s
    public void init () {
        s = new String ("Hello World!");
    }
    // paint method is called to draw applet context
    // paint a series of strings
    public void paint (Graphics g) {
        for (i = 25; i < 150; i+=25) {
            g.drawString (s, i, i);
        }
    }
}
```

This simple applet will "draw" a series of five Hello World! strings down and across to the right (see Figure 2.4). This applet illustrates the use of the import statement, class declaration, Java primitives, and two methods—init() and paint().

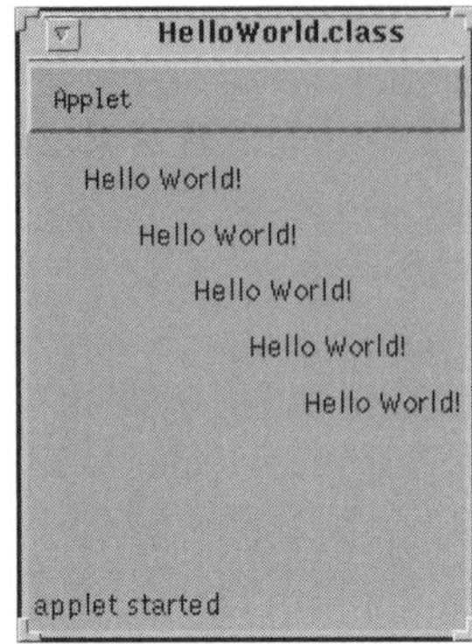

Figure 2.4: The Hello World! applet

STATEMENTS AND COMMENTS

Java statements make up a Java applet or application. Each statement in Java is terminated with a semicolon (;). Methods can contain several statements and are identified by an opening and closing brace.

Comments can be placed on a separate line or at the end of a line. Comments are very useful for making a code section clearer to the reader. At a minimum, add a comment to any line or lines of code that perform something tricky. There are three comment styles:

```
// this is a comment
/* This is the C style comment - and can extend
over multiple lines */
/** This is a documentation comment */
```

Putting these together, here is a simple add method:

```
/* The add method adds two numbers and
   returns the result */
public int add (int x, int y) {
    int n;
    n = x + y;  // Here the numbers are added
    return n;
}
```

IMPORT STATEMENT

The import statement in Java is used to let the compiler know where to look for a class name. The import statement includes the keyword *import* and the name of a Java package to search during compilation. In Java, packages are collections of class files, like a library in other languages. You may specify a particular class within a package name, or use an asterisk to wildcard the entire package. For example:

```
import java.awt.*;
import java.applet.Applet;
```

These statements indicate that the compiler should search the entire java.awt package for a class reference and the Applet class within the java.applet package. Within the paint() method, the Graphics class was referenced:

```
public void paint (Graphics g) {
```

The compiler will search through the java.awt package for the Graphics class and find it there.

CLASS DECLARATIONS

In Java, every program, applet, or application must start by declaring the name of a class to load and execute. When creating applets, you will almost always use the syntax shown in the declaration of the HelloWorld class:

```
public class HelloWorld extends Applet {
```

This declaration indicates that you wish to create a new class called HelloWorld, which will inherit from the Applet class. This single declaration gives you access to all of the functionality of an applet, including several methods like init() and paint().

JAVA PRIMITIVE TYPES

Everything in Java is an object type except primitive types. Primitive types include Boolean, byte, char, short, int, long, float, and double. A variable of each of these types can be declared by using the name of the primitive in front of the variable. Each primitive type can store a value (or number) that is representative of the type in which it is stored. For example, integers (int) can store numbers between –2,147,483,648 and 2,147,483,647. In most languages, strings are also represented by primitive types as character arrays. In Java, strings are objects. In HelloWorld, a String object *s* is declared:

```
String s;
```

This object does not contain any characters until the init method:

```
public void init () {
    s = new String ("Hello World!");
}
```

Once init is completed, the String object *s* will point to the characters "H-e-l-l-o-(space)-W-o-r-l-d-!".

APPLET METHODS

Applet methods are part of the hierarchy of methods that are inherited from the Applet class. Each method is called by the browser (or by the AppletViewer). By overriding each method you can control the behavior of the applet during execution in a browser.

The Init() Method The HelloWorld applet uses two applet methods, perhaps the most common: init() and paint(Graphics g). The init() method is guaranteed to complete first, before any other method is run. This method is a good place to initialize applet variables. Also, the init() method is only run once—when the applet is first loaded—so be careful not to put any code that needs to be executed more than once into the init() method.

The Paint(Graphics g) Method When the browser loads and executes an applet class like HelloWorld, the browser creates a drawing context for the applet to work with. The paint(Graphics g) method is called whenever the applet drawing context needs to be refreshed. The paint() method is the primary way for the applet to draw onto its drawing context. When the browser calls paint(), a reference to the Graphics context class is passed to the applet. The Graphics class defines a number of drawing routines, including drawing of lines, circles, squares, polygons, and so on, and both GIF and JPEG images. For complete information on the methods available in the Graphics class, consult the Java API.

The Start() and Stop() Methods The start() method is called whenever the HTML page that contains the applet is first visited (or first run in the AppletViewer). The start() method is a good method to use for reinitializing applet variables or starting a background task for an applet, such as playing an audio file.

The stop() method is the converse to start()—it is called when the applet is no longer viewable; for example, when the browser moves to a different page. The stop() method is a good method for halting background tasks, like a looping audio file.

The Repaint() and Update(Graphics g) Methods The update() method is called by the browser whenever there is a need to refresh the applet. In essence, this happens whenever the applet is partially covered by another window or receives some other refresh event. This method is implemented by the browser to perform four tasks:

- Set the background color to the default background color (typically the browser default background color).

- Draw a filled rectangle of the background color over the applet drawing context.
- Set the foreground (drawing) color to the default foreground color (typically black).
- Call paint.

The default behavior of update() is to clear any current drawing on the drawing context and start over by calling paint(). It can be a wise idea to override this method if you are planning to draw a number of images (for example, in an animation):

```
// Override update to prevent screen clear
public void update (Graphics g) {
    // just call paint
    paint (g)
}
```

Now the update() method (when called) will not clear the background or change color settings, and instead will just call the paint() method.

The repaint() method is your main control over when update() and paint() get called. It is possible to force an update by making a call to repaint(). This is very useful in animations like the Spinner applet shown in Figure 2.5. Here is an example of an applet that rotates six different colors through four lines, giving the impression that the drawing is spinning:

```
import java.awt.*;
import java.applet.*;
// Spinner rotates colors through lines
public class Spinner extends Applet {
    // Create four arrays of points for the lines, x1, y1, x2, y2
    int x1[] = { 0, 5, 25, 45 };
    int y1[] = { 25, 5, 0, 5 };
    int x2[] = { 50, 45, 25, 5 };
    int y2[] = { 25, 45, 50, 45 };
    int index = 0, c = 0;
    // An array of colors to use in the spinner
    Color clist[] = { Color.blue, Color.red, Color.green, Color.yellow,
Color.white, Color.cyan };
    // Paint the first line, then schedule an update
    public void paint (Graphics g) {
        g.drawLine (x1[index], y1[index], x2[index], y2[index]);
        repaint();
    }
    // during update, set the next set of points
```

```
    // and the color
    public void update (Graphics g) {
        index++; c++;
        if (index >= x1.length) index = 0;
        if (c >= clist.length) c = 0;
        // set the drawing color from the list
        g.setColor (clist[c]);
        paint (g);
    }
}
```

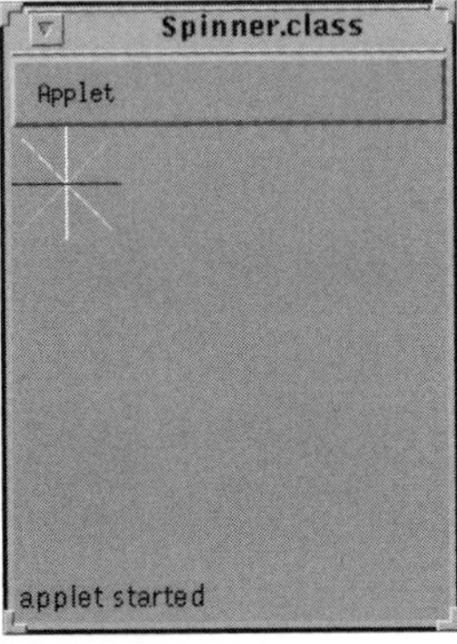

Figure 2.5: The Spinner applet

JAVA ARRAYS

In the Spinner applet you'll notice that the coordinates of the lines and the list of colors use two square braces in their declaration:

```
int x1[]...
Color clist[]...
```

These are called *array declarations.* Arrays in Java are created and stored as objects. You will access an individual element of an array object the same way it's done in other languages:

```
g.setColor (clist [c]);
```

However, the array is stored in Java as an object, and thus also stores the length of the array as an instance variable:

```
if (c >= clist.length) c = 0;
```

Arrays may either be created implicitly, by declaring the elements that the array will contain, as in Spinner:

```
int x1[] = { 0, 5, 25, 45 };
```

or explicitly, by declaring the array and then using the new operator to create locations for the array:

```
String s[];
s = new String [3];
s[0] = "Tom";
s[1] = "Dick";
s[2] = "Harry";
```

Once created, any attempt to access beyond the end of the array will create a runtime error. Arrays may not be declared statically:

```
int x[10];  // Will create a compiler error
```

JAVA FLOW CONTROL

There are five flow control statements in Java. These are common to other languages as well:

- if/else statement

```
if (c > 10) {
    c = 0;
}
else {
    c++;
}
```

- switch/case

```
switch (n) {
    case 0:
        i = 10;
        break;
    case 5:
        i = 0;
        break;
    default:
        i = 5;
}
```

- for loop

```
for (int i = 0; i < 10; i++ ) {
    s = s + i;
}
```

- while loop

```
le (n > 20) {
 d = d + n * 10;
    n--;
}
```

- do/while loop

```
do {
    s = s + n;
} while (s < 100);
```

NETWORKING—CONNECTING APPLETS VIA SOCKETS

So far you have seen Java applets and applications that are basically stand-alone programs. In all of the examples, the programs don't interact with one another. However, Java is a network-centric language, and one of its appealing features is the ability to create an applet or application that communicates with another applet or application. This makes it possible to access a back-end database with an applet, set up remote "chat" sessions between applications, or even use a remote server to perform high-speed calculations for a low-performance client computer.

WHAT IS A SOCKET?

A *socket* is the end point of a communication link between two processes. There are two distinct socket types under Java: TCP (Transport Control Protocol) and UDP (User Datagram Protocol). Sockets can be used to make connections between processes that are running on a single machine (intranet) and between processes on two different machines (Internet). When the socket is a TCP-type socket and runs over the Internet Protocol (IP), it is referred to as a TCP/IP socket. Both types of sockets communicate by collecting data into a block of bytes called a packet. The actual content of the packet depends upon the socket type used.

In general, you should consider using TCP sockets exclusively. A TCP socket represents a connection-oriented service—a connection is made to another process and the communication is guaranteed to transfer data in the correct order. TCP also resends any part of the message that becomes damaged or lost. A good analogy for a TCP socket is a conversation by telephone. The phones represent the socket connections, and the people conversing can make sure the "data" is received in order and that no part of the message is lost. If the message becomes garbled, the listener can request that the other person "resend."

UDP sockets represent a connectionless service. While they operate with less overhead than TCP sockets, this savings is more than offset by the unreliable nature of this service. Every UDP packet contains all of the information needed to get the data to the recipient, including the recipient's name (port number) and address. UDP socket communications are analogous to sending a series of messages by postcard. If you were to write a long message to your friend in the United States from South America by sending each part of the message on a single postcard, could you guarantee that the postcards would arrive in order? Or even in the same week? This is the unreliable nature of UDP sockets.

SECURITY RESTRICTIONS

In the first chapter of this book you saw how the security features of Java keep applets from doing damage to your system. Unfortunately, these same features may keep your applet from doing what you want it to. Under the Netscape Navigator browser version 2.0, applets are only allowed to reconnect to the host server from which they originated. For most applications, this is enough, but bear this in mind when you design your applet communication system.

A SIMPLE CLIENT/SERVER SOCKET SYSTEM

To create a socket and use it to communicate between two processes, you will need to create a client and server that communicate over an established protocol. In the following example, the client is an applet and the server is an application. The server-side application should always be running in order to receive the client's request. The socket system works as follows:

1. The server runs first and registers with a port number and service type (TCP or UDP).
2. The server then waits (listens) for any client request on the port number.
3. When the client makes a request, the server establishes a connection with the client and opens the server-side socket.
4. The client also establishes the connection with the server host on the port number.

5 Both client and server may now create stream handles to communicate back and forth.

Client Side Here is the client-side Java source file. This is an applet, which would be included on an HTML page served from the same system that is running the simpleServer (below) in a background process:

```
/*
 * TCP/IP simple client--Echo back the servers output
 */
import java.awt.*;
import java.net.*;
import java.io.*;
import java.applet.*;
// This client opens a socket to the server and reads
// the string sent
public class appletClient extends Applet {
    int c;
    Socket s;
    InputStream sIn;
    String x;
    // Open the connection to the server and read until done
    public void init () {
        x = new String ();
        // Attempt to make a connection to the server
        try {
            // Open our connection to server at port 8000
            s = new Socket("blueline",8000);
            // Get an input file handle from the socket
            // and read the input
            sIn = s.getInputStream();
            while ((c = sIn.read()) != -1) {
                x += (char)c;
            }
            // When the EOF is reached, just close the
            // connection and exit
            s.close();
        } catch (IOException e) {
            // No connection made!
            x = "Error: Server not responding";
        }
    }
    // Paint whatever you get from the server
    public void paint (Graphics g) {
        g.drawString (x, 25, 25);
```

```
    }
}
```

The appletClient class (see Figure 2.6) uses two methods: init() and paint(). In init() it attempts to connect to the server and open a socket. In this example code the server and port number are hard-coded to *blueline* and *8000*, but could have used Java param tags instead. Once the connection is established, the client reads all of the characters the server sends until it reads the end-of-file (EOF) character (–1). Once the EOF is read, the client closes the connection (on the client side). The paint() method then draws the contents of the x string. Note that if a connection cannot be made—for example, if the server is not running—then the client will report an error message: *Error: Server not responding.*

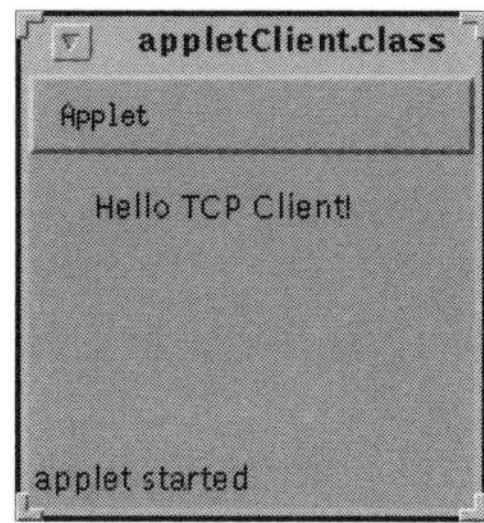

Figure 2.6: The appletClient applet

Server Side Here is the code for the server side of this example:

```
/*
 * TCP/IP Simple Server
 */
import java.awt.*;
import java.net.*;
import java.io.*;
// This is a Java application - and is meant to run
// on the system that serves the web page containing
// appletClient.
class simpleServer {
    public static void main(String args[]) throws IOException {
        ServerSocket s=(ServerSocket) null;
        Socket s1;
        String sendString = "Hello TCP Client!\n";
        int slength;
        OutputStream s1out;
        // Request a service on socket 8000
        try {
```

```
                s = new ServerSocket(8000);
                System.out.println ("Ready for client request...");
            } catch (IOException e) { }
            // Run the listen/accept loop forever
            while (true) {
                // Wait here and listen for a connection
                s1=s.accept();
                System.out.println ("Sending to client...");
                // Get an output file handle associated with
               // the socket
                slout = s1.getOutputStream();
                // Send our string!
                slength = sendString.length();
                for (int i=0; i<slength; i++) {
                    slout.write((int)sendString.charAt(i));
                }
                  // Close the connection, not the server socket
                s1.close();
            }
        }
}
```

The server side is an application. The simpleServer application is run from the server machine. The server must be running before the client applet runs and is started by someone else:

```
java simpleServer
```

This starts the application and runs the main() method.

Within the main() method of the application, the server registers a port number (8000) with the TCP service. It then enters a forever while loop, listening for any client attempting to connect to the service registered at port 8000 for this server. If a client makes a request, the simpleServer opens an output stream and sends the string *Hello TCP Client!*, one character at a time. It then closes the connection to the client (but not the service connection) and loops back to wait for another client connection attempt.

GOING FURTHER

This section just scratches the surface of what is possible with sockets. For more information and examples, take a look at Gamelan's Network and Communication section on http://www.gamelan.com.

MULTITHREADING

A *thread* is a single path through a program flow. Consider the following activities involved in the process of making a cake:

1. Get the eggs, flour, milk, and cake mix.
2. Mix the ingredients in a bowl.
3. Turn the oven on to 350 degrees.
4. Wait for the oven to reach temperature.
5. Pour the mixture into a cake tin.
6. Put the cake tin into the oven.
7. Wait for 40 minutes.
8. Make the frosting.
9. Take the cake out and cool.
10. Frost the cake.

This process is a single thread of execution. In this outline of activities things happen in a specific order, one after another. For some events, this makes sense. It is simply not possible to pour the mixture into a cake tin before getting out the ingredients. Note, however, that there are periods of slack time in some of the events where some other task could be accomplished in order to speed up the end result. *Multithreading* is a technique where part of the slack time in the overall execution is used to perform other tasks, creating the impression that multiple tasks are happening simultaneously.

Figure 2.7 shows a multithreaded version of the cake bake, with two threads of execution, thread A and B. Note that there is still only one cook, but the slack time is used more effectively.

In a single-thread cake bake there are ten sequential activities, and two involve waiting for a long period of time (long in the world of the CPU, that is). In the multithreaded version, with two threaded tasks there is a maximum of seven sequential activities; and while the cake mix is being mixed, the oven is heating, and while the cake is baking, the frosting is being made.

In Java programs, as in real life, it is possible to create multiple threads that are not related to a single task. While the cake was baking for 40 minutes, it probably would have been possible to have another thread that took care of cleaning the mixing bowl, getting the laundry, or mowing the lawn.

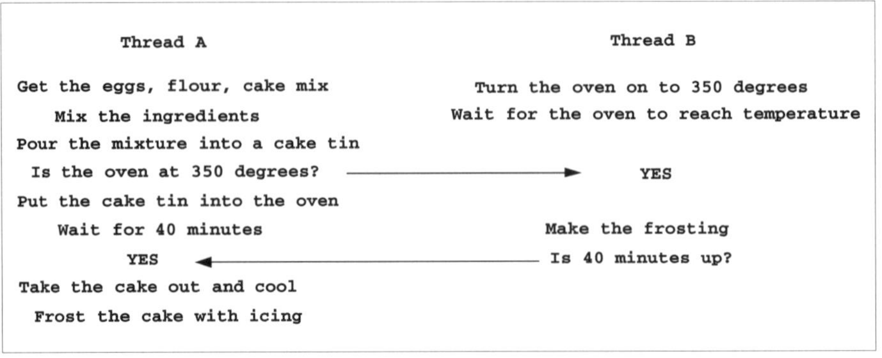

Figure 2.7: Multithreaded cakemaking

THREAD PRIORITY AND PREEMPTION

Now consider what might happen if the phone rings while you're in the middle of mixing the cake batter. You will stop mixing and answer the phone. The phone task is considered higher priority and will preempt the current cake mix task. Java's multithreading model supports preemptive scheduling. When a thread of higher priority is ready to run, that thread is given execution context and other threads of lower priority are made to wait.

Threads of equal priority are scheduled in a round-robin fashion. If you have three threads of equal priority (A, B, and C), then A will run until it quits or is blocked, followed by B, then C.

Note: Win32 machines have a slightly different implementation: Threads of equal priority will time-slice.

JAVA MULTITHREADING

Java applets are by default multithreaded. The garbage collector is its own thread running at a low priority, and there are other system-level threads created on your behalf. Creating your own threads in Java applets is a matter of making use of the Thread class in the java.lang package.

In this example, you will see a Java applet that creates several threads that each run at the same priority and do the same amount of work:

```
import java.applet.*;
// A Simple thread test program
// creates three threads
```

```
public class simpleThread extends Applet {
    workThread t1, t2, t3;
    // Initialize three thread object
    public void init () {
        t1 = new workThread (1000, "Thread 1");
        t2 = new workThread (500, "Thread 2 ");
        t3 = new workThread (2000, "Thread 3");
    }
    // Start each of the three threads by
    // calling the start method of each thread
    public void start () {
        t1.start();
        t2.start();
        t3.start();
    }
}
// The workThread class
// subclassed from Thread, this class will
// print a message to the system console when
// started, an one when exiting
class workThread extends Thread {
    int sleep_time;
    String thread_name;
    // workThread constructor:
     // passed two arguments: a sleep time (in milliseconds)
    //                     a thread name (String)
    public workThread (int stime, String Tname) {
        sleep_time = stime;
        thread_name = Tname;
    }
    // The run method is the body of this thread
    // run is called through threadobj.start()
    public void run () {
        // Echo a start message
         System.out.println ("inside thread " + thread_name);
        // Sleep for a bit
        try {
            sleep (sleep_time);
        } catch (InterruptedException e) { }
        // Echo an exit message
        System.out.println ("exiting thread " + thread_name);
    }
}
```

Note that this single source file contains two classes: the simpleThread applet class and the workThread class.

The simpleThread class creates three thread objects (t1, t2, and t3), and then starts these in order. Each workThread object is passed two arguments, a sleep interval time and a string name. These are stored in instance variables as part of the object. When the simpleThread class executes, the three threads each run in turn, first printing their entry message, then sleeping for the sleep time interval, then printing their exit message. The output looks like this:

```
inside thread Thread 1
inside thread Thread 2
inside thread Thread 3
exiting thread Thread 2
exiting thread Thread 1
exiting thread Thread 3
```

Thread 2 finishes first because it has the shortest sleep interval, just 500 milliseconds, followed by Thread 1 at 1,000ms, and then Thread 3 at 2,000ms.

USING THE RUNNABLE INTERFACE

With Java, it is almost always possible to write a program with more than one technique. This is very true of threads in applets. The Runnable interface is a special class in Java. An *interface* is an abstract class with methods that must be implemented. The Runnable class, for example, has a single run method that must be overridden. However, the Thread class also implements the Runnable interface, which means you implement the functionality of Threads by implementing this "shared" class, Runnable.

Here is an example of the Spinner applet, rewritten to implement Runnable:

```
import java.awt.*;
import java.applet.*;
// Spinner rotates colors through lines
public class Spinner2 extends Applet implements Runnable {
    Thread spin;
    // Create four arrays of points for the lines,
    // x1, y1, x2, y2
    int x1[] = { 0, 5, 25, 45 };
    int y1[] = { 25, 5, 0, 5 };
    int x2[] = { 50, 45, 25, 5 };
    int y2[] = { 25, 45, 50, 45 };
    int index = 0, c = 0;
    // An array of colors to use in the spinner
    Color clist[] = { Color.blue, Color.red, Color.green, Color.yellow,
Color.white, Color.cyan };
    // Run method - constantly calls repaint,
    // sleeping for an interval
    public void run () {
```

```
        while (true) {
            try {
                Thread.sleep (100);
            } catch (InterruptedException e) { }
        index++; c++;
        if (index >= x1.length) index = 0;
        if (c >= clist.length) c = 0;
            repaint ();
        }
    }
    // Paint the first line, then schedule an update
    public void paint (Graphics g) {
        g.drawLine (x1[index], y1[index], x2[index], y2[index]);
    }
    // during update, set the next set of points,
    // and the color
    public void update (Graphics g) {
        // set the drawing color from the list
        g.setColor (clist[c]);
        paint (g);
    }
    // Create the thread in start
    public void start () {
        spin = new Thread (this);
        spin.start();
    }
    // Stop thread as we leave the page
    public void stop() {
        spin stop ();
        spin = null
        {
}
```

This version of Spinner uses the start() method to create a thread that allows the run method to control the behavior of the color changes. Note that the start() method calls the Thread constructor with *this* as an argument. The keyword *this* in Java refers to the object instance itself, in other words, the Spinner2 class object. Effectively we are creating a thread object that uses the run method in the applet as its own, "converting" the applet into a thread.

GOING FURTHER

There are quite a few sources for more information about the inner workings of threading in Java, but you should definitely check out Doug Lea's Java Concurrency Mechanics home page at http://g.oswego.edu/dl/pats/javaconc.html. And of course, for great examples of multithreaded applets in action, there is a wealth of code at the Gamelan Web page, at http://www.gamelan.com/.

JavaScript

JavaScript (formerly LiveScript) is a scripting language that allows you to modify properties of pre-existing objects. Unlike Java, JavaScript does not allow you to create new objects. It is not a script version of Java, and, as of this writing, it is a Netscape-only feature. JavaScript programs are written into HTML pages and may be read and executed only by Netscape Navigator 2.0 browsers. JavaScript allows you to integrate scripts into the HTML page that runs on the user's or client's machine. When someone browses your page where you have written a JavaScript, the script is executed from their browser on their machine. Before Java, the main focus of Web processing was the Common Gateway Interface (CGI). With CGI, processing requests can be made through scripts written to run on the server. The user interacts with CGI through HTML forms. Java can be used to create user interfaces that run on the client side, but Java is more difficult to learn than CGI. JavaScript is positioned between CGI and Java as a front-end to Java applications, by handling a number of the interactive features required and leaving Java to perform more elaborate tasks.

There are a number of differences between Java and JavaScript. Here are the most notable:

- In JavaScript scripts are immediately interpreted in the browser, whereas Java applets are compiled to class files.
- JavaScript can define objects but not classes of objects.
- JavaScript does not support object inheritance.
- JavaScript does not require the strong type declarations that Java does.
- JavaScript allows different HTML tags and elements to interact with each other.

Despite these differences, JavaScript can do a lot for you with less overhead than Java, particularly if you need to create dynamic forms. With JavaScript, it is possible to change the way a form looks, depending upon how the user selects checkboxes, radio buttons, or text input fields.

JAVASCRIPT IN 30 SECONDS

JavaScript's real power is the simple application of forms to local functions or calculations without the need for complex server-based scripts. JavaScript utilizes a new tag named SCRIPT. All of the text placed between a <SCRIPT> and </SCRIPT> tag pair is executed as JavaScript. The tag pair may be placed in the HEAD section of the HTML page, in which case it is executed before the page is loaded, or it may reside in the BODY section. Scripts may also be located in files and executed through an SRC tag:

```
<SCRIPT> LANGUAGE="Javascript">
<SRC="http://myserver:80/~home/calc.js">
</SCRIPT>
```

Note: Loading JavaScript files via the SRC tag is not yet implemented in Netscape Navigator; it should be available in a later release. The use of the .js extension is arbitrary, and is used to differentiate Java class files from JavaScript files.

Rather than belabor the syntax of the language, here is a small sample calculator created in JavaScript:

```
<HTML>
<HEAD>
<TITLE>Simple calculator</TITLE>
<SCRIPT LANGUAGE="Javascript">
function addNum (form, x, y) {
    form.result.value = eval(x) + eval(y);
}
function subNum (form, x, y) {
    form.result.value = eval(x) - eval(y);
}
function multNum (form, x, y) {
    form.result.value = eval(x) * eval(y);
}
function divNum (form, x, y) {
    form.result.value = eval(x) / eval(y);
}
</SCRIPT>
</HEAD>
<BODY>
<H1> A simple calculator in JavaScript </H1>
<HR>
<P><H3>
<FORM>
Simple calculator:<BR>
Value 1: <INPUT NAME="val1" TYPE="text" VALUE="" SIZE=5><BR>
Value 2: <INPUT NAME="val2" TYPE="text" VALUE="" SIZE=5><BR>
Result:  <INPUT NAME="result" TYPE="text" VALUE="" SIZE=5><BR>
<INPUT TYPE="button" VALUE="Add" onClick="addNum(this.form,
form.val1.value, form.val2.value)">
<INPUT TYPE="button" VALUE="Subtract" onClick="subNum(this.form,
form.val1.value, form.val2.value)">
```

```
<INPUT TYPE="button" VALUE="Mutliply" onClick="multNum(this.form,
form.val1.value, form.val2.value)">
<INPUT TYPE="button" VALUE="Divide" onClick="divNum(this.form,
form.val1.value, form.val2.value)">
<HR>
</H3>
</FORM>
</BODY>
</HTML>
```

This simple example (shown in Figure 2.8) illustrates the use of the text and button types available in JavaScript, and the embedding of the working part of the script in the HEAD section of the page. It takes two values entered in the first two text fields and then applies either addition, subtraction, multiplication, or division based upon the function button selected.

This sample calculator is extremely simple—it does no error checking, including division by zero, but it demonstrates the ease with which simple input-based applications can be created with JavaScript. For more exotic calculators, including a 1040EZ tax calculator, surf to http://www.c2.org/~andreww/javascript/calc.html.

GOING FURTHER

Since much of JavaScript syntax is similar to Java, and this book is really about Java, we'll leave the task of learning JavaScript to you. Consider the following sources of information:

The JavaScript Authoring Guide	http://home.netscape.com/eng/mozilla/Gold/handbook/javascript/index.html
A presentation on JavaScript by Frank Hecker	http://www.access.digex.net/~hecker/netscape/majug/javascript/
JavaScript Tutorial via Windows Online Help	http://www.jchelp.com/javahelp/javahelp.htm
The JavaScript FAQ	http://www.his.com/~smithers/freq/beta/
An Index to JavaScript information	http://www.c2.org/~andreww/javascript/index.html

The use of JavaScript is growing rapidly, and there are a number of great examples on Gamelan—http://www.gamelan.com.

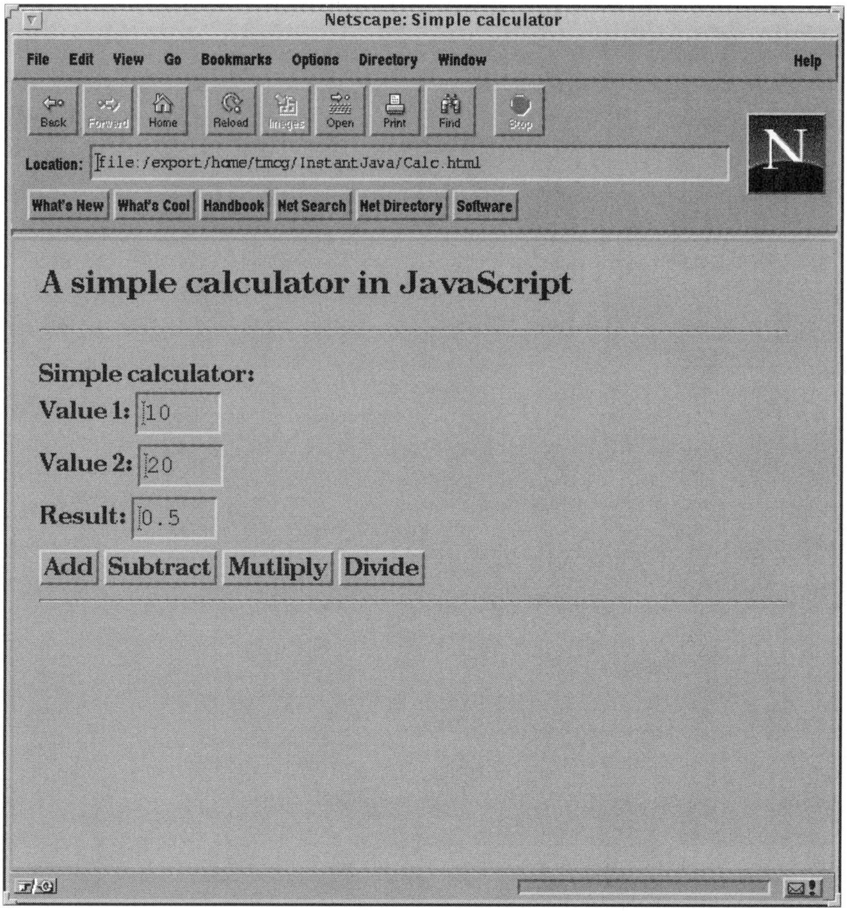

Figure 2.8: A JavaScript calculator

Basic Customizable Applets

How this chapter is organized

HelloWorld applet

Input and output from files in Java

Animation applet

Ticker applet

PlaySound applet

Chapter 3

In this chapter, we'll assume that you have read the first two parts of this book and have a basic understanding of Java syntax and object-oriented concepts. We'll review the basics here, but to gain a good understanding of the source code, we recommend that you go back and read the sections that precede this if you have not already done so.

To refresh your memory, here are some basic Java terms that you should be familiar with at this point:

Applet A Java program that can be accessed from a Web page with an HTML APPLET tag.

Class The basic unit of programming in Java. Each new type of object that you wish to define in a Java program should be enclosed within a new class of its own. When each separate piece of functionality in a program is done inside a separate class, you have clean encapsulation.

Method Each class consists of a set of functions, called methods in object parlance. Methods can be class methods or instance methods. A *class method* is defined by declaring the method to be static. There is only one copy of the class method for all copies of the class running in a particular program. This is different from an instance method, where you have one copy of the method (conceptually) for each time you create a new variable of that type.

Object An instance of a particular class. You can have many objects of one class in a particular Java applet.

Inheritance If you're writing a new class that makes a modification to the behavior of an existing class in Java, you can tell Java that your class "extends" the existing class. This means that your class inherits from the existing class. Your class then has access to all the functions of the existing class. All the applets described in this chapter inherit from the Applet class, which already exists in Java.

Interface A collection of definitions of functions that can be implemented in several ways. Once an interface is defined, Java classes can then be said to "implement" the interface, which means that they implement each of the functions in the interface definition.

Thread An independent process within the Java virtual machine. Threads are used pervasively within Java. If you want your class to be run as a separate thread within the Java virtual machine, it must implement the Runnable interface, which means that you must have a run() method in your class.

The applets we'll discuss in this chapter represent some of the useful things that you can do with Java on your Web page. We've chosen these applets in part because of how easy they are to use and customize.

How this chapter is organized

The description for each applet is divided into four sections: Class Hierarchy, Flow of Control, Source Code with Annotations, and a last section featuring customizations to the applet.

CLASS HIERARCHY

The Class Hierarchy section contains a diagram of the inheritance tree for the applet. While this may not be particularly important for the applets that we present here, since they all have relatively few classes, it is important to start thinking in terms of class hierarchies in the object-oriented world of Java.

The Class Hierarchy section will also help you understand the concept of encapsulation, which is one of the basic concepts of object-oriented programming. Encapsulation refers to the division of functionality into various classes, so that each class does one thing and does it well. This is an important idea in the world of objects and we try to reinforce it here with the use of these class hierarchy diagrams, which define what the classes within each applet are and what function each class performs.

FLOW OF CONTROL

When you look at the source code for an applet, it is useful to have a picture of the order in which the code is executed. The flow of control diagram for each applet walks us through the applet as it performs its tasks. Before you begin reading and customizing the source code, it is essential to know which part of the applet you want to customize to achieve the particular modification in functionality that would satisfy your needs. This will save you time when you want to make a simple modification to the behavior already in the applet.

SOURCE CODE WITH ANNOTATION

We've included the complete source code for each applet along with detailed annotations. Each new feature and important customization is defined and explained as it occurs in the code.

CUSTOMIZATION WITH PARAMETERS

This section is particularly important for Webmasters who are interested in configuring and customizing the applets for their own use. Each applet described allows itself to be configured by reading in parameters from the HTML file from which it is called. You can change these parameters to reflect your particular needs. You do not have to worry about altering the source code if all your needs can be met by changing the parameter values in the HTML file.

Now that you some idea of the structure of each description, on to the applets themselves.

HelloWorld applet

The purpose of describing the HelloWorld, one of Java's simplest applets, is to provide an understanding of the infrastructure that Java provides for each applet that you write or modify. Since the HelloWorld applet is simple, it allows us to concentrate on Java's support structure.

CLASS HIERARCHY

The HelloWorld Applet *inherits* (gets basic functionality) from the Applet class, which already exists in Java. The Applet class encapsulates the basic functions that an applet may be called upon to perform in its lifetime. Some of these functions include initializing variables, reading parameters, and starting and stopping the applet. This class is provided as a convenience to programmers so that all they need to do is modify the existing functionality to fit the needs of their particular program.

Figure 3.1 shows the inheritance hierarchy (the path all the way to the root of the Java class tree) of HelloWorld. Note that all the classes above HelloWorld have already been provided by Java. These classes provide various functions that HelloWorld uses without having to worry about implement them. These include creating the initial applet window and painting the letters on the screen. All you need to do is to add a few lines of code to one of the methods in the existing Applet class in order to change the behavior of the Applet class and make it display the "Hello World" string on the screen.

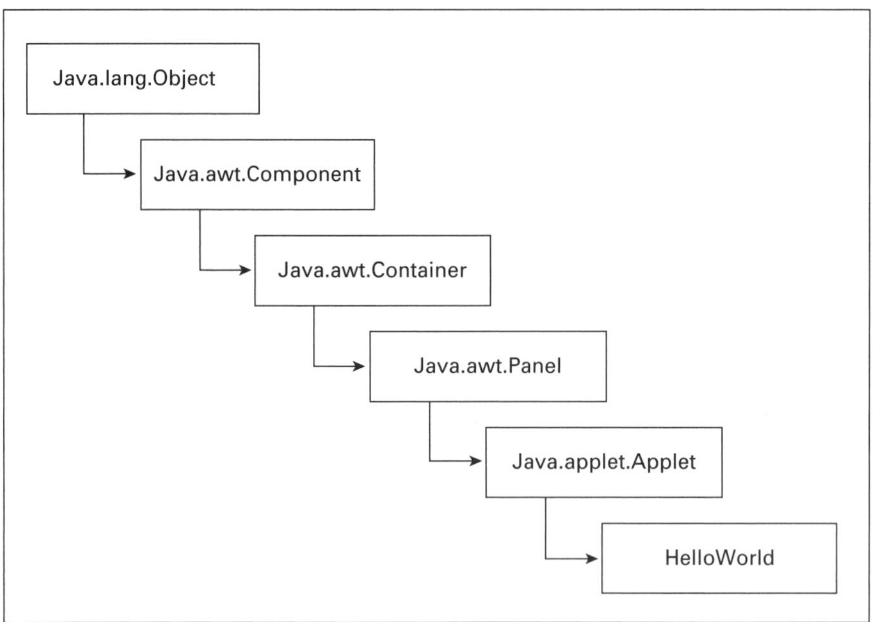

Figure 3.1: Class hierarchy of HelloWorld

As you can see from Figure 3.1, the Object class is the base class for HelloWorld. In fact, the Object class is the base class for all Java programs, and it has methods that perform housekeeping duties common to all classes. Since the HelloWorld class inherits from, or *extends*, Applet, it also has access to all the methods (functions) in class Applet as well as to all classes up the Java class tree to Object.

FLOW OF CONTROL IN HELLOWORLD APPLET

To understand the flow of control inside any applet, it is important that we first gain an understanding of the applet's implicit functions—that is, those provided to our applet by the basic Java Applet class and all the classes above it in the Java class tree. Once we know the functionality we are beginning with, we can then decide where to make the modifications necessary for our applet. Here we outline the methods of the Applet class. Keep these in mind as you go through the source code in this chapter, since each and every applet *overrides* (changes the functionality from what it was in the basic Applet class) at least one of these methods.

The Java Applet Class and Its Methods The *init()* method does the following things:

- It initializes variables.
- It reads parameters specified in the HTML APPLET tag. Parameters are read in with another method in the applet class, getParameter().

The *start()* method, on the other hand, performs those tasks that need to be done every time the user accesses the applet page. While the init() function is only invoked once when the applet is called the first time, the start() function is called every time a user follows a link to the page that includes the APPLET tag. After the first time that user accesses the page, Java saves the state of the applet as it was when the user left the page and reloads the applet when the user gets back to the page. This is efficient since the work that goes into initializing the applet and loading it into the Java virtual machine is not redone every time the applet needs to be run.

The *stop()* method is exactly the opposite of start(); it stops the applet when the user leaves the page that contains the applet. The default behavior in Java is to stop an applet when you leave a page and start the applet when you access it again.

The *destroy()* method is used by applets to perform a final clean-up (in other words, to reclaim space used by variables in the applet) before the applet exits.

FLOW OF CONTROL IN HELLOWORLD

First, the init() function resizes the applet window to a desired size. Since there are no parameters to read in from the HTML APPLET tag, there are no calls to getParameter(). A modification that you could try is to make the string that is displayed a parameter that the HelloWorld applet reads rather than being hard-coded in the Applet code.

Control then passes to the paint() function, which does the actual drawing on the screen—in this case, the words *Hello World*. The paint() function is implemented in the Java.awt.Component class in the Java class tree. The Component class is three levels above the HelloWorld class, but the HelloWorld class does not care where the paint() method resides; it merely calls the method with the string that it wants to draw.

After the paint() method has finished, control returns to the user and the applet waits for user events such as a key press or mouse click.

SOURCE CODE WITH ANNOTATION

Listing 3.1 shows the source code for the HelloWorld applet.

Listing 3.1: Source code for HelloWorld

```
import java.awt.Graphics;
public class HelloWorld extends java.applet.Applet {

        public void init() {
            resize(150,25);
    }

    public void paint(Graphics g) {
        g.drawString("Hello world!", 50, 25);
    }
}
```

This line includes the Graphics class and all its methods for use in HelloWorld. The Graphics class is used to draw the HelloWorld string.

The *public* keyword makes HelloWorld accessible from other packages either directly or through an import statement.

The *extends* keyword defines the inheritance relationship. In this case, HelloWorld inherits from Applet. This means we're going to take advantage of the existing functionality in java.applet.Applet as a starting point for HelloWorld.

The Applet class also has an init() method, which is empty. Here we override that method and include a resize() statement in ours to make the applet window a certain size upon initialization.

The paint method from the Component class is modified here to draw the "Hello World" string on the screen. The two numbers are the coordinates that determine where the string should appear relative to the applet window. 0,0 is taken as the upper-left-hand corner.

MAJOR CUSTOMIZATION POINTS

The HelloWorld applet can be customized to display any message in any size window that will fit on your display. It is included here mostly to give you a basic understanding of the structure around the applet. Knowing this structure will help when we move on to more complex applets that do a lot more and can be customized in a number of ways.

INPUT AND OUTPUT FROM FILES IN JAVA

The AliasEdit applet reads data from a file and displays it for the user to edit. Once the user has edited the data, the applet then saves the data in the same file. This is a simple form of input and output from Java, but it is surprisingly useful for a wide variety of tasks on your Web site. For almost any kind of persistent state (information about users who have connected to your Web site previously) that you want to keep, storing the data in files is a good option. At the end of this chapter, you should be able to display, edit, and save files using applets.

The specific file that AliasEdit displays and edits is a mail alias. A mail alias file consists of two entries per line, separated by a colon. The left side of the colon is the alias and the right side is the address to which the alias points.

All files are represented inside a Java applet with streams. A *stream* is nothing more than a Java name for a physical sequence of bits. You can have streams that you read from (streams that already have a sequence of bits waiting to be read) or streams that you write to (streams that are waiting for you to send them a sequence of bits that they will then write to a file or elsewhere). You can use various kinds of streams in Java, depending on what form your data is in. The list below is not exhaustive, but should give you a general idea of what streams to use for the most common kinds of data.

- *FileInputStream* and *FileOutputStream* should be used when you have data in files that you want to read and write.
- *DataInputStream* and *DataOutputStream* are used for reading and writing text to files line by line.
- *BufferedInputStream* and *BufferedOutputStream* are used when you want to read or write large amounts of data. The data is stored in a buffer in memory for fast access and is only read or written when the buffer is full.

CLASS HIERARCHY FOR ALIASEDIT.JAVA

As shown in Figure 3.2, the AliasEdit class is the main class in the AliasEdit applet. This class has objects of two different types inside it. The AliasFile object encapsulates all the tasks that we expect to perform with the file. This includes opening, loading, saving, and closing the file. The AliasForm object represents all the user interface objects that you see on the screen. It is the GUI portion of the applet. The AliasEdit Applet divides itself neatly into these two portions. This also makes it simpler for you to customize this applet for use on your own Web site.

FLOW OF CONTROL IN ALIASEDIT APPLET

The methods for the three classes in the AliasEdit applet appear below the class names. As you can see in Figure 3.3, there are two distinct paths of flow control. The applet follows the first path when it is first initialized. The applet then waits for user events and performs tasks that depend on the action the user takes.

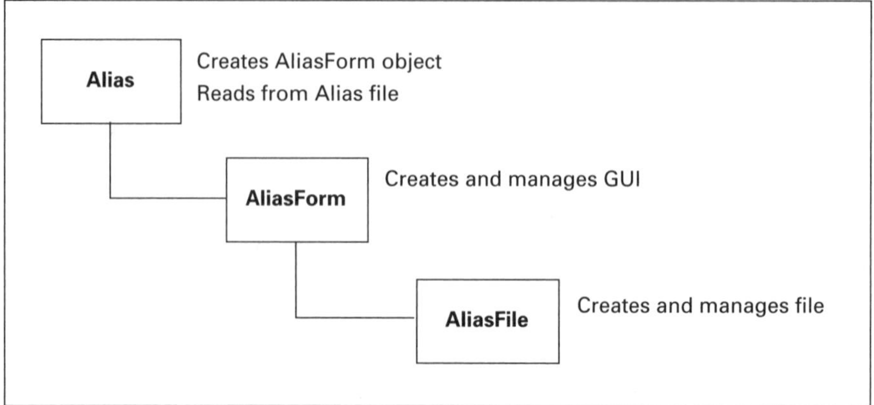

Figure 3.2: Class hierarchy for the AliasEdit applet

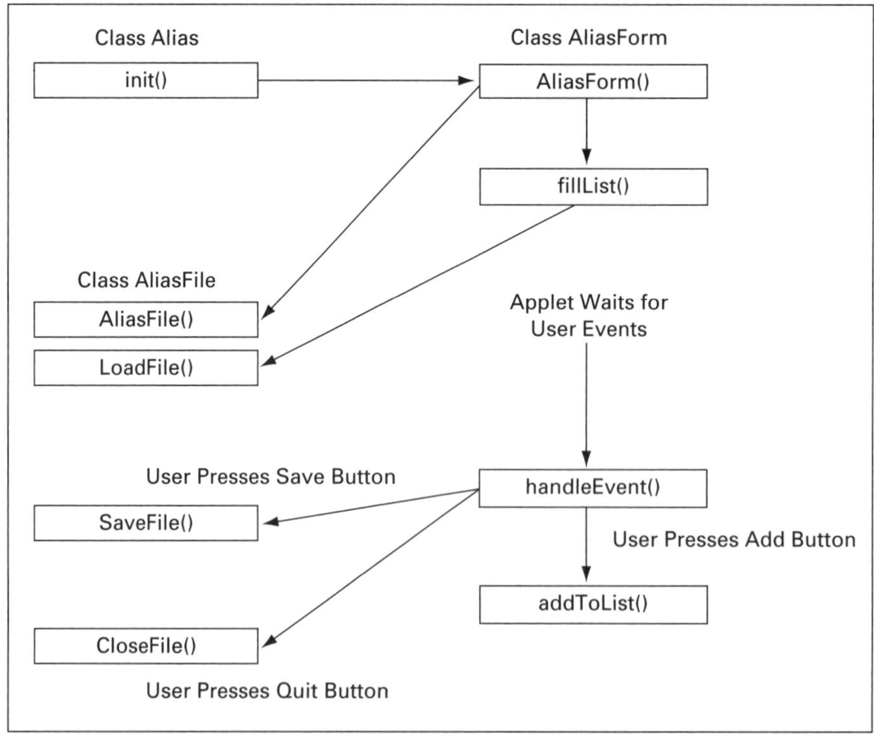

Figure 3.3: Flow of Control in AliasEdit

ANNOTATED SOURCE CODE

Listing 3.2 shows the complete source code, with annotations, for the AliasEdit applet.

Listing 3.2: Source code for Alias edit

```
import java.awt.*;
import java.io.*;
import java.lang.*;
import java.applet.*;
```

The usual includes for the java built-in classes that we want to use in our applet

```
public class Alias extends Applet {

  public void init() {
        String InputFile;
        String OutputFile;

        InputFile = getParameter("inputfile");
        OutputFile = getParameter("outputfile");

            AliasForm form = new AliasForm("Alias Edit", InputFile, OutputFile);
        form.fillList();
    }
}
```

Init() has two tasks: to get the parameters from the HTML file, and to create the top-level classes that the applet needs. In our case, the top level class is AliasForm.

AliasFile has responsibility for the file that contains all the aliases.

```
class AliasFile {

    FileInputStream infile;
    DataInputStream indata;
    FileOutputStream outfile;
    DataOutputStream outdata;
    String buffer;
```

The FileInputStream class is used as an intermediary to get to a DataInputStream, which lets the user read the data in line by line. You can easily “stack” streams in Java to achieve the kind of behavior that you want. More on this later in the source code.

```
   public AliasFile(String InputFileName) {
        try {
            infile = new FileInputStream(InputFileName);
            indata = new DataInputStream(infile);
        } catch (Exception e) {
        }
    }
```

This is the constructor for this class. The input streams are created here. The output streams are not created here, because the same file is used for input and output and creating an output stream would destroy the file before we have had a chance to read from it.

```
    public void LoadFile(List list) throws IOException {

       String line;
       int i = 0, count = 0;
        while ((line = indata.readLine()) != null) {
```

Read the data from the DataInputStream and use the list object on the GUI to display the data.

Listing 3.2: Source code for Alias edit (Continued)

```
            list.addItem(line);
        }
    }

    public void SaveFile(List list, int rows, String OutputFileName) {

      try {
      outfile = new FileOutputStream(OutputFileName);
      outdata = new DataOutputStream(outfile);
      } catch (IOException e) {
      }


     for (int i = 0; i < rows; i++) {
                buffer = list.getItem(i);
                try {
                outdata.writeBytes(buffer);
                outdata.writeBytes("\n");
                } catch (IOException e) {
                }
        }
    }

    public void CloseFile() {

            try indata.close(); catch (IOException e);
            try outdata.close(); catch (IOException e);
            try infile.close(); catch (IOException e);
            try indata.close(); catch (IOException e);
    }

}

class AliasForm extends Frame {

    MenuBar menubar;
    Menu file, help;
    Button add, build, clear, quit;
    Choice choice;
    CheckboxGroup profiles, export;
    TextField recipient, alias, count;
    List aliasList;
    int currentindex;
    Panel panel1, panel2;
    Panel buttonpanel;
    AliasFile aliasFile;

    String inaliasdb;
    String outaliasdb;
```

Creating the Output streams here in the SaveFile() method makes it safe to destroy the file, since we know we're going to save over it anyway.

We write out a newline character after every line we get from the list, since the newlines are not part of the string that we read from the list.

Java maintains a good policy of enclosing each open and close of an input or output stream in a try block. Doing this means that the application will always exit gracefully and never die because a file could not be opened or closed.

These are all the user interface components that make up the GUI. These will be described as we encounter them in the class.

The input and output files used for loading and saving the data

Listing 3.2: Source code for Alias edit (Continued)

```
GridBagLayout gridbag = new GridBagLayout();

public AliasForm(String title, String inaliasdb, String outaliasdb) {

    super(title);
    this.inaliasdb = inaliasdb;
    this.outaliasdb = outaliasdb;
    aliasFile = new AliasFile(inaliasdb);

    menubar = new MenuBar();
    this.setMenuBar(menubar);
    file = new Menu("File");
    file.add(new MenuItem("New"));
    menubar.add(file);
    help = new Menu("Help");
    help.add(new MenuItem("Index"));
    menubar.add(help);
    menubar.setHelpMenu(help);


    add = new Button("Add");
    build = new Button("Save and Build");
    clear = new Button("Clear");
    quit = new Button("Quit");

    recipient = new TextField(20);
    alias = new TextField(20);
    count = new TextField(5);
    recipient.setEditable(true);
    aliasList = new List(10,false);


panel1 = new Panel();
    panel2 = new Panel();
    buttonpanel = new Panel();


    panel1.setLayout(gridbag);
    panel2.setLayout(gridbag);
    buttonpanel.setLayout(new FlowLayout());
    buttonpanel.setLayout(gridbag);


    Font listFont = new Font("Helvetica", Font.PLAIN,12);
    aliasList.setFont(listFont);
```

The GridBagLayout() is among the most flexible provided by Java. It allows you to specify where each element will appear independently.

The superclass for AliasForm is frame that has a constructor that expects a string as its argument. This string becomes the title for the frame. It appears on the bar at the top of the window.

Create the components that make up the user interface for the alias form

Breaking the user interface into panels gives us more control over what component goes where and makes it easier to group components.

This sets the layouts for the panels. We had already decided to use gridbag, since it offers us the most flexibility in placing components.

This is where we choose a more readable font for the list.

Listing 3.2: Source code for Alias edit (Continued)

The constrain() method is overloaded here. There are three different methods with the same name, but a different number of arguments. This gives us flexibility as to which one to call. If we don't want to specify all the arguments, the ones left out will assume default values.

```
constrain(panel1, new Label("Recipient"),0,0,1,1);
constrain(panel1, recipient, 1,0,1,1);
constrain(panel1, new Label("Alias"), 0,1,1,1);
constrain(panel1, alias, 1,1,1,1);
constrain(panel1, new Label("Max. Characters"),2,1,1,1);
constrain(panel1, count, 3,1,1,1);
```

The three labels and text fields are placed in panel 1. (See comment for GridBagLayout explanation.)

The arguments in the above constrain() function are name of panel, name of component, row of component, column of component, no. of cells in width of component, and no. of cells in height of component.

```
constrain(panel2, new Label("File:"),0,0,1,1);
constrain(panel2, aliasList,0,1,40,1, GridBagConstraints.BOTH,
        GridBagConstraints.CENTER, 1.0,0.0,1,1,1,1);
```

The arguments in the call to constrain in the above line are name of panel, component, and x and y coordinates (0,1 means second row and first entry). The fill (HORIZONTAL, VERTICAL, NONE, BOTH) specifies whether the component should try to fill up all the space in either direction. The anchor specifies where in the panel the component should sit. The numbers with the decimal are the weights (border thickness) for the component. Then we have the four numbers that specify the insets for the component.

```
constrain(buttonpanel, add, 0,0,1,1, GridBagConstraints.NONE,
        GridBagConstraints.CENTER,0.3,0.0,0,0,0,0);
constrain(buttonpanel, build, 1,0,1,1, GridBagConstraints.NONE,
        GridBagConstraints.CENTER,0.3,0.0,0,0,0,0);
constrain(buttonpanel, clear, 2,0,1,1, GridBagConstraints.NONE,
        GridBagConstraints.CENTER,0.3,0.0,0,0,0,0);
constrain(buttonpanel, quit, 3,0,1,1, GridBagConstraints.NONE,
        GridBagConstraints.CENTER, 0.3,0.0,0,0,0,0);

this.setLayout(gridbag);
```

Set the layout for the whole form to be gridbag ("this" refers to the current object).

```
constrain(this, panel1, 0,0,1,1, GridBagConstraints.VERTICAL,
        GridBagConstraints.NORTHWEST, 0.0, 1.0, 10,10,5,5);
constrain(this, panel2, 0,1,1,1, GridBagConstraints.BOTH,
        GridBagConstraints.CENTER, 1.0,1.0, 10,10,5,10);
constrain(this, buttonpanel, 0,2,2,1, GridBagConstraints.HORIZONTAL,
        GridBagConstraints.CENTER, 1.0,0.0, 5,0,0,0);


    super.pack();
    super.show();
}
```

Send a message to the super class of AliasForm (Frame) to pack all the components within it and show them on the screen.

```
public void fillList() {
    try {
    aliasFile.LoadFile(aliasList);
    } catch (Exception e) {
    }
}
```

Fill the list with the data from the alias file. Since the file is the responsibility of the AliasFile class, the fillList() method merely calls the LoadFile() method in class AliasFile with the name of the list to fill in.

Listing 3.2: Source code for Alias edit (Continued)

```
    public void addToList() {
        aliasList.addItem(recipient.getText());
    }


public boolean handleEvent(Event evt) {

        if (evt.target == build) {
            aliasFile.SaveFile(aliasList, aliasList.getRows(), outaliasdb);
        }
        else if (evt.target == quit) {
            System.exit(0);
        }
        else if (evt.target == clear) {
            recipient.setText("");
            alias.setText("");
            count.setText("");
        }
        else if (evt.target == add) {
            addToList();
        }
        else if (evt.id == Event.LIST_SELECT) {
           currentindex = aliasList.getSelectedIndex();
           recipient.setText(aliasList.getItem(currentindex));
        }
        return true;
    }


    void constrain(Container container, Component component,
                      int grid_x, int grid_y, int grid_width,
                      int grid_height, int fill, int anchor,
                      double weight_x, double weight_y, int top,
                      int left, int bottom, int right)
    {

        GridBagConstraints c = new GridBagConstraints();
        c.gridx = grid_x; c.gridy = grid_y;
        c.gridwidth = grid_width; c.gridheight = grid_height;
        c.fill = fill; c.anchor = anchor;
        c.weightx = weight_x; c.weighty = weight_y;
        if (top+bottom+left+right>0) {
            c.insets = new Insets(top, left, bottom, right);
        }

        GridBagLayout gb = (GridBagLayout) container.getLayout();
```

The handleEvent() method handles all the user events after the applet is initialized. The general mode of operation here is to check which area of the GUI the event occurred in and do the task that is relevant.

If the user clicks on the Save and Build button, this saves the file to disk. The build portion is unimplemented.

This is the base constrain method; the other two call this one after filling in the missing arguments with defaults.

Set the values for the GridbagConstraints

This line gets us the GridBag Layout that the panel is using.

Listing 3.2: Source code for Alias edit (Continued)

```
            gb.setConstraints(component, c);
        container.add(component);
    }
```

Add the component to the panel after setting the constraints to what the component wants.

```
    void constrain(Container container, Component component,
                        int grid_x, int grid_y, int grid_width,
                        int grid_height)
    {

        constrain(container, component, grid_x, grid_y, grid_width,
                grid_height, GridBagConstraints.NONE,
                GridBagConstraints.NORTHWEST,
                0.0,0.0,0,0,0,0);
    }
```

This calls the constrain method above with the left out arguments filled in.

```
void constrain(Container container, Component component,
               int grid_x, int grid_y, int grid_width,
int grid_height, int top, int left, int bottom, int right)
    {

        constrain(container, component, grid_x, grid_y, grid_width,
                grid_height, GridBagConstraints.NONE,
                GridBagConstraints.NORTHWEST,
                0.0,0.0, top, left, bottom, right);
    }

}
```

This calls the constrain method above with the left-out arguments filled in.

CUSTOMIZING THE APPLET WITH PARAMETERS

There are two parameters that can be customized on the Input/Output applet: the input file and the output file. You can specify which input file to read from and which output file to write to. Note that in our example, both files were the same. Here are some other customizations you might want to try:

- Filter the data and look for certain words. This can be done using a FilterInputStream class.
- Use a relational database instead of a flat file. In this case, you will only need to modify the LoadFile and SaveFile methods in the AliasFile class to call the relevant query methods for your database. Commercial implementations of Java API's for Sybase, Oracle, and Informix already exist.

ANIMATION APPLET

The animation applet is the most complicated applet we'll explain in this book. It may seem unapproachable, but if you follow the flow of control outlined below, you will see that the parts of the applet that you would really want to customize for your own use are easy to understand.

CLASS HIERARCHY OF THE ANIMATION APPLET

As you can see from Figure 3.4, the animation applet is an extension of the Applet class. This applet implements the Runnable interface, which allows it to run as a separate thread.

> **NOTE** An applet is said to implement an interface if it implements all the methods specified in the interface. For the Runnable interface, only one method, run(), needs to be implemented.

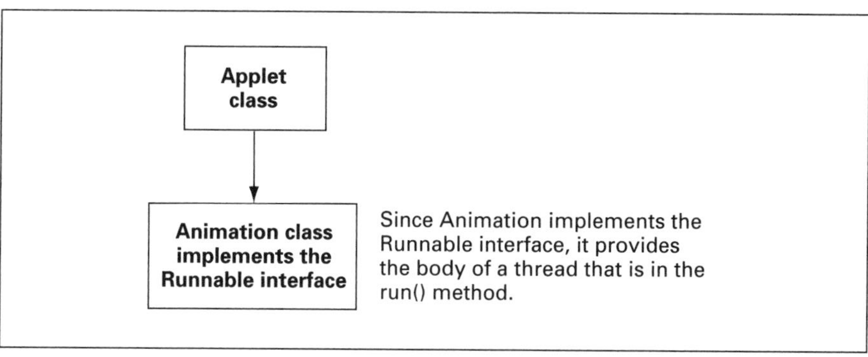

Figure 3.4: Class hierarchy of the animation applet

FLOW OF CONTROL WITHIN THE ANIMATION APPLET

Figure 3.5 shows the flow of control in the animation applet. The first method called in the applet is, as usual, init(). The init() method reads in and parses the parameters that are used in the HTML file for customizing the applet. The flow of control figure offers a relatively high-level view; this was done intentionally to give you a feel for the basic pieces of any animation in Java and not be bogged down by the details of this particular applet.

The start(), run(), and paint() loop is common to every animation that you will write in Java. While the handling of user event via a handleEvent() method may not seem like an essential part of an animation applet, it is important to give the user of the animation the control to start and stop the animation.

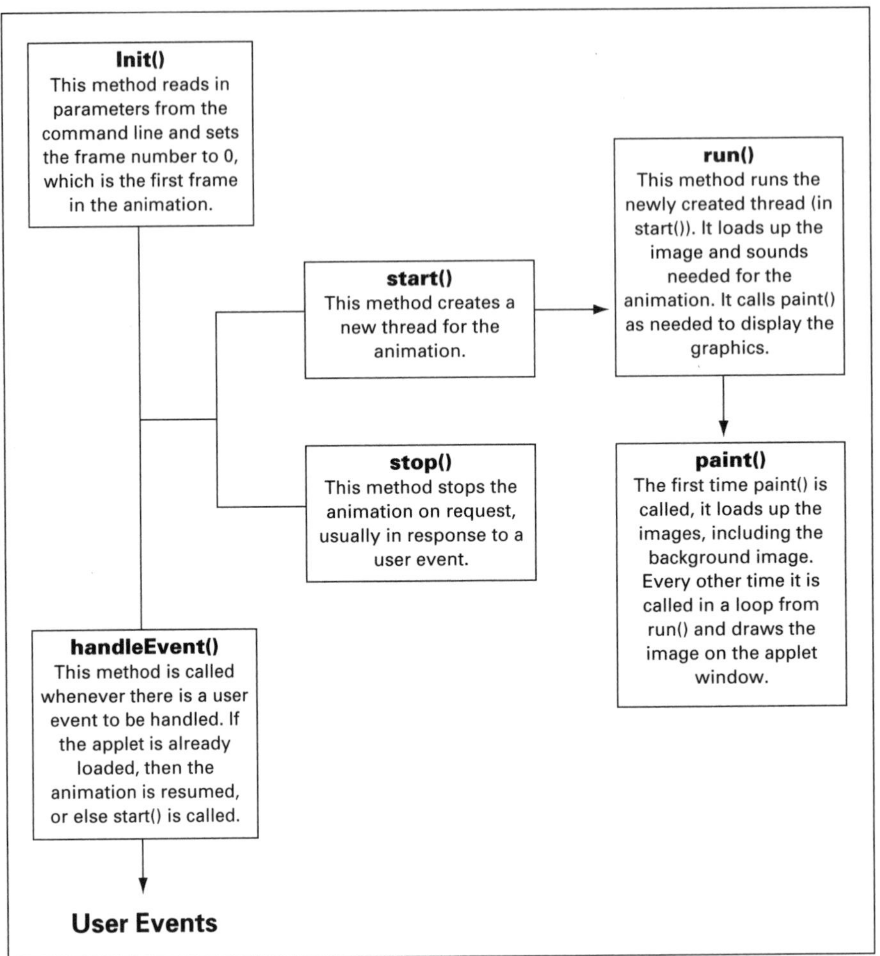

Figure 3.5: Flow of control in the animation applet

SOURCE CODE WITH ANNOTATIONS

There are three basic parts to this animation applet: a series of image files that together form the pieces of the animation; the position of each image within the animation; and the time that each image has to stay on the screen as part of the animation. There may or may not be an audio portion associated with each image. There may also be a soundtrack associated with the whole animation and not with any particular image in the animation.

What follows next is a review and analysis of the code from Animator.java. We'll point out the various places where you can customize the applet inside the source code. At the end of the source code annotation section, we'll tell you how to use parameters from within an HTML file to customize the applet without ever touching the source code. This is something to keep in mind when you write an applet. The best way to customize an applet is through the parameters, so make sure you give yourself and other users of your applet every opportunity to customize various aspects of the applet through the parameters.

Listing 3.3 shows the complete code listing for the animation applet.

Listing 3.3: Source code for Animator.java

```
import java.io.InputStream;
import java.awt.*;
import java.awt.image.ImageProducer;
import java.applet.Applet;
import java.applet.AudioClip;
import java.util.Vector;
import java.util.Hashtable;
import java.util.Enumeration;
import java.io.File;
import java.net.URL;
import java.net.MalformedURLException;

/**
 * An applet that plays a sequence of images, as a loop or a one-shot.
 * Can have a soundtrack and/or sound effects tied to individual frames.
 *
 * author Herb Jellinek
 */

public class Animator extends Applet implements Runnable {
    /* The images, in display order (Images). */
    Vector images = null;

    /**
     * Duration of each image (Integers, in milliseconds).
     */
    Hashtable durations = null;

    /**
     * Sound effects for each image (AudioClips).
     */
    Hashtable sounds = null;

    /**
     * Position of each image (Points).
     */
```

"Runnable" means Animator implements run() and stop() methods.

Think of a hashtable as a list of pairs. Here it maps each graphic to how long it must stay on the screen as part of the animation.

Listing 3.3: Source code for Animator.java (Continued)

```
Hashtable positions = null;
/**
 * Background image URL, if any.
 */
URL backgroundImageURL = null;
/**
 * Background image, if any.
 */
Image backgroundImage = null;
/**
 * Start-up image URL, if any.
 */
URL startUpImageURL = null;
/**
 * Start-up image, if any.
 */
Image startUpImage = null;
/**
 * The soundtrack's URL.
 */
URL soundtrackURL = null;
/**
 * The soundtrack.
 */
AudioClip soundtrack;
/**
 * Largest width.
 */
int maxWidth = 0;

/**
 * Largest height.
 */
int maxHeight = 0;

/**
 * Was there a problem loading the current image?
 */
boolean imageLoadError = false;

/**
 * The directory or URL from which the images are loaded
 */
URL imageSource = null;

/**
 * The directory or URL from which the sounds are loaded
 */
URL soundSource = null;
```

This tells the applet how big to make the frame in which the animation will be displayed. It needs to be big enough to show the largest image.

Listing 3.3: Source code for Animator.java (Continued)

```
/**
 * The thread animating the images.
 */
Thread engine = null;

/**
 * The current loop slot - index into 'images.'
 */
int frameNum;

/**
 * frameNum as an Object - suitable for use as a Hashtable key.
 */
Integer frameNumKey;

/**
 * The current X position (for painting).
 */
int xPos = 0;

/**
 * The current Y position (for painting).
 */
int yPos = 0;

/**
 * The default number of milliseconds to wait between frames.
 */
public static final int defaultPause = 3900;

/**
 * The global delay between images, which can be overridden by
 * the PAUSE parameter.
 */
int globalPause = defaultPause;

/**
 * Whether or not the thread has been paused by the user.
 */
boolean userPause = false;

/**
 * Repeat the animation?  If false, just play it once.
 */
boolean repeat;

/**
 * Load all images before starting display, or do it asynchronously?
```

This tells us which frame we're currently on.

Listing 3.3: Source code for Animator.java (Continued)

```
    */
    boolean loadFirst;
    /**
     * The offscreen image, used in double buffering
     */
    Image offScrImage;

    /**
     * The offscreen graphics context, used in double buffering
     */
    Graphics offScrGC;

    /**
     * Can we paint yet?
     */
    boolean loaded = false;

    /**
     * Was there an initialization error?
     */
    boolean error = false;

    /**
     * What we call an image file in messages.
     */
    final static String imageLabel = "image";

    /**
     * What we call a sound file in messages.
     */
    final static String soundLabel = "sound";

    /**
     * Print silly debugging info?
     */
    boolean debug = false;

    /**
     * Info.
     */
    public String getAppletInfo() {
     return "Animator Applet by Herb Jellinek";
    }

    /**
     * Parameter Info
     */
    public String[][] getParameterInfo() {
     String[][] info = {
```

Listing 3.3: Source code for Animator.java (Continued)

```
        {"imagesource", "url", "a directory"},
        {"startup", "url", "displayed at startup"},
        {"background", "url", "displayed as background"},
        {"startimage", "int", "start index"},
        {"endimage", "int", "end index"},
        {"pause", "int", "milliseconds"},
        {"pauses", "ints", "milliseconds"},
        {"repeat", "boolean", "repeat or not"},
        {"positions","coordinates", "path"},
        {"soundsource","url", "audio directory"},
        {"soundtrack","url", "background music"},
        {"sounds","urls","audio samples"},
    };
    return info;
    }

    /**
     * Print silly debugging info.
     */
    void dbg(String s) {
     if (debug) {
         System.out.println(s);
     }
    }

final int setFrameNum(int newFrameNum) {
     frameNumKey = new Integer(frameNum = newFrameNum);
     return frameNum;
    }


public synchronized boolean imageUpdate(Image img, int infoFlags,
                 int x, int y,
        int width, int height) {
       if ((infoFlags & ERROR) != 0) {
              imageLoadError = true;
     }

     notifyAll();
     return true;
}

    void updateMaxDims(Dimension dim) {
          maxWidth = Math.max(dim.width, maxWidth);
          maxHeight = Math.max(dim.height, maxHeight);
    }

    /**
     * Parse the IMAGES parameter.  It looks like
```

"Synchronized" means that this method does things that make it undesirable for it to be called simultaneously by two routines. (See note at the end of code.)

Listing 3.3: Source code for Animator.java (Continued)

```
     * 1|2|3|4|5, etc., where each number (item) names a source image.
     *
     * Returns a Vector of image file names.
     */
    Vector parseImages(String attr) {
          Vector result = new Vector(10);
          for (int i = 0; i < attr.length(); ) {
              int next = attr.indexOf('|', i);
              if (next == -1) next = attr.length();
              String file = attr.substring(i, next);
              result.addElement(file);
              i = next + 1;
          }
          return result;
    }

    /**
     * Fetch the images named in the argument, updating
     * maxWidth and maxHeight as we go.
     * Is restartable.
     *
     * @return URL of the first bogus file we hit, null if OK.
     */
    URL fetchImages(Vector images) {
         for (int i = 0; i < images.size(); i++) {
         Object o = images.elementAt(i);
         if (o instanceof URL) {
                 URL url = (URL)o;
                 tellLoadingMsg(url, imageLabel);
                 Image im = getImage(url);
                 try {
                     updateMaxDims(getImageDimensions(im));
                 } catch (Exception e) {
                     return url;
                 }
                 images.setElementAt(im, i);
                     }
                 }
                 return null;
    }

    /**
     * Parse the SOUNDS parameter.  It looks like
     * train.au||hello.au||stop.au, etc., where each item refers to a
     * source image.  Empty items mean that the corresponding image
     * has no associated sound.
     *
     * @return a Hashtable of SoundClips keyed to Integer frame numbers.
     */
```

"Fill the images vector with the images that were specified in the images parameter."

Listing 3.3: Source code for Animator.java (Continued)

```
    Hashtable parseSounds(String attr, Vector images)
    throws MalformedURLException {
          Hashtable result = new Hashtable();

          int imageNum = 0;
          int numImages = images.size();
          for (int i = 0; i < attr.length(); ) {
              if (imageNum >= numImages) break;

              int next = attr.indexOf('|', i);
              if (next == -1) next = attr.length();

              String sound = attr.substring(i, next);
              if (sound.length() != 0) {
                    result.put(new Integer(imageNum),
                               new URL(soundSource, sound));
              }
              i = next + 1;
              imageNum++;
          }

          return result;
    }

    /**
     * Fetch the sounds named in the argument.
     * Is restartable.
     *
     * @return URL of the first bogus file we hit, null if OK.
     */
URL fetchSounds(Hashtable sounds) {
     for (Enumeration e = sounds.keys() ; e.hasMoreElements() ;) {
         Integer num = (Integer)e.nextElement();
         Object o = sounds.get(num);
         if (o instanceof URL) {
                 URL file = (URL)o;
                 tellLoadingMsg(file, soundLabel);
                 try {
                     sounds.put(num, getAudioClip(file));
                 } catch (Exception ex) {
                     return file;
                 }
         }
     }
     return null;
    }
    /**
     * Parse the PAUSES parameter.  It looks like
     * 1000|500|||750, etc., where each item corresponds to a
```

This is a common Java idiom for creating a loop around some data that you already have. You can create an object of the off class enumeration and use hasMoreElements() to traverse the data.

Listing 3.3: Source code for Animator.java (Continued)

```
     * source image.  Empty items mean that the corresponding image
     * has no special duration, and should use the global one.
     *
     * @return a Hashtable of Integer pauses keyed to Integer
     * frame numbers.
     */
Hashtable parseDurations(String attr, Vector images) {
     Hashtable result = new Hashtable();

     int imageNum = 0;
     int numImages = images.size();
     for (int i = 0; i < attr.length(); ) {
         if (imageNum >= numImages) break;

         int next = attr.indexOf('|', i);
         if (next == -1) next = attr.length();

         if (i != next - 1) {
                 int duration = Integer.parseInt(attr.substring(i, next));
                 result.put(new Integer(imageNum), new Integer(duration));
         } else {
                 result.put(new Integer(imageNum),
                    new Integer(globalPause));
         }
         i = next + 1;
         imageNum++;
     }
     return result;
    }
    /**
     * Parse a String of form xxx@yyy and return a Point.
     */
    Point parsePoint(String s) throws ParseException {
     int atPos = s.indexOf('@');
     if (atPos == -1) throw new ParseException("Illegal position: "+s);
     return new Point(Integer.parseInt(s.substring(0, atPos)),
      Integer.parseInt(s.substring(atPos + 1)));
    }
    /**
     * Parse the POSITIONS parameter.  It looks like
     * 10@30|11@31|||12@20, etc., where each item is an X@Y coordinate
     * corresponding to a source image.  Empty items mean that the
     * corresponding image has the same position as the preceding one.
     *
     * @return a Hashtable of Points keyed to Integer frame numbers.
     */
Hashtable parsePositions(String param, Vector images)
  throws ParseException {
     Hashtable result = new Hashtable();
```

Listing 3.3: Source code for Animator.java (Continued)

```
    int imageNum = 0;
    int numImages = images.size();
    for (int i = 0; i < param.length(); ) {
        if (imageNum >= numImages) break;

        int next = param.indexOf('|', i);
        if (next == -1) next = param.length();
        if (i != next) {
                result.put(new Integer(imageNum),
                   parsePoint(param.substring(i, next)));
        }
        i = next + 1;
        imageNum++;
    }
    return result;
}

/**
 * Get the dimensions of an image.
 * @return the image's dimensions.
 */
synchronized Dimension getImageDimensions(Image im)
throws ImageNotFoundException {
      // Get the width of the image.
      int width;
      int height;

      while ((width = im.getWidth(this)) < 0) {
          try {
                 wait();
          } catch (InterruptedException e) { }
          if (imageLoadError) {
                  throw new ImageNotFoundException(im.getSource());
          }
      }

      // Get the height of the image.
      while ((height = im.getHeight(this)) < 0) {
          try {
                  wait();
          } catch (InterruptedException e) { }
          if (imageLoadError) {
                  throw new ImageNotFoundException(im.getSource());
          }
      }

      return new Dimension(width, height);
```

This method is synchronized because we don't want two routines resizing the image at the same time.

Listing 3.3: Source code for Animator.java (Continued)

```
    /**
     * Stuff a range of image names into a Vector.
     * @return a Vector of image URLs.
     */
    Vector prepareImageRange(int startImage, int endImage)
    throws MalformedURLException {
          Vector result = new Vector(Math.abs(endImage - startImage) + 1);
          if (startImage > endImage) {
              for (int i = startImage; i >= endImage; i--) {
                      result.addElement(new URL(imageSource, "T"+i+".gif"));
              }
          } else {
              for (int i = startImage; i <= endImage; i++) {
                      result.addElement(new URL(imageSource, "T"+i+".gif"));
              }
          }
          return result;
    }


   /* Initialize the applet.  Get parameters.
     */
    public void init() {

     try {

String param = getParameter("IMAGESOURCE");
        imageSource = (param == null) ? getDocumentBase() : new
URL(getDocumentBase(), param + "/");
        dbg("IMAGESOURCE = "+param);

        param = getParameter("PAUSE");
        globalPause =
        (param != null) ? Integer.parseInt(param) : defaultPause;
        dbg("PAUSE = "+param);

        param = getParameter("REPEAT");
        repeat = (param == null) ? true : (param.equalsIgnoreCase("yes") ||
param.equalsIgnoreCase("true"));

        int startImage = 1;
        int endImage = 1;
        param = getParameter("ENDIMAGE");
        dbg("ENDIMAGE = "+param);
        if (param != null) {
               endImage = Integer.parseInt(param);
               param = getParameter("STARTIMAGE");
               dbg("STARTIMAGE = "+param);
```

First method to get called in any applet. Used to parse parameters.

Exception handler for all errors encountered in getting parameters.

Listing 3.3: Source code for Animator.java (Continued)

```
                    if (param != null) {
                        startImage = Integer.parseInt(param);
                    }
                    images = prepareImageRange(startImage, endImage);
        } else {
                    param = getParameter("STARTIMAGE");
                    dbg("STARTIMAGE = "+param);
                    if (param != null) {
                        startImage = Integer.parseInt(param);
                        images = prepareImageRange(startImage, endImage);
                    } else {
                        param = getParameter("IMAGES");
                        if (param == null) {
                                showStatus("No legal IMAGES, STARTIMAGE, or
                                    ENDIMAGE "+ "specified.");
                                return;
                        } else {
                                images = parseImages(param);
                        }
                    }
        }
        param = getParameter("BACKGROUND");
        dbg("BACKGROUND = "+param);
        if (param != null) {

    backgroundImageURL = new URL(imageSource, param);
        }

        param = getParameter("STARTUP");
        dbg("STARTUP = "+param);
        if (param != null) {
                startUpImageURL = new URL(imageSource, param);
        }

        param = getParameter("SOUNDSOURCE");
        soundSource = (param == null) ? imageSource : new
URL(getDocumentBase(), param + "/");
        dbg("SOUNDSOURCE = "+param);

        param = getParameter("SOUNDS");
        dbg("SOUNDS = "+param);
        if (param != null) {
                sounds = parseSounds(param, images);
        }

        param = getParameter("PAUSES");
        dbg("PAUSES = "+param);
        if (param != null) {
                durations = parseDurations(param, images);
```

Creates a new URL object to store background image.

Listing 3.3: Source code for Animator.java (Continued)

```
        }

        param = getParameter("POSITIONS");
        dbg("POSITIONS = "+param);
        if (param != null) {
               positions = parsePositions(param, images);
        }

        param = getParameter("SOUNDTRACK");
        dbg("SOUNDTRACK = "+param);
        if (param != null) {
               soundtrackURL = new URL(soundSource, param);
        }
    } catch (MalformedURLException e) {
        showParseError(e);
    } catch (ParseException e) {
        showParseError(e);
    }
    setFrameNum(0);
   }
```

Two kinds of exceptions can occur in getting parameters: badly formed URLs and parsing errors. These exceptions are thrown in each case.

This is the line that gets us going. It sets the frame vector to 0, which is where we start. This line is also the last line in the init() method. The start() method gets called next.

```
void tellLoadingMsg(String file, String fileType) {
    showStatus("Animator: loading "+fileType+" "+abridge(file, 20));
   }

   void tellLoadingMsg(URL url, String fileType) {
          tellLoadingMsg(url.toExternalForm(), fileType);
   }

   void clearLoadingMessage() {
    showStatus("");
   }

   /**
    * Cut the string down to length=len, while still keeping it readable.
    */
   static String abridge(String s, int len) {
          String ellipsis = "...";

          if (len >= s.length()) {
              return s;
          }

          int trim = len - ellipsis.length();
          return s.substring(0, trim / 2)+ellipsis+
              s.substring(s.length() - trim / 2);
```

Listing 3.3: Source code for Animator.java (Continued)

```
    }

    void loadError(URL badURL, String fileType) {
          String errorMsg = "Animator: Couldn't load "+fileType+" "+
              badURL.toExternalForm();
           showStatus(errorMsg);
           System.err.println(errorMsg);
           error = true;
           repaint();
    }

    void showParseError(Exception e) {
           String errorMsg = "Animator: Parse error: "+e;
           showStatus(errorMsg);
           System.err.println(errorMsg);
           error = true;
           repaint();
    }

    void startPlaying() {
           if (soundtrack != null) {
               soundtrack.loop();
           }
    }

    void stopPlaying() {
           if (soundtrack != null) {
               soundtrack.stop();
           }
    }

    /**
     * Run the animation. This method is called by class Thread.
     * @see java.lang.Thread
     */
    public void run() {
           Thread me = Thread.currentThread();

           me.setPriority(Thread.MIN_PRIORITY);

           if (! loaded) {
               try {
                     // ... to do a bunch of loading.
                     if (startUpImageURL != null) {
                         tellLoadingMsg(startUpImageURL, imageLabel);
                         startUpImage = getImage(startUpImageURL);
                         try {
                              updateMaxDims(getImageDimensions(startUpImage));
               } catch (Exception e) {
```

The heart of any applet that implements the Runnable interface This method controls the animation, since it belongs to the animation thread and not the main applet thread.

If there is a starting image, load it up.

Listing 3.3: Source code for Animator.java (Continued)

```
            loadError(startUpImageURL, "start-up image");
        }
        resize(maxWidth, maxHeight);
        repaint();
    }

    if (backgroundImageURL != null) {
        tellLoadingMsg(backgroundImageURL, imageLabel);
        backgroundImage = getImage(backgroundImageURL);
        repaint();
        try {
              updateMaxDims(
              getImageDimensions(backgroundImage));
        } catch (Exception e) {
              loadError(backgroundImageURL, "background image");
        }
    }

    URL badURL = fetchImages(images);
    if (badURL != null) {
        loadError(badURL, imageLabel);
        return;
    }

    if (soundtrackURL != null && soundtrack == null) {
        tellLoadingMsg(soundtrackURL, imageLabel);
        soundtrack = getAudioClip(soundtrackURL);
        if (soundtrack == null) {
              loadError(soundtrackURL, "soundtrack");
              return;
        }
    }

    if (sounds != null) {
        badURL = fetchSounds(sounds);
        if (badURL != null) {
              loadError(badURL, soundLabel);
              return;
        }
    }
    clearLoadingMessage();
    offScrImage = createImage(maxWidth, maxHeight);
    offScrGC = offScrImage.getGraphics();
    offScrGC.setColor(Color.lightGray);

    resize(maxWidth, maxHeight);
    loaded = true;
    error = false;
} catch (Exception e) {
```

The repaint() method ends up calling the paint() method, which does the real work of drawing on the screen.

Get the images all ready to go by loading them into an images vector. A *vector* is a list of elements of any type.

This is the off-screen image and graphics context used in double buffering to reduce flicker.

Listing 3.3: Source code for Animator.java (Continued)

```
                error = true;
                e.printStackTrace();
            }
        }
        if (userPause) {
            return;
        }
        if (repeat || frameNum < images.size()) {
            startPlaying();
        }

        try {
            if (images.size() > 1) {
                while (maxWidth > 0 && maxHeight > 0 && engine == me) {
                    if (frameNum >= images.size()) {
                        if (!repeat) {
                            return;
                        }
                        setFrameNum(0);
                    }
                    repaint();

                    if (sounds != null) {
                        AudioClip clip =
                            (AudioClip)sounds.get(frameNumKey);
                        if (clip != null) {
                            clip.play();
                        }
                    }

                    try {
                            Integer pause = null;
                            if (durations != null) {
                                pause = (Integer)durations.get(frameNumKey);
                            }
                            if (pause == null) {
                                Thread.sleep(globalPause);
                            } else {
                                Thread.sleep(pause.intValue());
                            }
                    } catch (InterruptedException e) {
                        // Should we do anything?
            }
            setFrameNum(frameNum+1);
        }
            }
        } finally {
            stopPlaying();
        }
```

- `startPlaying();` — This starts the audio loop, which plays the soundtrack.
- `if (frameNum >= images.size()) {` — Check to see if the animation is done
- `if (!repeat) {` — If it is not repeating, then it is done.
- `setFrameNum(0);` — If it's repeating, then set frame to 0.
- `setFrameNum(frameNum+1);` — This is the increment for the main loop of the animation that runs with the run() method. Incrementing the frame number then lets the paint() method work on the next frame.
- `stopPlaying();` — If the animation is not repeating, stop the audio as well.

Listing 3.3: Source code for Animator.java (Continued)

```
}

/**
 * Paint the current frame.
 */
public void paint(Graphics g) {
 if (error || !loaded) {
     if (startUpImage != null) {
         g.drawImage(startUpImage, 0, 0, this);
     } else {
         if (backgroundImage != null) {
             g.drawImage(backgroundImage, 0, 0, this);
         } else {
             g.clearRect(0, 0, maxWidth, maxHeight);
         }
     }
 } else {
     if ((images != null) && (images.size() > 0)) {
            if (frameNum < images.size()) {
                if (backgroundImage == null) {
                       offScrGC.fillRect(0, 0, maxWidth, maxHeight);
                } else {
                       offScrGC.drawImage(backgroundImage, 0, 0, this);
                }

                Image image = (Image)images.elementAt(frameNum);
                Point pos = null;
                if (positions != null) {
                       pos = (Point)positions.get(frameNumKey);
                }
                if (pos != null) {
                       xPos = pos.x;
                       yPos = pos.y;
                }
                offScrGC.drawImage(image, xPos, yPos, this);
                g.drawImage(offScrImage, 0, 0, this);
            } else {
                // no more animation, but need to draw something
                dbg("No more animation; drawing last image.");
                g.drawImage((Image)images.lastElement(), 0, 0, this);
            }
     }
 }
 }

 /**
  * Start the applet by forking an animation thread.
  */
```

The paint() method actually does the drawing part of the animation.

This part of paint() loads images for the first time or if there was an initialization error.

This part deals with the next frame as the main loop in run() increments frameNum.

Load up background image to off screen.

Set positions for the next image. These are then arguments to drawImage.

Listing 3.3: Source code for Animator.java (Continued)

```
    public void start() {
        if (engine == null) {
            engine = new Thread(this);
            engine.start();
     }
    }

    /**
     * Stop the insanity, um, applet.
     */
    public void stop() {
        if (engine != null && engine.isAlive()) {
            engine.stop();
        }
            engine = null;
    }

    /**
     * Pause the thread when the user clicks the mouse in the applet.
     * If the thread has stopped (as in a non-repeat performance),
     * restart it.
     */
    public boolean handleEvent(Event evt) {
        if (evt.id == Event.MOUSE_DOWN) {
            if (loaded) {
                if (engine != null && engine.isAlive()) {
                    if (userPause) {
                        engine.resume();
                        startPlaying();
                    } else {
                        engine.suspend();
                        stopPlaying();
                    }
                    userPause = !userPause;
                } else {
                    userPause = false;
                    setFrameNum(0);
                    engine = new Thread(this);
                    engine.start();
                }
            }
            return true;
        } else {
            return super.handleEvent(evt);
        }
    }
}
class ParseException extends Exception {
    ParseException(String s) {
```

This gets called right after init(). Instantiate a new thread with the current object as the target, and then start it off. This will eventually call run().

Override of handleEvent that resumes or starts the applet

If engine was not initialized yet, start it off from the start of the thread. Engine is the thread that runs the animation.

If the applet was not loaded, let the super class of Animator handle this event.

Listing 3.3: Source code for Animator.java (Continued)

```
        super(s);
    }
}

class ImageNotFoundException extends Exception {
    ImageNotFoundException(ImageProducer source) {
        super(source+"");
    }
}
```

Synchronized Methods A method is usually labeled as "synchronized" when it does things that need to be done serially, that is, one at a time. It would then be undesirable for that method to be called by two routines at the same time. By using the keyword *synchronize* in the method title, the Java interpreter is told to make sure that the method is not called simultaneously by more than one routine. The interpreter does this by associating a *monitor* with the routine. When the routine calls notifyAll(), the monitor then notifies all other routines waiting to call the synchronized routine that it is now safe for them to do so. What really happens then is that all the routines waiting on the synchronized method fight it out among themselves as to who will be the next one to call the method.

PARAMETER CUSTOMIZATIONS FROM HTML FILES

An animation consists of images and sounds. The animation applet allows you to customize both of these parts without changing the source code. The only changes that need to be made are to the HTML file that drives the applet. Most well-written applets will let you change the important parameters from the HTML file.

Customizing Images To substitute your own images in the animation, you need to change two parameters in the animation.html:

```
<param name=imagesource value="images/Globe">
```

and

```
<param name=endimage value=7>
```

The *imagesource* parameter tells the Java interpreter that the image source is a directory called images/Globe. This is a relative path from the directory in which the HTML resides. You can specify a different path by using the codebase parameter, which should point to the base directory of your applet. The images are named as T1.gif, T2.gif, and so on. Following this scheme will make your images portable, since Sun follows this convention for all their images.

The *endimage* parameter lets the applet know when to stop and redo the animation. The number 7 points to T7.gif. The images are thus numbered from T1 to T7.

Customizing Sounds To substitute your own sound, you can change up to three parameters in the animation.html file:

```
<param name=soundsource value="audio">
<param name=soundtrack value=spacemusic.au>
```

and

```
<param name=sounds value="1.au|2.au|3.au|4.au|5.au|6.au|7.au">
```

The *soundsource* parameter points to a directory relative to the directory in which the HTML file resides. You can change this with the *codebase* parameter, which points to a base directory for your applet.

The *sounds* parameter consists of a series of audio files that you can associate with each image of your animation. The audio files must be numbered the way they are above unless you make source code changes.

The *soundtrack* parameter gives you the option of specifying either a file or a URL for a sound file as the soundtrack for your animation. This soundtrack will start playing when your animation starts and will repeat as long as the animation runs. You can have both a soundtrack parameter and a sounds parameter to play two sounds at once. This may be useful when you want to have background music and a voiceover for specific images in a animation.

Customizing Image Duration, Position, and Repeat The repeat parameter,

```
<param name=repeat value="true">
```

is true by default. If you would like to change it so your animation runs only once, you can set it to false.

The pauses parameter,

```
<param name=pauses value="1000|1000|||||750">
```

tells the applet how long to keep each image in the animation on the screen. The values are in milliseconds, so the first image will stay on for 1 second, as will the second image. The || symbol tells the applet to use the global default for the duration of the image. The last image will stay for three quarters of a second.

The positions parameter,

```
<param name=positions value="30@10|50@10|90@10|||||">
```

specifies where on the screen your images will appear. Make sure that your applet window is big enough to handle the coordinates that you put in here.

This can be done by changing the width and height parameters, as shown below. The numbers represent *x* and *y* coordinates, with the upper-left corner being 0,0.

TICKER APPLET

Tickers are among the most commonly used applets on Web pages. Ticker applets are different from the animation applet presented in the last section. In an animation, a series of images is displayed on the screen in some order. Each image stays on the screen for a period of time specified by the animator. In a ticker applet, one image is redrawn incrementally a number of times.

CLASS HIERARCHY FOR TICKER

The ticker applet, like all other applets that we have seen, inherits from the basic Applet class in Java. As you can see from Figure 3.6, there is only one public class in the ticker applet, which is the main Ticker class. There are two other classes are not visible to the outside world and are available only to the Ticker class. These classes are TickerText and TickerTextAttributes.

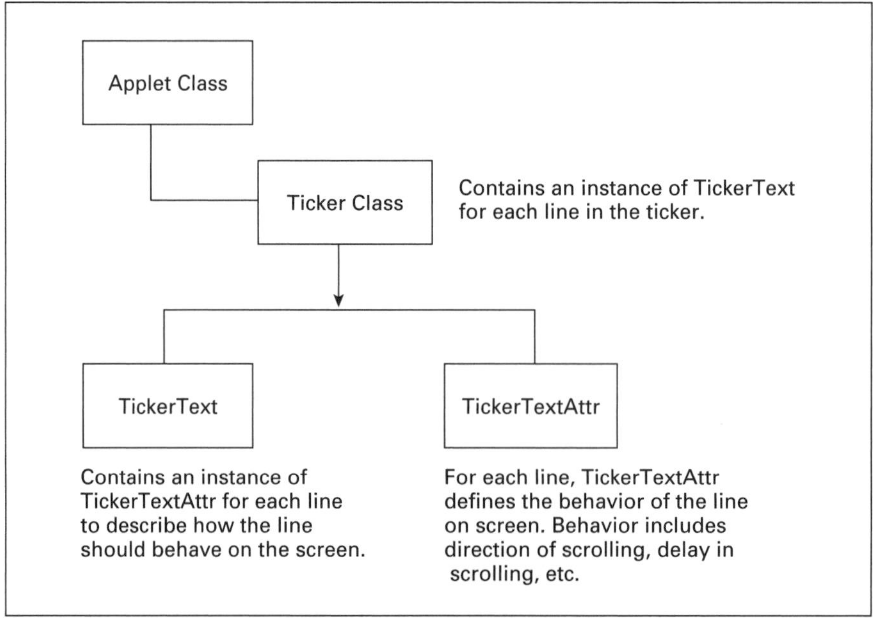

Figure 3.6: Class hierarchy for ticker applet

The TickerText class encapsulates each line of text in the ticker. So, for each line in the ticker, we create an object of type TickerText. TickerTextAttributes encapsulates the properties of each line in the text. An object of class TickerTextAttr is created for every line in the ticker.

FLOW OF CONTROL WITHIN TICKER APPLET

The init() method reads in all the parameters and calls createAnimatedTexts(). This method creates an object of type TickerText and TickerTextAttr for each line in the ticker, as mentioned in the class hierarchy. Once these objects have been created, the start() method in the Ticker class is called. This happens because Ticker is a subclass of Applet, whose default behavior is to call its start() method. The start() method in this case creates a new Thread(), with the Ticker object itself as the argument, and it calls the start() method of the Thread class. The start() method in the Thread() class always searches for and calls the run() method, which the class Ticker has implemented. This idiom of creating a Thread() with the calling object itself as the argument is away of getting around the lack of multiple inheritance in Java. Our program needs to be a subclass of Applet to be run as an applet, yet it needs to run as a separate thread without becoming a subclass of Thread, because Java does not allow a class to be a subclass of two different classes. Figure 3.7 does not show all these interactions, since they are not useful in understanding the basic operational loop of a ticker in Java. The run() method in class Ticker calls repaint(), which calls update(). In any application that draws and updates the screen, the methods that need to be modified are update() and paint().

SOURCE CODE WITH ANNOTATIONS

Listing 3.4 shows the complete source code for the ticker applet, along with annotations.

Listing 3.4: Source code for ticker applet

```
/*
 * Ticker class and program.
 * Amit Bhatiani
 * Ideas and code borrowed from Tom Wendt and Jan Andersson
*/

import java.applet.*;
import java.awt.*;
import java.util.*;
import java.lang.*;
import java.net.*;
```

Here are the familiar import directives. These are classes we're going to need in this applet.

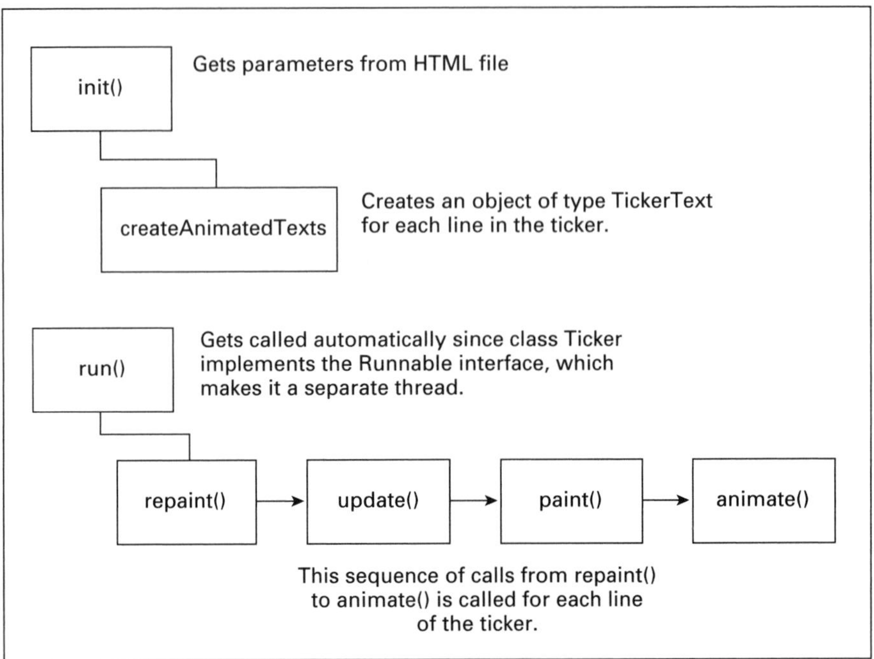

Figure 3.7: Flow of control in the ticker applet

Listing 3.4: Source code for ticker applet (Continued)

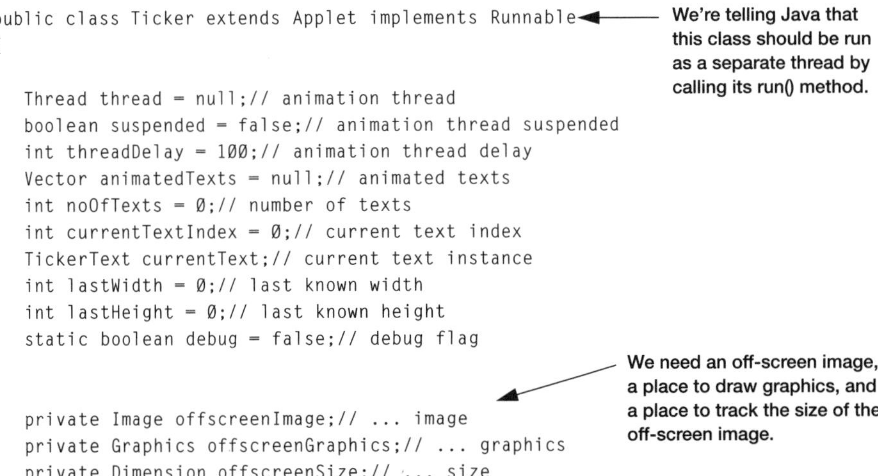

```
public class Ticker extends Applet implements Runnable
{

   Thread thread = null;// animation thread
   boolean suspended = false;// animation thread suspended
   int threadDelay = 100;// animation thread delay
   Vector animatedTexts = null;// animated texts
   int noOfTexts = 0;// number of texts
   int currentTextIndex = 0;// current text index
   TickerText currentText;// current text instance
   int lastWidth = 0;// last known width
   int lastHeight = 0;// last known height
   static boolean debug = false;// debug flag


   private Image offscreenImage;// ... image
   private Graphics offscreenGraphics;// ... graphics
   private Dimension offscreenSize;// ... size
```

We're telling Java that this class should be run as a separate thread by calling its run() method.
We need an off-screen image, a place to draw graphics, and a place to track the size of the off-screen image.

Listing 3.4: Source code for ticker applet (Continued)

```
Color fg;
Color bg;
Image img;

/**
 * Init applet
 */
public void init()
{
  String lines[] = initLineParameters();

  // get color parameters
  fg = readColor(getParameter("fgColor"), Color.black);
  bg = readColor(getParameter("bgColor"), getBackground());
  setBackground(bg);
  setForeground(fg);

  // get font parameters
  String fontName = getParameter("font");
  if (fontName == null)
  fontName = "TimesRoman";
  String fontSize = getParameter("size");
  if (fontSize == null)
  fontSize = "22";
  int size = Integer.valueOf(fontSize).intValue();
  Font font = new Font(fontName, Font.BOLD, size);

  // get animation thread delay time
  String par = getParameter("delay");
  if (par != null)
  threadDelay = Integer.valueOf(par).intValue();

  // get deltax/deltay movement
  int deltax = 6;
  int deltay = 2;
  par = getParameter("deltax");
  if (par != null)
  deltax = Integer.valueOf(par).intValue();
  par = getParameter("deltay");
  if (par != null)
  deltay = Integer.valueOf(par).intValue();


  // get delimiters string
  String delim = getParameter("delim");
  try {
  img = getImage(new URL(getDocumentBase(), "snap.gif"));
  } catch (Exception e) {
  }
```

Read all the text lines that we have specified in the HTML file and put them into an array called lines[]

Gets font parameters from the HTML file and creates a new object of class Font with which to set the font

The delay parameter defines how long each ticker string must stay on the screen.

Deltax and deltay define how far to move the ticker text in the x and y direction each time through the ticker loop.

Listing 3.4: Source code for ticker applet (Continued)

```
    // create animated texts
    createAnimatedTexts(lines, font, fg, bg, deltax, deltay, delim);
}

/**
* Init unparsed line parameters
*/
protected String[] initLineParameters()
{
    String par;
    // get unparsed line parameters
    dbg("get line parameters...");
    String lines[] = new String[10];
    for (int i=0; i<10; i++) {
    String parName = "line" + i;
    par = getParameter(parName);
    lines[i] = par;
    dbg("  " + parName + ":" + par);
    }
    if (lines[0] == null) {
    // assume no line parameter provided; use default
    lines[0] = "<20>" + getAppletInfo();
    }
    return lines;
}

/**
* Applet Info.
*/
public String getAppletInfo() {
    return "Ticker Applet...Stand By";
}

/**
 * Parameter Info.
 */
public String[][] getParameterInfo() {
    // More should be added...
    String[][] info = {
    {"line0",   "string", "Message line 0" },
    {"linen",   "string", "Message line <n>" },
    {"line9",   "string", "Message line 9" },
    {"delim",   "string", "Delimiter string (<>)" },
    {"font",    "string", "Message font (TimesRoman)" },
    {"size",    "int",    "Message font size (22)" },
    {"delay",   "int",    "Animation delay time in millisec. (100)" },
    {"deltax",      "int",
           "No of pixels to move horizontally for each animation (2)" },
    {"deltay",      "int",
```

This function creates an object of type TickerText for each line in the ticker. All the arguments to this function are parameters used by TickerText objects.

This routine takes the parameters specified by line1, line2, and so on in the HTML file and stuffs them into an array called lines for further use by the applet.

This prints out parameter info when asked: This is useful for new users of the applet.

Listing 3.4: Source code for ticker applet (Continued)

```
            "No of pixels to move vertically for each animation (1)" },
        {"fgColor", "hex",     "Foreground Color" },
        {"bgColor", "hex",     "Background Color" },
        };
        return info;
    }

    /**
     * Convert a Hexadecimal String with RGB-Values to Color
     * Uses aDefault, if no or not enough RGB-Values
     */
    public Color readColor(String aColor, Color aDefault) {
        if ((aColor == null) ||
         (aColor.charAt(0) != '#') ||
         (aColor.length() != 7 )) {
        return aDefault;
        }

        try {
        Integer rgbValue = new Integer(0);
        rgbValue = Integer.valueOf(aColor.substring(1, 7), 16);
        return new Color(rgbValue.intValue());
        }
        catch (Exception e) {
        return aDefault;
        }
    }

    /**
     * Create animated texts
     */
    public void createAnimatedTexts(String lines[], Font font,
          Color fg, Color bg,
          int deltax, int deltay,
          String delim)
    {
        noOfTexts = 0;
        animatedTexts = new Vector(10);
        dbg("Creating Animated Text...");
        for (int i=0; i<10; i++) {
        if (lines[i] == null)
           break;
        dbg("  " + lines[i]);
           animatedTexts.addElement(
              new TickerText(
              this, lines[i], font, fg, bg, deltax, deltay, delim));
        noOfTexts++;
        }
```

For each ticker string that we previously read into the array lines, create an object of type TickerText. CurrentTextIndex points to the string being shown.

Listing 3.4: Source code for ticker applet (Continued)

Start with the first line. The array goes from 0 to 9.

```
        currentTextIndex = 0;
        currentText = (TickerText)
        animatedTexts.elementAt(currentTextIndex);
    }

    /**
     * Animate the texts
     */
    public void animate(Graphics g) {
        // update current text
        if (currentText.update(g)) {
        // done; get next text
        currentTextIndex++;
        if (currentTextIndex >= noOfTexts)
            currentTextIndex = 0;
        currentText = (TickerText)
            animatedTexts.elementAt(currentTextIndex);
        currentText.reset(lastWidth, lastHeight);
        }
    }

    /**
     * Paint the graphics
     */
    public void paint(Graphics g) {
        if (lastWidth != size().width || lastHeight != size().height) {
        lastWidth = size().width;
        lastHeight = size().height;
        // reset Animated Text item
         currentText.reset(lastWidth, lastHeight);
        }
        animate(g);
    }

    /**
     * Update off-screen graphics
     *
     */
     public final synchronized void update (Graphics theG)
     {
        Dimension d = size();
        if((offscreenImage == null) || (d.width != offscreenSize.width) ||
        (d.height != offscreenSize.height)) {
        offscreenImage = createImage(d.width, d.height);
        offscreenSize = d;
        offscreenGraphics = offscreenImage.getGraphics();
        offscreenGraphics.fillRect(0,0,d.width-1, d.height-1);
        offscreenGraphics.setFont(getFont());
```

This calls the update() method in class TickerText, which actually does the drawing and the moving of the text.

Move on to the next string by incrementing the index. If we're done with all the strings, set index back to 0 to start repeating the ticker sequence. Reset the width and height of the ticker area if the outside window changed.

Paint() checks to see of the outside window size changed. If so, it resets the inside text drawing area to the same size. It then calls animate().

The update() method is called by repaint(). It does the double-buffering by creating the actual image off screen first and then drawing it all at once on the screen. This reduces flicker and makes the ticker smoother.

Listing 3.4: Source code for ticker applet (Continued)

```
        }
        offscreenGraphics.setColor(getBackground());
        offscreenGraphics.fillRect(0,0,d.width, d.height);
        paint(offscreenGraphics);
        theG.drawImage(offscreenImage, 0, 0, this);
    }

    /**
     * Run the loop. This method is called by class Thread.
     */
    public void run() {
        Thread.currentThread().setPriority(Thread.MIN_PRIORITY);
        while (thread != null) {
        repaint();
        try {Thread.sleep(threadDelay);}
        catch (InterruptedException e){}
        }
    }

    /*
     * Start the applet by forking an animation thread.
     */
    public void start() {
        if (thread == null) {
        thread = new Thread(this);
        thread.start();
        }
    }

    /**
     * Stop the applet. The thread will exit because run() exits.
     */
    public void stop() {
        thread = null;
    }

    /**
     * Suspend/Resume
     */
    public boolean mouseDown(Event evt, int x, int y) {
        // handle Suspend/Resume
        if (suspended) {
        thread.resume();
        }
        else {
        thread.suspend();
        }
        suspended = !suspended;
        // show version
```

The body of the thread. The run() method gets called first. It calls repaint(), which calls update(). (annotation pointing to `while (thread != null) {`)

Create a new thread and call its start() method. That, in turn, calls run(), which holds the body of the thread. (annotation pointing to `if (thread == null) {`)

Listing 3.4: Source code for ticker applet (Continued)

```
      if (suspended)
      showStatus(getAppletInfo());
      return true;
   }

   /**
    * Simple debug...
    */
   static public void dbg(String str) {
      if (debug) {
      System.out.println("Debug: " + str);
      System.out.flush();
      }
   }
}

/**
 * Attributes of Ticker Animated Text
 */
class TickerTextAttr
{
     // scroll styles:
   static final int NONE = 0;// no scrolling (default)
   static final int LEFT = 1;// scroll left
   static final int RIGHT = 2;// ... right
   static final int UP = 3;// ... up
   static final int DOWN = 4;// ... down
     // text styles:
   static final int NORMAL = 0;// normal (default)
   static final int NERVOUS = 1; // "nervous" text
                 // IMAGE?
   static final int IMAGE = 5;

   String msg = "";// message line
   String image;        // if image, then we need a string to store the image
location.
   String delimiters = "<>";// used delimiters (default is "<>")
   int startScroll = NONE;// start scroll style
   int endScroll = NONE;// end scroll style
   int showDelay = 10;// start delay
   int endDelay = -1;// end delay
   int style = NORMAL;// text style

   public TickerTextAttr(String line, String delim)
   {
      if (delim != null) {
      // used specified delimiter
      delimiters = delim;
      }
```

Each TickerText object contains an object of type TickerTextAttr to store the scroll direction, delay, and other parameters for each string in the ticker.

Listing 3.4: Source code for ticker applet (Continued)

```
      parse(line);
   }

   public String msg()
   {
      return msg;
   }

   public int startScroll()
   {
      return startScroll;
   }

   public int endScroll()
   {
      return endScroll;
   }

   public int showDelay()
   {
      return showDelay;
   }

   public int endDelay()
   {
      return endDelay;
   }

   public int style()
   {
      return style;
   }

   void parse(String line)
   {
      StringTokenizer st = new StringTokenizer(line, delimiters);
      boolean gotText = false;
      while (st.hasMoreTokens()) {
      int scroll = -1;
      String token = st.nextToken();
      // parse scroll style
      if (token.equalsIgnoreCase("left"))
            scroll = LEFT;
      if (token.equalsIgnoreCase("right"))
            scroll = RIGHT;
      if (token.equalsIgnoreCase("up"))
            scroll = UP;
      if (token.equalsIgnoreCase("down"))
            scroll = DOWN;
```

For each line, read the attributes specified in the HTML file and assign them to variables

Determines which way to scroll to get the text on and off the screen. StartScroll is the direction of scrolling to begin showing the text and endScroll is the direction to end showing the text.

Listing 3.4: Source code for ticker applet (Continued)

```
if (scroll >= 0) {
   if (!gotText)
      startScroll = scroll;
   else
      endScroll = scroll;
   continue;
}

// parse text style
if (token.equalsIgnoreCase("nervous")) {
   style = NERVOUS;
   continue;
}

if (token.equalsIgnoreCase("image")) {
   style = IMAGE;
   continue;
}
// check if integer, if so assume delay value
boolean isInt = true;
for (int i=0; i<token.length(); i++) {
   int digit = Character.digit(token.charAt(i), 10);
   if (digit < 0) {
      // not a digit
      isInt = false;
      break;
   }
}

if (style == IMAGE) {
   // we have an image
   gotText = true;
   image = token;
}
if (isInt) {
   try {
      if (!gotText)
 showDelay = Integer.parseInt(token);
      else
 endDelay = Integer.parseInt(token);
   } catch (NumberFormatException ne) {}
   continue;
}
else {
   // assume text string parsed
   if (!gotText) {
      msg = token;
      gotText = true;
   }
```

Read in the delay while the string is being shown and the delay after it's been shown.

Listing 3.4: Source code for ticker applet (Continued)

```
      }
     }
   }

}

/**
 * TickerText - Ticker Animated text class
 */
class TickerText
{
                        // states:
   static final int START = 0;// start sequence
   static final int SHOW = 1;// show sequence
   static final int END = 2;// end sequence
   static final int DONE = 3;// done sequence
   int state = START;// animate state
   TickerTextAttr attr;// attributes
   char chars[];// the characters
   int noOfChars;// number of characters
   int xPos[];// the x positions
   int yPos[];// the y positions
   boolean visible[];// flags set to true if character visible
   int delayCount = 0;// used to delay for a while
   int width;// the applet width
   int height;// the applet height
   int textHeight;// text height
   int lineHeight;// text line height
   Color bg;// background color
   Color fg;// foreground color
   Font font;// font
   int maxWidth;// max width
   int charWidth;
    int currXPos = 0;
   int xStart;// starting X pos
   int yStart;// starting Y pos
   int deltax;// x distance to move
   int deltay;// y distance to move
   String msg = "";
   Image image;
   int msgWidth = 0;

   public TickerText(Ticker appl, String line,
            Font font, Color fg, Color bg,
            int deltax, int deltay, String delim)
   {
      this.font = font;
      this.fg = fg;
      this.bg = bg;
```

We create a TickerText object for each string of the ticker that is specified in the HTML file.

Listing 3.4: Source code for ticker applet (Continued)

```
this.deltay = deltay;
this.deltax = deltax;
// parse message line and init attributes
attr = new TickerTextAttr(line, delim);

appl.dbg("Parsed Attributes:");
appl.dbg("        msg:" + attr.msg());
appl.dbg(" startScroll:" + attr.startScroll());
appl.dbg("   endScroll:" + attr.endScroll());
appl.dbg("   showDelay:" + attr.showDelay());
appl.dbg("    endDelay:" + attr.endDelay());
appl.dbg("       style:" + attr.style());
appl.dbg("deltay:" + deltay + " deltax:" + deltax);

if (attr.msg() != "")
{
msg = attr.msg();
image = getImage(new URL(jattr.image();
noOfChars = msg.length();
chars = new char[noOfChars];
msg.getChars(0, noOfChars, chars, 0);
xPos = new int[noOfChars];
yPos = new int[noOfChars];
visible = new boolean[noOfChars];
FontMetrics fm = appl.getFontMetrics(font);
msgWidth = fm.stringWidth(msg);
if (attr.style() == TickerTextAttr.NERVOUS)
// need some extra space here!
textHeight = 4 + font.getSize();
else
textHeight = font.getSize();
lineHeight = font.getSize();

int currYPos = fm.getAscent();
boolean escape = false;
boolean newLine = false;
for (int i = 0; i < noOfChars; i++) {
if (escape) {
   // we already have an escape character
   if (chars[i] == 'n') {
      // got "\n" - line break; i.e line really consists
      // of more than one line
      chars[i-1] = ' ';
      chars[i] = ' ';
      newLine = true;
   }
   escape = false;
}
else if (chars[i] == '\\') {
```

Create an attributes object for this string that we're currently in. Remember, each TickerText object is a string in the ticker.

We set the length of the text and define xPos and yPos to be integer arrays with size equal to the length of the ticker text. These arrays are used to determine if all the text has been shown on the screen. The height and width of the string must be known in order to determine when the text is off and on the screen.

Listing 3.4: Source code for ticker applet (Continued)

```
        // escaped characted; wait for next character
        escape = true;
     }
     else {
        if (newLine) {
           // we have a new line
           textHeight += deltay * 2 + font.getSize();
           currXPos = fm.charsWidth(chars, 0, i);
           System.out.println("currXPos = " + currXPos);
           currYPos += fm.getDescent() + fm.getAscent();
           newLine = false;
        }
        xPos[i] = fm.charsWidth(chars, 0, i) - currXPos;
        maxWidth = Math.max(maxWidth, xPos[i]);
        yPos[i] = currYPos;
     }
     }
     }
     else {
       // we have an image to deal with
     }
  }

  /**
   * Reset width and height
   */
  void reset(int width, int height)
  {
     this.width = width;
     this.height = height;
     int scroll = attr.startScroll();
     switch (scroll) {
     case TickerTextAttr.NONE:
        xStart = (width-maxWidth)/2;
        yStart = height/2;
        break;
     case TickerTextAttr.LEFT:
     if (deltax <=4) {
        xStart = width-deltax;
     } else {
        xStart = width-4;
     }
        yStart = height/2;
        break;
     case TickerTextAttr.RIGHT:
     if (deltax <= 4) {
        xStart = -msgWidth;
     } else {
        xStart = -msgWidth;
```

We have to set the height of the text accordingly if it consists of more than one line.

If we want to restart the scrolling of the ticker text, the reset() method restores the text to its original position, depending on which direction the scrolling is supposed to move.

Listing 3.4: Source code for ticker applet (Continued)

```
      }
        yStart = height/2;
        break;
      case TickerTextAttr.UP:
        xStart = (width-maxWidth)/2;
        yStart = height;
        break;
      case TickerTextAttr.DOWN:
        xStart = (width-maxWidth)/2;
        yStart = 0-textHeight;
        break;
      }
      state = START;
      Ticker.dbg("State: START");
  }

   /**
   * Update method for AnimatedText
   */
  boolean update(Graphics g)
  {
      move();
      paint(g);
      if (state == DONE && delayCount < 0)
      return true;// we are done!
      else
      return false;
  }

  /**
   * Move characters
   */
  void move()
  {
      switch (state) {
      case START:
         // start sequence
         boolean switchState = false;
         int scroll = attr.startScroll();
         if (scroll == TickerTextAttr.NONE) {
            // no animation; just switch state
            switchState = true;
         }
         else {
            // some kind of animation; check if all characters displ.
           if (textDisplayed(scroll)) {
           // yupp; switch state
           switchState = true;
            }
```

This method gets called from the main Ticker class. It in turn calls move() and paint(). It also checks if the current text is done displaying and if it has been displayed for the delay period specified.

We haven't shown the ticker text yet. Check to see if we have a string and if it has been displayed. Setting switchState to true means that we can start checking what's visible and set the delayCount.

Listing 3.4: Source code for ticker applet (Continued)

```
        }
        if (switchState == true) {
           // switch state
           updateVisible();
           state = SHOW;
           Ticker.dbg("State: SHOW");
           delayCount = attr.showDelay();
        }
        else {
           // just move text (scroll)
           moveText(scroll);
           updateVisible();
        }
        break;

     case SHOW:
        // show sequence
        if (delayCount-- < 0) {
           // switch state
           state = END;
           Ticker.dbg("State: END");
        }
        break;

     case END:
        // end sequence
        // check if all characters still visible
        if (updateVisible() == 0 ||
           attr.endScroll() == TickerTextAttr.NONE) {
           // none visible or no end animation; switch state
           state = DONE;
           Ticker.dbg("State: DONE");
           delayCount = attr.endDelay();
           return;
        }
        else {
           moveText(attr.endScroll());
        }
        break;

     case DONE:
        // done sequence; just delay
        delayCount--;
        break;
     }
  }

  /**
   * Return true if (all) text is displayed
```

The text is visible; we're going to keep updating how much of it is visible and changing the state variable to denote that the we're currently SHOWING the text.

We have finished showing all the text; now it's time to go through the delay at the end. This is in the DONE part of the case statement.

Listing 3.4: Source code for ticker applet (Continued)

```
 */
boolean textDisplayed(int scroll)
{
   switch (scroll) {
   case TickerTextAttr.LEFT:
      // scrolling left
      if (maxWidth > width) {
         // text is wider that applet width
        if (maxWidth+xStart < width-4*deltax)
           return true;
      }
      else {

         int appletEndPoint = 0;
         int textEndPoint = xStart+msgWidth;
         if (textEndPoint <= appletEndPoint)
            return true;
      }
      break;

   case TickerTextAttr.RIGHT:
      // scrolling right
      if (maxWidth > width) {
         // text is wider that applet width
         if (xPos[0]+xStart > 4*deltax)
            return true;
      }
      else {
         int appletEndPoint = width;
         int textEndPoint = xStart;
         if (textEndPoint >= appletEndPoint)
            return true;
      }
      break;

   case TickerTextAttr.UP:
      // scrolling up
      if (yStart <= (height-textHeight)/2)
         return true;
      break;

   case TickerTextAttr.DOWN:
      // scrolling down
      if (yStart >= height+textHeight)
         return true;
      break;
   }
   return false;
}
```

For each direction of scrolling, check if we have shown all the text.

Listing 3.4: Source code for ticker applet (Continued)

```
/**
 * update array with flags if characters are visible. Return
 * number of visible characters.
 */
int updateVisible()
{
   int visibleCount = 0;

   for (int i = 0; i < noOfChars; i++) {
   visible[i] = (xPos[i]+xStart > 0 &&
         xPos[i]+xStart < width &&
         yPos[i]+yStart+lineHeight > 0  &&
         yPos[i]+yStart-lineHeight < height);
   if (visible[i])
      visibleCount++;
   }
   return visibleCount;
}

void moveText(int scroll)
{
   switch (scroll) {
   case TickerTextAttr.LEFT:
      xStart -= deltax;
      System.out.println("xStart LEFT = " + xStart);
      break;
   case TickerTextAttr.RIGHT:
      xStart += deltax;
      System.out.println("xStart RIGHT = " + xStart);
      break;
   case TickerTextAttr.UP:
      yStart -= deltay;
      break;
   case TickerTextAttr.DOWN:
      yStart += deltay;
      break;
   }
}

/**
 * Paint characters
 */
void paint(Graphics g)
{
 Dimension d = size();
 if (msg != null) {
   g.setFont(font);
   g.setColor(fg);
```

Checks to see if the whole string has been shown on the screen. When this returns 0, it means that there are no characters on the screen.

Sets new *x* and *y* positions for the ticker text, depending on the direction of the scrolling

This does the actual drawing of the text on the screen.

Listing 3.4: Source code for ticker applet (Continued)

```
      g.drawString(msg, xStart, yStart);
    } else {
      g.drawImage(image, xStart, yStart, d.width(), d.height(), null);
    }
  }
}
```

CUSTOMIZING WITH PARAMETERS

The ticker applet is a good example of how an applet can allow its behavior to be customized. Almost every action of every line in the ticker can be controlled from the HTML file. Here is a sample list of the parameters that can be specified for the ticker applet.

Foreground color	<param name="fgColor" value= "#AA00AA">
Background color	<param name="bgColor" value= "#123456">
Lines of the ticker. (For each line, you can specify a begin and end delay. You can also specify a begin and end scroll direction.)	<param name="line0" value= "Ticker line 1<15>">
	<param name="line1" value= "<left>Ticker line 2<5>">
	<param name="line2" value= "<down>Ticker line 3<10><up>">
	<param name="line3" value= "<10>Ticker line 4 <30>">
Speed of the ticker in vertical and horizontal directions	<param name="deltax" value="6">
	<param name="deltay" value="3">
Size of the font of the ticker	<param name="size" value="18">

PLAYSOUND APPLET

The PlaySound applet is not a large applet. It is included here because we forsee audio clips as being an essential part of any Web site. This applet is a good place to start when you need to add a sound to your web page.

CLASS HIERARCHY OF THE PLAYSOUND APPLET

PlaySound again inherits from java.applet.Applet. The Applet methods that it overrides are init() and stop().

FLOW OF CONTROL WITHIN PLAYSOUND APPLET

The Java interpreter passes control to init(). Init() sets up the user interface and waits for user events. As you can see from Figure 3.8, the only kind of event that PlaySound recognizes is a button press. When the user clicks on the "Hit me" or the "stop" button, the action() method is called. Action() checks to see which button has been pressed and starts or stops the sound it is playing based on whether the "Hit me" or "stop" button was pressed. It calls Play-Next() to play the audio clip and stop() to finish.

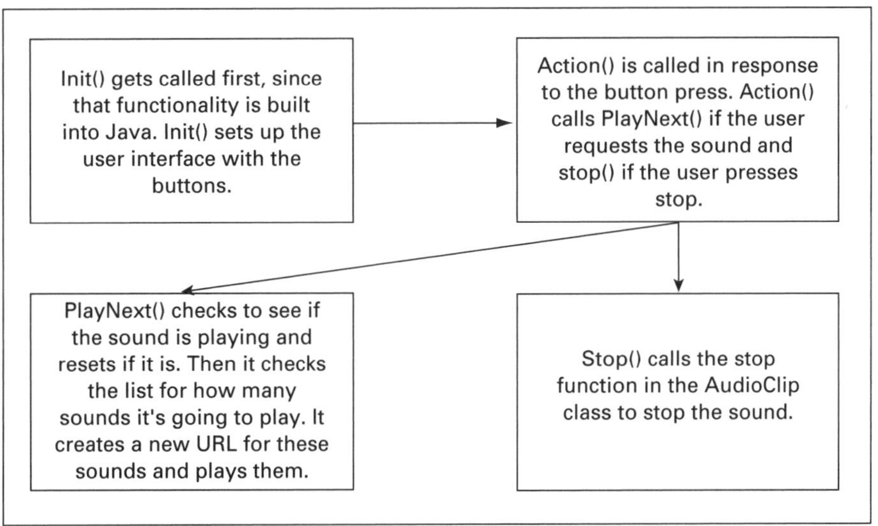

Figure 3.8: Flow of control within the PlaySound applet

SOURCE CODE WITH ANNOTATIONS

Listing 3.5 shows the source code for the PlaySound applet, along with annotations.

Listing 3.5: Source code for PlaySound

```
import java.awt.*;
import java.net.*;
import java.applet.*;
```

Import all classes in awt, net, and applet for use within this applet.

```
public class PlaySound extends Applet {

// String that holds the file name for the audio file
 private String sounds;

// String that holds the name of the button to be
// pressed for sound.

private String myButtonName;

// A panel is a container object for the two buttons.

    private Panel myPanel;

// The two buttons

    private Button myButton;
    private Button myButton2;

    private int index;
```

The number of the sound

```
 // The current audioClip.

    private AudioClip audio;

    public void playNext() {
      try {
```

This method parses the audio clip line from the parameters and tries to play the audio clips inside a "try" block. This is necessary because Java will not let you open an URL without catching the exception arising from a malformed URL.

Listing 3.5: Source code for PlaySound (Continued)

```
            if (audio != null) {
                audio.stop();
            audio = null;
        }
```

If something is playing, this stops it and sets the audioClip back to null.

```
String url = sounds;
```

The sounds variable is the URL into which we retrieve the current sound.

```
    if (sounds.indexOf('|') >= 0) {
          int start = index;
          if ((index = sounds.indexOf('|', index)) < 0) {
              url = sounds.substring(start);
              index = start;
          } else {
              url = sounds.substring(start, index++);
          }
              }
          if (url.length() > 0) {
          audio = getAudioClip(new URL(getDocumentBase(), url));
          audio.play();
        }
      } catch (Exception e) {
     }
    }


    public void init() {

     sounds = getParameter("snd");
     if (sounds == null) {
         sounds = "/audio/spacemusic.au";
     }
     myButtonName = getParameter("buttonname");
     if (myButtonName == null) {
         myButtonName = "Hit me";
     }

   myPanel = new Panel();
    myPanel.setLayout(new GridLayout(2,1));

    add(myPanel);
```

This looks for the delimiter in the URL and separates the sounds.

This turns the URL into an audio clip that can be played and plays it.

Listing 3.5: Source code for PlaySound (Continued)

```
    myButton = new Button(myButtonName);
    myButton2 = new Button("Stop");
    myPanel.add(myButton);
    myPanel.add(myButton2);
    resize(100,60);
    myPanel.show();
    }

    public void stop() {
     if (audio != null) {
         audio.stop();
         audio = null;
     }
    }


// This is the method that gets called whenever an
// event takes place and if there is no special
// method for that event.

    public boolean action(Event evt, Object arg) {

       // If the button is "Hit me" then start the
       // audio clip. If it's "Stop", then stop
       // playing the audio.

     if ("Hit me".equals(arg))
         playNext();
     if ("Stop".equals(arg))
         audio.stop();
     return true;
    }

}
```

The user interface is created just to facilitate the playing of the audio clip. There is no reason for the reader to create another interface that plays the same sound.

CUSTOMIZATION WITH PARAMETERS

The PlaySound applet can be customized with the following parameters:

snd: This parameter will tell the applet which sound or series of sounds to play. Each sound needs to be separated by a vertical bar (|) if there is more than one.

Buttonname: This parameter names the button that the user will hit to play the sound. The sound can be turned off with the Stop button.

Using and Modifying Applets on the CD-ROM

Chapter 4

We have provided you with a sampling of applets so that you can get an idea of how applets work, look at the source code for each applet and, if you would like, customize them for yourself. Many of the applets we have provided can be easily customized without having to change the source code at all, through the use of parameter tags. These applets provide a broad range of examples of how Java can be used, and all of these appear on the CD that is included with this book.

Each applet description contains the following:

- A brief description of what the applet does
- An explanation of the parameter tags
- The HTML used to place the applet on a Web page
- A screen shot of the applet

THE ALARM CLOCK

Creator: Man Kam Kwong
E-Mail: kwong@mcs.anl.gov
This alarm clock applet is a digital clock that allows you to set any alarm time by using either your keyboard or the buttons provided in the applet. Twenty seconds before alarm time, the clock face on the Web page turns from white to cyan. At alarm time, the clock face turns from cyan to red for 30 seconds. There is a small counter that tells you how much time (in seconds) is left before the alarm goes off.

HTML FOR THE ALARM CLOCK

To embed this applet in your Web page, use the following code:

```
<applet code="AClock3.class" width=260 height=180>
</applet>
```

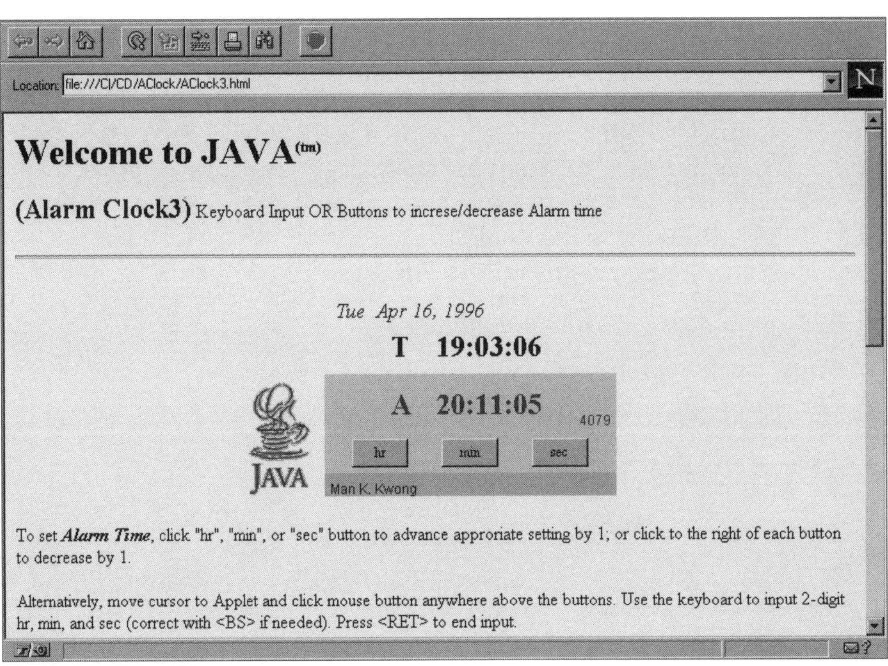

Asternoid

Creator: Ben Sigelman
E-mail: sigelman@crocker.com

Asternoid is an asteroids clone, with many advanced features and great source code. The basic idea is to move your ship around and destroy all the asternoids. As in the arcade game, if you hit a ship it will break into smaller pieces. The mouse starts, pauses, and restarts the game.

The main keyboard commands for moving the ship are

Left	J
Right	L
Thrust	K
Shoot	Space bar
Shield	Z

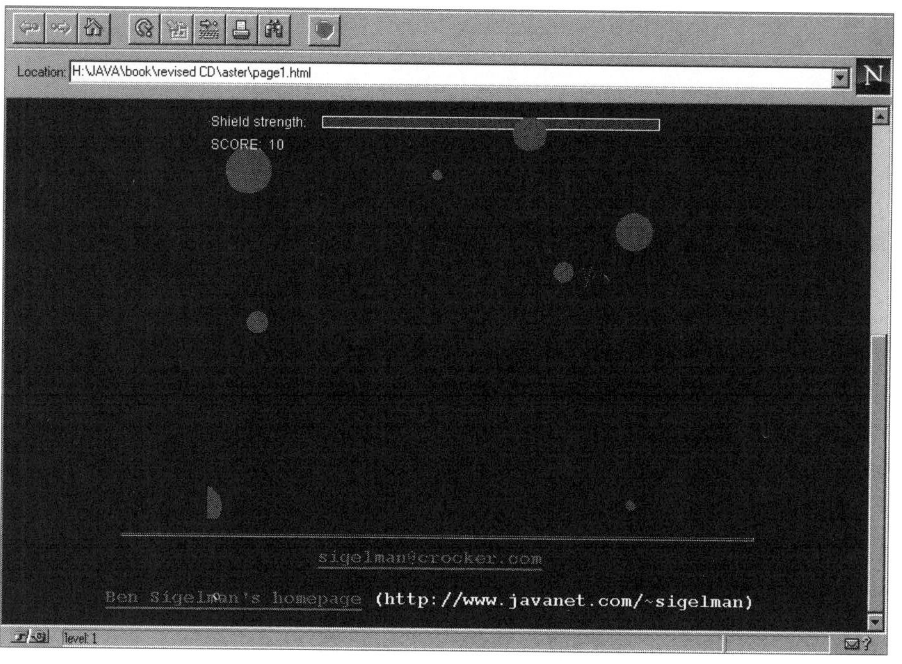

PARAMETERS

Through parameters you can specify the width and height of the playing area, for example,

```
<APPLET CODE="aster" WIDTH=400 HEIGHT=350>
```

HTML FOR ASTERNOID

To embed this applet in your Web page, use the following code:

```
<APPLET CODE="aster" WIDTH=400 HEIGHT=350>
<param name=wid value=400>
<param name=hei value=350>
</APPLET>
```

Celebrity Painter (v2.0)

Creator: Jeff Orkin
E-mail: jeff@demonsys.com

Celebrity Painter allows artists and nonartists alike to paint portraits using facial features of celebrities. Rather than picking from a palette of colors, users pick from a palette of famous faces. They can paint with Madonna's eyes, Jim Carrey's mouth, and Bill Clinton's nose. Here's how:

1. Choose a celebrity brush from the list box.
2. Hold down the left mouse button while slowly rubbing where the facial features should appear.
3. If you make a mistake, click on the eraser and rub off unwanted areas, or click Clear to erase the whole image. You can add as many celebrities and portraits as you want just by using the parameter tags.

Celebrity Painter makes use of a variety of Java classes. It uses the awt for the interface, the ImageConsumer class to get the pixel color values of an image, and the Canvas to paint on. Celebrity Painter employs a double buffer to keep track of what's been painted so far.

To add a David Letterman portrait, for example, follow these steps:

1. Add a parameter line to the applet tag in the HTML that has the next sequential brush number and a name:

   ```
   <PARAM NAME=brush4 VALUE="David Letterman">
   ```

2. Provide a 160-pixel-by-200-pixel jpeg of the celebrity, with a file name that matches the name string without spaces; for example, DavidLetterman.jpg.
3. Provide a 40 pixel-by-50 pixel jpeg of the celebrity, with a file name that matches the name string without spaces plus the characters *BR*; for example, DavidLettermanBR.jpg.

HTML FOR CELEBRITY PAINTER

To add this applet to your Web page, use the following code:

```
<APPLET CODE=CelebrityPainter.class WIDTH=300 HEIGHT=200>
    <PARAM NAME=brush1 VALUE="Drew Barrymore">
    <PARAM NAME=brush2 VALUE="Jim Carrey">
    <PARAM NAME=brush3 VALUE="Bill Clinton">
    <PARAM NAME=brush4 VALUE="Cindy Crawford">
    <PARAM NAME=brush5 VALUE="Harrison Ford">
```

```
    <PARAM NAME=brush6 VALUE="Bill Gates">
    <PARAM NAME=brush7 VALUE="Janet Jackson">
    <PARAM NAME=brush8 VALUE="Lisa Kudrow">
    <PARAM NAME=brush9 VALUE="David Letterman">
    <PARAM NAME=brush10 VALUE="Madonna">
    <PARAM NAME=brush11 VALUE="Demi Moore">
    <PARAM NAME=brush12 VALUE="Matthew Perry">
    <PARAM NAME=brush13 VALUE="Brad Pitt">
    <PARAM NAME=brush14 VALUE="Colin Powell">
    <PARAM NAME=brush15 VALUE="Cybill Shepherd">
    <PARAM NAME=brush16 VALUE="Alicia Silverstone">
    <PARAM NAME=brush17 VALUE="OJ Simpson">
</APPLET>
```

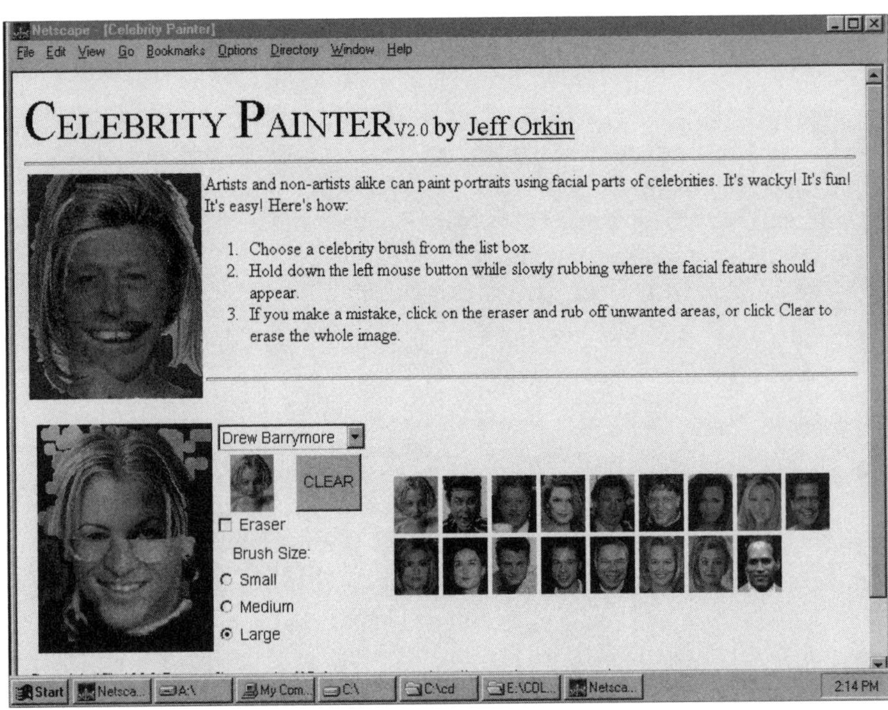

THE CHALKBOARD APPLET

Creator: TESSERACT Information Solutions Inc.

The Java Graffiti Chalkboard is a community chalkboard that allows users to leave their mark on a Web page. The commercial version of this applet communicates with a server called JAAS (Java Advanced Applet Server), and allows the user to load and save images and share the chalkboard in real-time over the Internet (in other words, people can play tic-tac-toe over the Net). The applet that comes with this book has the networking components disabled. For more information on this applet, please visit http://www.tisinc.com.

There are two sections to the Graffiti Chalkboard applet: the Chalkboard and the Tools palette. The Chalkboard is self-explanatory. The Tools palette allows you to vary the size of your chalk. The long black rectangle on the top of the toolbar is an eraser. If you press the eraser button, the chalk turns black. To restore the chalk to white, press the eraser again.

If you want to use the Load Chalkboard and Save Chalkboard buttons on the chalkboard, you will need the JAAS server (please see the applet on the CD for more information). Pressing the *C* key will clear the chalkboard.

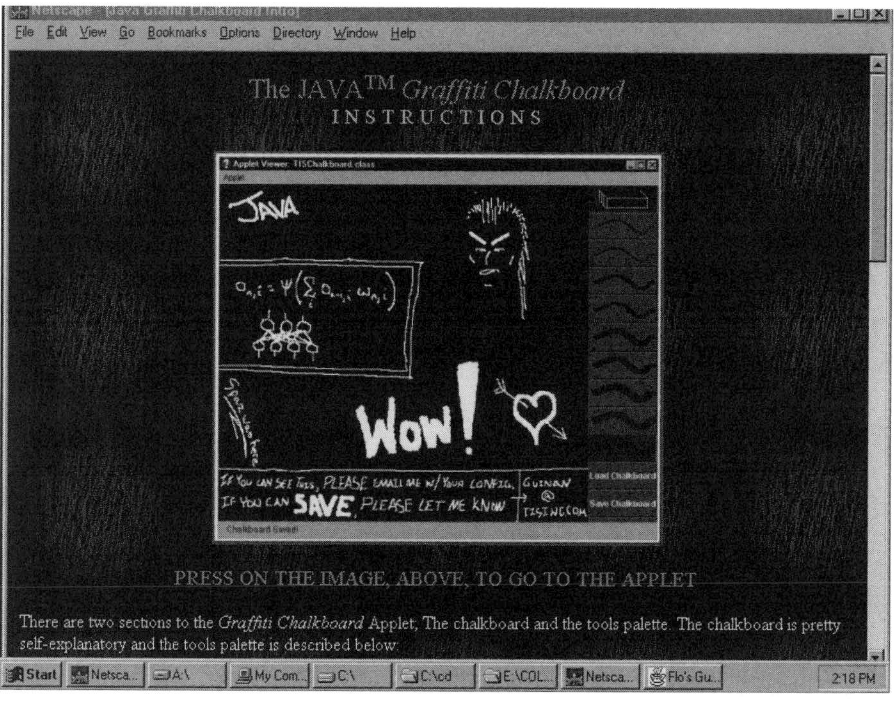

The Java Graffiti Chalkboard consists of three main classes and several auxiliary classes. The main classes are TISChalkboard.class (the applet), CBCanvas.class (the Chalkboard), and CBChalk.class (the Tools palette). Both the Chalkboard and the Tools palette use double buffering, and all controls are custom (not awt components). The non-JAAS-enabled version of this applet can only be used at 640-by-480 size.

HTML FOR THE CHALKBOARD APPLET

To embed this applet in your Web page, use the following code:

```
<applet code=TISChalkboard.class width=640 height=480 ALIGN=MIDDLE></applet>
```

THE KZMDCLOCK

Creator: Alessandro Aldo "Kazuma" Garbagnati
E-Mail: kazuma@energy.it

The KzmDClock is a digital clock that shows the time and, if the user requests it, the date every five seconds. The user can define the colors and the dimensions of the display.

In KzmDClock the base of the applet is a thread that updates the clock every five seconds. The LEDs are preconfigured as a polygon in the init() part of the source code. A paint() procedure is called every second, and updates every digit by redrawing the seven LEDs.

PARAMETERS

Here are the parameters for the clock.

Parameter	Description	Tag
Dimension: (big or small, default=big)	The dimension of the clock. The one you see on the page is big, the default. Big is 214 pixels (width) by 60 pixels (height), and the small size is 115 pixels (width) by 34 pixels (height).	`<PARAM NAME= "dimension" VALUE="big">`
Border: (yes or no, default=no)	Show the border of the applet	`<PARAM NAME= "border" VALUE="yes">`
ShowDate: (yes/no, default=yes)	Display the date for 3 seconds every 5 seconds	`<PARAM NAME= "showdate" VALUE="yes">`
DateFormat: (default=mdy, m=month d=day y=year)	Show the date in the format defined	`<PARAM NAME= "showdate" VALUE="yes">`
BackColor: (R G B, default=0 0 0) Determine the color of the scrollable area, the rectangle		`<PARAM NAME="backcolor" VALUE="0 0 0">`

Parameter	Description	Tag
ForeColor: (R G B, default=128 0 0)	The color of the LEDs	`<PARAM NAME="forecolor" VALUE="128 128 0">`

HTML FOR KZMDCLOCK

To embed this applet in your Web page, use the following code:

```
<APPLET CODE="KzmDClock" WIDTH=214 HEIGHT=60>
    <PARAM NAME="dimension" VALUE="big">
    <PARAM NAME="border" VALUE="yes">
    <PARAM NAME="showdate" VALUE="yes">
    <PARAM NAME="dateformat" VALUE="mdy">
    <PARAM NAME="backcolor" VALUE="0 0 0">
    <PARAM NAME="forecolor" VALUE="128 128 0">
</APPLET>
```

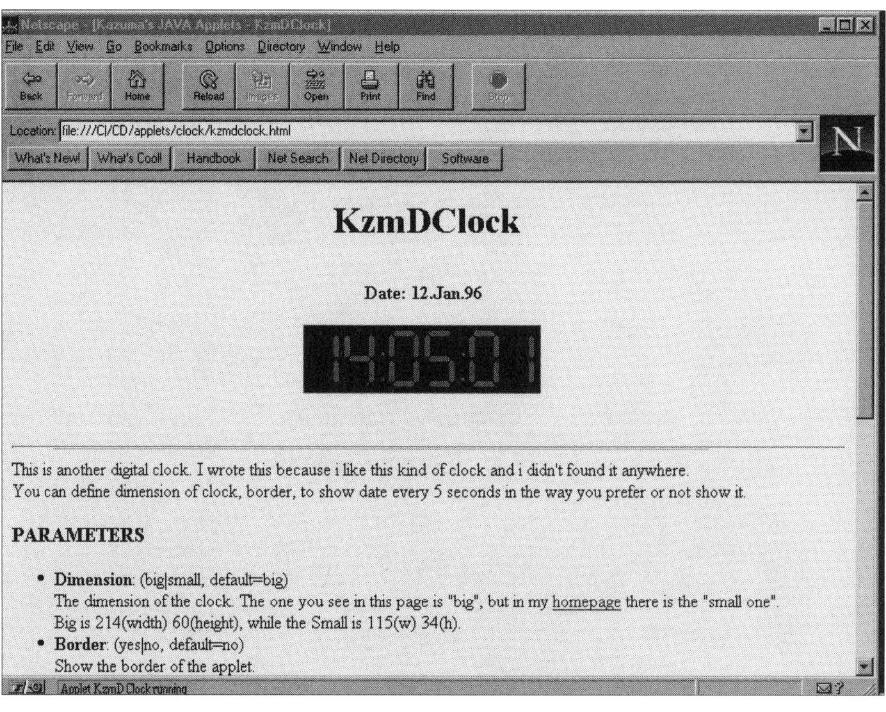

Color Sampler

Creator: Man Kam Kwong
E-Mail: kwong@mcs.anl.gov

The Color Sampler allows you to search for a particular color and see both how the color will appear in your browser and the RGB triplet for that color. On the left are five TextFields where you may specify the color names to be displayed. The sixth TextField is used to specify a color by its RGB values, in the format *128,128,128* or *100 200 250* and converts these values to hexidecimal format.

You may choose which color palette should be matched, either the Netscape (the N button) palette or the X11-Xwindows (the X button) palette. (In other words, if you enter the word *purple* and press the N button, the applet will display its match of the word purple and its RGB value.)

When the input is a string of letters, such as *tel*, the Color Sampler displays the color whose name starts with *tel* (or its closest match).

If the input starts with a period, such as *.yell*, the Color Sampler displays the first color (alphabetically after the last match) whose name contains *exactly* the letters *yell*.

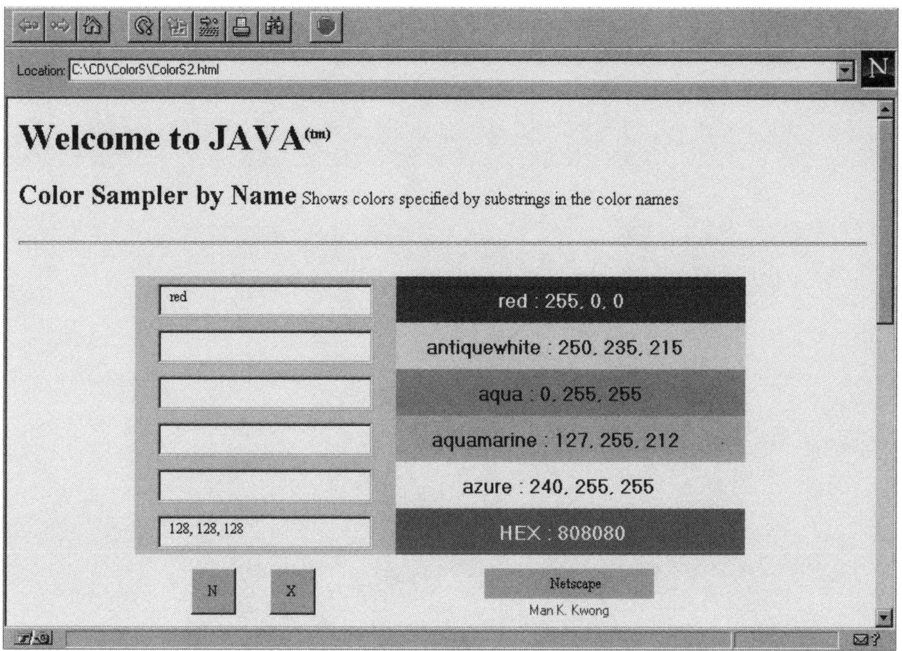

If the input is just a period, the same substring for the previous TextField is used, and the next match is displayed.

When the Return key is pressed, substring matches advance to the next match.

NOTE On monitors having only 256 colors, the actual color displayed for the "color" chosen by the user may be an approximation.

HTML FOR THE COLOR SAMPLER

To embed this applet in your Web page, use the following code:

```
<applet code="ColorS2.class" width=540 height=300>
</applet>
```

KzmFortune Scroller

Creator: Alessandro Aldo "Kazuma" Garbagnati (kazuma@energy.it)
Home page: http://www.energy.it/~kazuma/
The KzmFortune Scroller scrolls a message in a rectangular area on the screen. The user can define parameters such as speed, colors, delay, and the file name containing the messages. Every time the applet runs, it reads a random message and shows it on the screen.

KzmFortune is based on threads and input/output. The init part reads all the parameters and prepares all the variables. A routine reads a file from the server using a standard connection. A random number is then generated and chooses which line of the text will be printed on the screen. At least the run part runs the thread and every delay call paint to repaint the messages.

The Fortune applet is based on a scrolling applet and scrolls a message on the screen. The message is randomly read from a text file that must be present on the same directory as the applet.

PARAMETERS FOR KZMFORTUNE

Here are the parameters for this applet:

Parameter	Description	Tag
Font: (String, default=Arial)	The font name. The only restriction is that it must be written exactly as the system requires it to be (normally with the first letter capitalized)	`<PARAM NAME="font" VALUE="Arial">`
FontBold: (0/1, default=1)	If this value is 0, the font is bold; if it is 1 the font is bold.	`<PARAM NAME="fontbold" VALUE=0>`
FontSize: (Integer, default=12)	The size of the font	`<PARAM NAME="fontsize" VALUE=14>`
Shift: (Integer, default=5)	The shifting of the message	`<PARAM NAME="shift" VALUE=2>`
Delay: (Integer, default=50)	The delay between every shift	`<PARAM NAME="delay" VALUE=50>`

Parameter	Description	Tag
Rectangle: (X Y WIDTH HEIGHT, default=applet dimension)	The dimension of the scrollable area	`<PARAM NAME= "rectangle" VALUE= "4 4 350 20">`
Rect_Color: (R G B, default= 0 0 0)	The color of the scrollable area, the rectangle	`<PARAM NAME= "rect_color" VALUE="0 0 128">`
Text_Color: (R G B, default= 255 255 255)	The color of the message	`<PARAM NAME= "text_color" VALUE="0 255 255">`
FileName: (String, default= fortune.txt)	The name of the file containing the fortunes. If the file name is unreadable the applet doesn't work.	`<PARAM NAME= "filename" VALUE= "fortune.txt">`
FileLines: (int)	The number of fortunes in the file. Every fortune must be one line. If the number of lines is wrong, the message will be "NO FORTUNE."	`<PARAM NAME= "filelines" VALUE="5">`

HTML FOR KZMFORTUNE

To embed this applet in your Web page, use the following code:

```
<APPLET CODE="KzmFortune" WIDTH=354 HEIGHT=24>
      <PARAM NAME="font" VALUE="Arial">
      <PARAM NAME="fontbold" VALUE=0>
      <PARAM NAME="fontsize" VALUE=14>
      <PARAM NAME="shift" VALUE=2>
      <PARAM NAME="delay" VALUE=50>
      <PARAM NAME="rectangle" VALUE="4 4 350 20">
      <PARAM NAME="background" VALUE=1>
      <PARAM NAME="rect_color" VALUE="0 0 128">
      <PARAM NAME="text_color" VALUE="0 255 255">
      <PARAM NAME="filename" VALUE="fortune.txt">
      <PARAM NAME="filelines" VALUE="5">
</APPLET>
```

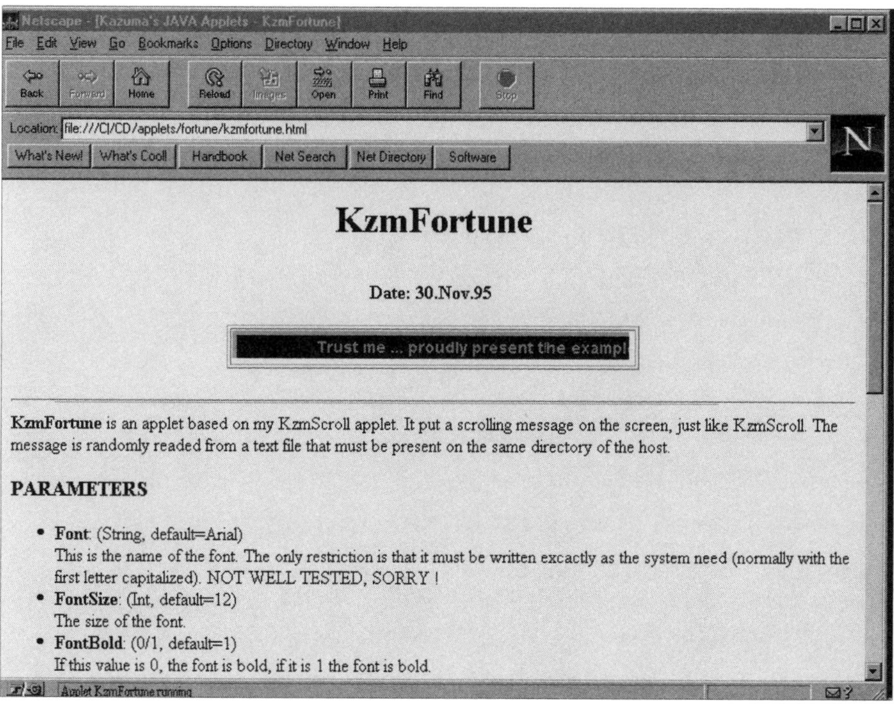
Netscape - [Kazuma's JAVA Applets - KzmFortune]
File Edit View Go Bookmarks Options Directory Window Help
Back Forward Home Reload Images Open Print Find Stop
Location: file:///C|/CD/applets/fortune/kzmfortune.html
What's New! What's Cool! Handbook Net Search Net Directory Software
KzmFortune
Date: 30.Nov.95
Trust me ... proudly present the exampl
KzmFortune is an applet based on my KzmScroll applet. It put a scrolling message on the screen, just like KzmScroll. The message is randomly readed from a text file that must be present on the same directory of the host.
PARAMETERS
Font: (String, default=Arial)
This is the name of the font. The only restriction is that it must be written excactly as the system need (normally with the first letter capitalized). NOT WELL TESTED, SORRY !
FontSize: (Int, default=12)
The size of the font.
FontBold: (0/1, default=1)
If this value is 0, the font is bold, if it is 1 the font is bold.
Applet KzmFortune running

A FROG'S LIGHT SNACK

Creator: Karl Hörnell
E-mail: karl@tdb.uu.se
This is a noninteractive applet that uses a simple animation for great results. It's one of the most practical applets we have found so far.

HTML FOR A FROG'S LIGHT SNACK

To embed this applet in your Web page, use the following HTML:

```
<applet code="frog.class" width=500 height=60>
</applet>
```

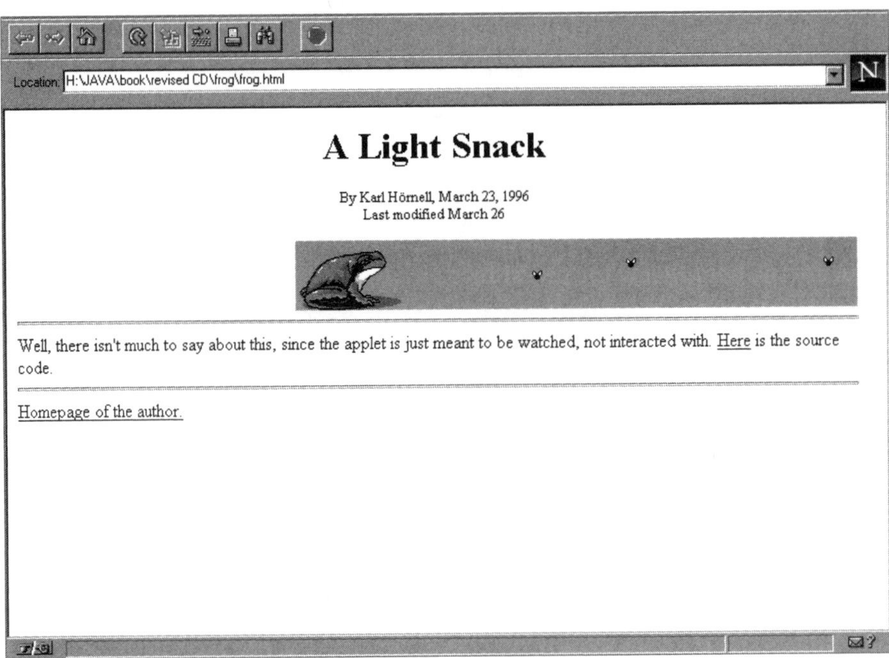

THE GUESTBOOK APPLET

Creator: Bill Giel
E-mail: rvdi@usa.nai.net
URL: http://www.nai.net/~rvdi/home.htm

Guestbook is an applet that invokes a pop-up applet window in which a page's viewer can optionally enter his name and e-mail address along with some comments. Guestbook then sends this information to the page's owner.

Guestbook simulates a server-based guest log, as an alternative to a "mailto" HTML form. Internally, it provides a good example of sending SMTP mail with Java. It could be used as a model to build a more exotic information form. Note that in order for guestbook to work, the homepage's server must permit a socket connection to the SMTP port, 25. Also, guestbook, and nearly all socket applets in general, may not function through network firewalls.

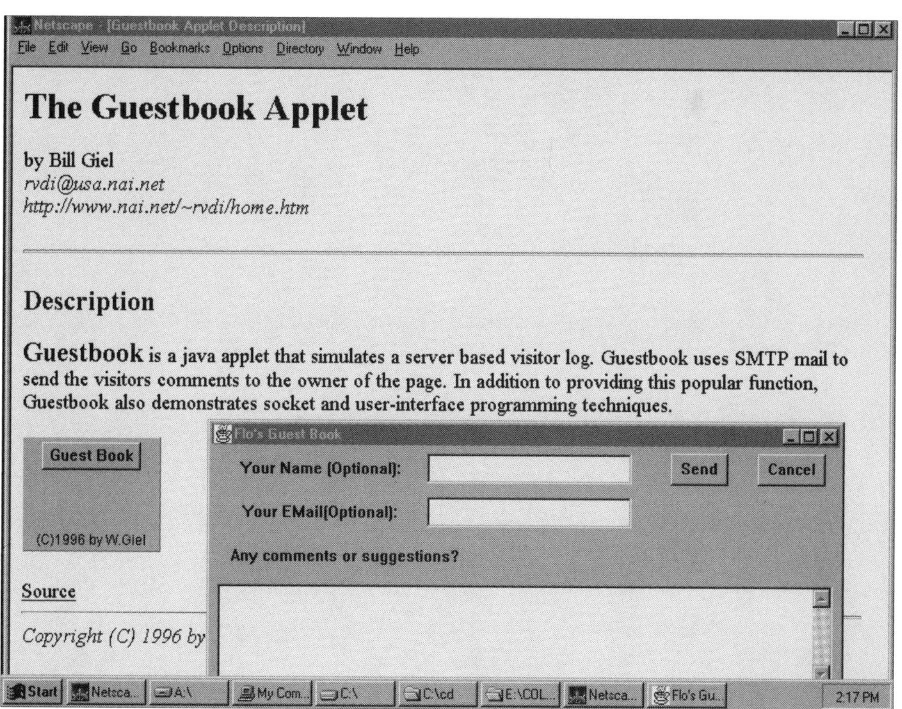

PARAMETERS

Use these parameters to modify the applet on your page:

Parameter Description	Tag
Substitute the page owner's e-mail address for the RECEIVER	`<param name=RECEIVER value= "flo@foo.bar.net">`
Substitute the small iconic image of your choice for IMAGEURL	`<param name=IMAGEURL value="icons155.gif">`
Substitute the title you want displayed in the guestbook pop-up for TITLE	`<param name=TITLE value= "Flo's Guest Book">`

HTML FOR GUESTBOOK

To embed this applet in your Web page, use the following HTML:

```
<applet code="guestbook.class" width=125 height=100>
    <param name=IMAGEURL value="icons155.gif">
    <param name=RECEIVER value="flo@foo.bar.net">
    <param name=TITLE value="Flo's Guest Book">
    </applet>
```

THE IMAGE MAP APPLET

Creator: Man Kam Kwong
E-mail: kwong@mcs.anl.gov

The image map applet allows the creator of a map to go far beyond the average image map program used by most Web servers. The applet enables the author to visually highlight the active area, change the color of the active text, display the URL of the link, and perform many other useful tasks not possible with the image map program alone.

PARAMETERS

You can modify this applet on your page using the following parameters:

Parameter Description	Tag
Create your own image in either the GIF or JPEG format.	`<param name="IMG" value="imm.gif">`
Modify text labels in the yellow cells (use the | symbol to indicate a line break)	`<param name="lab5" value="White|House">`
Specify the active image areas	`<param name= "area1" value="0 0 149 44 http://www.mcs.anl.gov/.../ Scroll.html">`

In the last item on this list, the first pair of integers describes the (x,y) coordinates of one of the corners, and the second pair describes the opposite corner. Up to 20 active areas can be specified. The labels and areas are numbered in the same (but otherwise arbitrary) order. Start with 1 (not 0). Areas must be numbered consecutively. If you specify area1, 2, 3, and 5, but not 4, then area5 will be lost. This, however, does not apply to labels. One can have an area without a label.

In our example, there are three such active rectangles, containing, respectively, name, e-mail, and the "Argonne" name. Because these areas are part of the image and cannot change color (like the labels in the yellow boxes), a red box is used to highlight the areas. You can ask for a highlighting box (in addition to highlighting the text) for labeled areas by adding an argument *b* after the http address in the area parameter. Replace *b* with *o* and you get a highlighting oval. (The active area is still rectangular). For example,

```
<param name="area5" value="0 179 152 222 http://www.whitehouse.gov b">
```

Other parameters you can supply include "fcolor" and "acolor", which are respectively the nonactive and active font colors of the labels. The defaults are blue (*b*) and red (*r*). The values are a single letter. Alternatively, you can specify the RGB values (in decimal, delimited by either a comma or a space). For example,

```
<param name="fcolor" value="b">
<param name="acolor" value="50, 100, 200">
```

You can also supply a font, such as "Dialog," "TimesRoman," "Courier," "Helvetica," or any other font name that Java can understand. It defaults to "Dialog" if the name is unknown (or misspelled). For example,

```
<param name="font" value="Dialog">
```

You can also choose the "style," which can be "bold," "italic," or "plain." For example,

```
<param name="style" value="bold">
```

You can choose the point size, which defaults to 14, through the following parameter:

```
<%param name="pointsize" value="12">
```

With "lineskip" you can control the spacing between lines in a label. The spacing is specified as a fraction of the font height. The default is "0.01." For example,

```
<%param name="lineskip" value="0.1">
```

To put the applet in "testing" mode, include the following line in your HTML:

```
<param name="xy" value="true">
```

If you do so, as the cursor moves over the image, the (x,y) coordinates of the cursor are displayed in the status bar to help you to identify the corners of the active areas. Also, in testing mode linking is disabled, even if the HREF of an active area has been specified. To get out of testing mode, either delete the above line, or simply add an % (or any other symbol) in front of the word *param* of the line you want to take out of testing mode.

HTML FOR IMAGE MAP APPLET

To embed this applet in your Web page:

```
<applet code="ImMap2.class" width=380 height=270>
<param name="IMG" value="imm.gif">
<%param name="pointsize" value="12">
<%param name="lineskip" value="0.1">
```

```
<% param name="xy" value="true">
<% param name="fcolor" value="100 255 0">
<param name="area1" value="0 0 152 44
http://www.mcs.anl.gov/home/kwong/JAVA/ImProc.html o">
<param name="area2" value="0 44 152 89
http://www.mcs.anl.gov/home/kwong/JAVA/AClock.html">
<param name="area3" value="0 89 152 134
http://www.mcs.anl.gov/home/kwong/JAVA/ColorM.html">
<param name="area4" value="0 134 152 179
http://www.mcs.anl.gov/home/kwong/JAVA/ColorS.html o">
<param name="area5" value="0 179 152 222 http://www.whitehouse.gov b">
<param name="area6" value="0 223 190 269
http://www.mcs.anl.gov/home/kwong/page1.html">
<param name="area7" value="191 223 379 269 mailto:kwong@mcs.anl.gov">
<param name="area8" value="180 170 365 222 http://www..anl.gov">
<param name="area9" value="188 22  293 127 http://www.mcs.anl.gov o">
<param name="lab1" value="Image|Processing">
<param name="lab2" value="Alarm Clock">
<param name="lab3" value="Color Matcher">
<param name="lab4" value="Color Sampler">
<param name="lab5" value="White|House">
</applet>
```

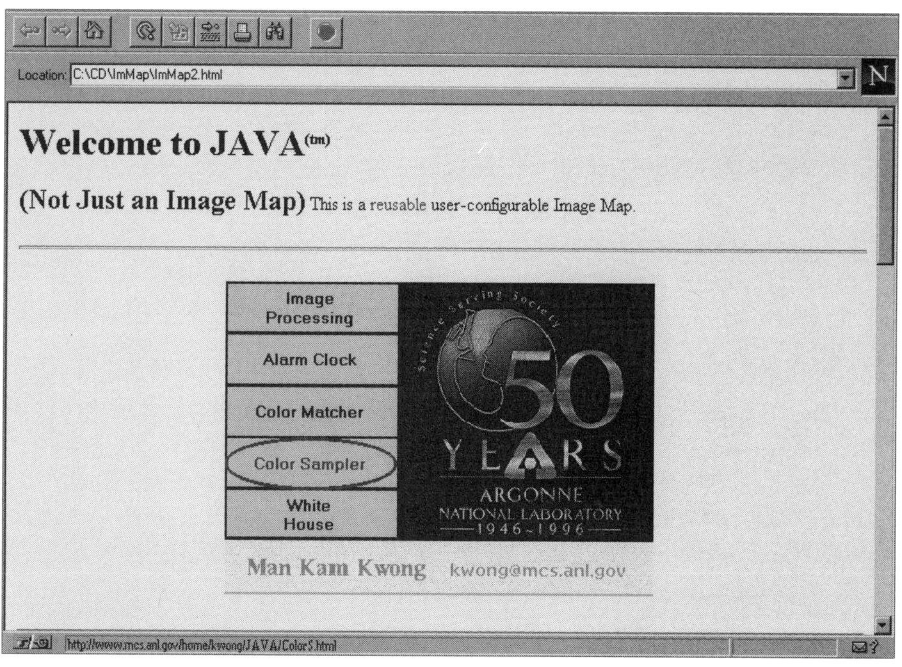

The JitterText applet

Author: Bill Giel
E-mail: rvdi@usa.nai.net
URL: http://www.nai.net/~rvdi/home.htm

JitterText is an applet that provides an animated and colorful display of a text string, and is useful for an alternative heading on a Web page. JitterText lets you control the jitter speed, the size of the display area (JitterText will optimize the font for the specified area), text, and background color, and whether or not you want random colors applied to the characters. If the viewer of the page clicks on the jittery text, JitterText suspends, and the text is displayed as a normal string. Clicking on the text again resumes the animated text display.

JitterText is an extensive hack of Dan Wyszynski's NervousText applet. It features text size optimizing, buffered animation to eliminate flicker, configurable speed and color option, and an improved "jitter" pattern. It uses a threaded timer to put the text in motion.

PARAMETERS

You can modify this applet on your Web page with the following parameters:

Parameter Description	Tag
Specify size of applet	<applet code="JitterText.class" width=350 height=60>
Specify the background color of the area	<param name=BGCOLOR value="000000">
Specify the color of the text	<param name=TEXTCOLOR value="FF0000">
Specify the text you would like displayed	<param name=TEXT value= "Java Applets">
Modify the speed of the applet	<param name=SPEED value=250>
Choose whether to apply a random color (1) or not (0)	<param name=RANDOMCOLOR value=1>

HTML FOR JITTERTEXT

To embed this applet on your Web page, use the following HTML:

```
<applet code="JitterText.class" width=350 height=60>
        <param name=BGCOLOR value="000000">
        <param name=TEXTCOLOR value="FF0000">
        <param name=TEXT value="Java Applets">
```

```
        <param name=SPEED value=250>
        <param name=RANDOMCOLOR value=1>
        <FONT SIZE=+2
COLOR=#FF0000>Java<SUP><SMALL>TM</SMALL></SUP>
Applets</FONT>
        </applet>
```

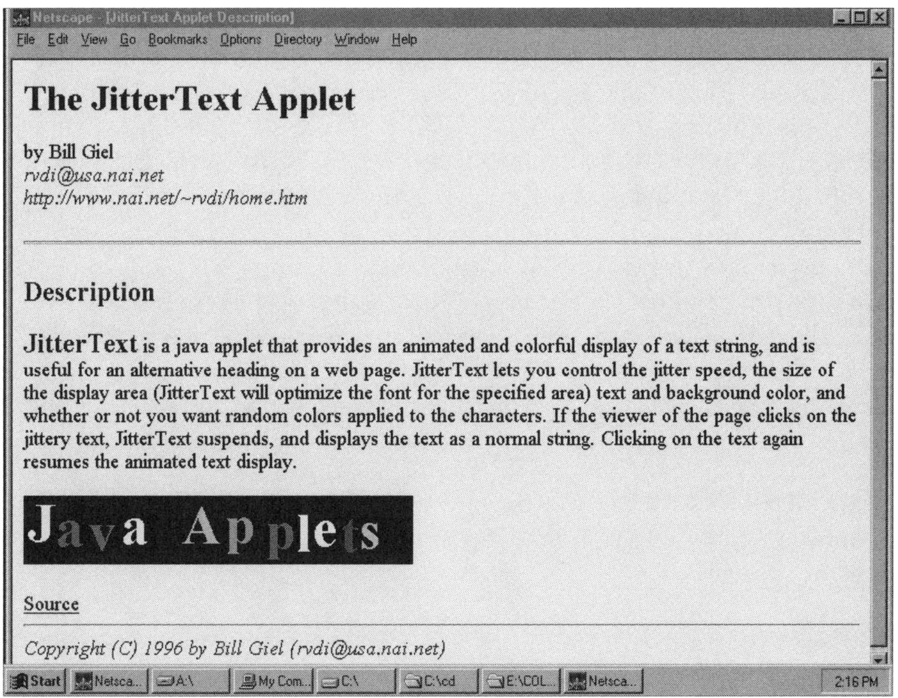

JAVA MASTERMIND

Creator: Karl Hörnell
E-mail: karl@tdb.uu.se

The Mastermind game is an example of a graphically pleasing Java applet that was created with very simple tools. The object of this game is to guess the sequence of four colored pegs that the computer has selected at random.

Here's how the applet works. First, you select the colors you want to appear in your game—the default set contains blue, green, red and yellow. For obvious reasons you are not allowed to select fewer than two. Clicking on a colored peg, which appears to the right of the board, will toggle the circle around it on and off, indicating whether it will be part of the color set from which the computer draws. Then press Start to begin.

You begin playing by filling the holes on the bottom row with colored pegs. Each time you have completed a guess (filled in all four holes), the computer responds by giving you one peg for each correct color—black if a guess was correct, white if a guess was incorrect. If you haven't managed to guess the sequence by your eighth guess, the computer reveals it to you and the game ends.

If you wish to start over, just press End to discontinue the game.

HTML FOR MASTERMIND

To embed this applet on your Web page, use the following HTML:

```
<applet code="mastermind.class" width=250 height=250>

</applet>
```

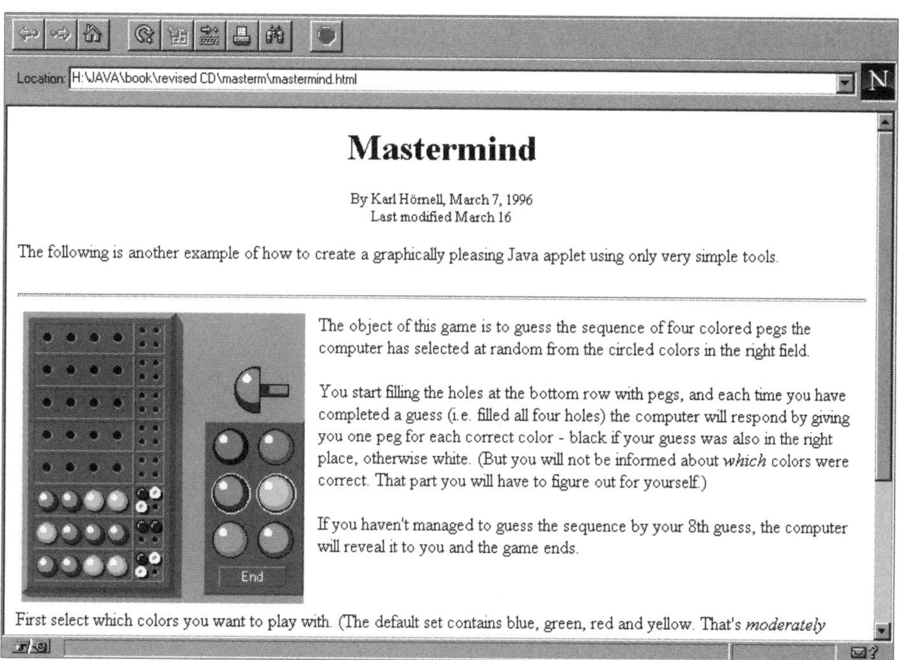
Location: H:\JAVA\book\revised CD\masterm\mastermind.html
Mastermind
By Karl Hörnell, March 7, 1996
Last modified March 16
The following is another example of how to create a graphically pleasing Java applet using only very simple tools.
The object of this game is to guess the sequence of four colored pegs the computer has selected at random from the circled colors in the right field.
You start filling the holes at the bottom row with pegs, and each time you have completed a guess (i.e. filled all four holes) the computer will respond by giving you one peg for each correct color - black if your guess was also in the right place, otherwise white. (But you will not be informed about which colors were correct. That part you will have to figure out for yourself.)
If you haven't managed to guess the sequence by your 8th guess, the computer will reveal it to you and the game ends.
End
First select which colors you want to play with. (The default set contains blue, green, red and yellow. That's moderately

CONTROL THE NUCLEAR POWER PLANT

Creator: Henrik Eriksson, Linköping University, Linköping, Sweden (Copyright © 1995).
E-mail: <her@ida.liu.se>

The control-room operators of the Kärnobyl nuclear power plant are telecommuting and are running the plant through the Web. However, the mean time between failure for the components of Kärnobyl is not great. The objective in this game is to try to keep the reactor stable when component failures occur.

To play, use sequence buttons 1–3 to run a failure-simulation sequence. The randomize button starts a random failure sequence. When a simulation sequence is running, you can control the state of valves and pumps by clicking on them. The moderator rods in the reactor can be moved by dragging them with the mouse.

HTML FOR NUCLEARPLANT

To embed this applet in your Web page, use the following HTML:

```
<applet code="NuclearPlant.class" width=680 height=473>
</applet>
```

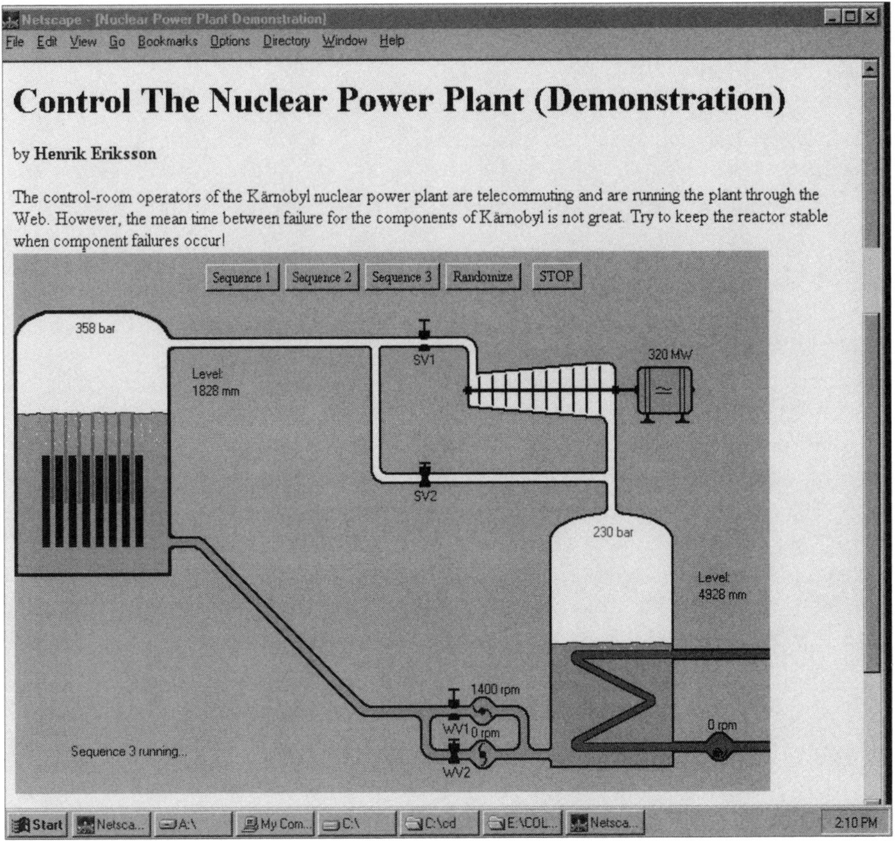
Netscape - [Nuclear Power Plant Demonstration]
File Edit View Go Bookmarks Options Directory Window Help
Control The Nuclear Power Plant (Demonstration)
by Henrik Eriksson
The control-room operators of the Kärnobyl nuclear power plant are telecommuting and are running the plant through the Web. However, the mean time between failure for the components of Kärnobyl is not great. Try to keep the reactor stable when component failures occur!
Sequence 1
Sequence 2
Sequence 3
Randomize
STOP
358 bar
Level:
1828 mm
SV1
320 MW
SV2
230 bar
Level:
4928 mm
1400 rpm
WV1
0 rpm
0 rpm
WV2
Sequence 3 running...
Start
Netsca...
A:\
My Com...
C:\
C:\cd
E:\COL...
Netsca...
2:10 PM

THE OPTION PRICER

Creator: Dr. Robert Lum

E-mail: robertl@intrepid.com

This applet provides a very easy way to price stock options. Just type in the price of the stock, its strike, the dividend yield to expiration, the cash interest rate until expiration, the volatility for the stock, and the time to expiration. The stock price and strike should be entered in dollars and cents. The dividend yield, interest rate, and volatility are measured in percentages per annum. The interest rate to use should be the treasury rate of the government debt (bond, note, or bill) of the same expiration as the option.

Next, select the units of time to measure the remaining expiration and then enter the time to expiration. Choose "call option" or "put option" radio button for the type of option, and whether the option is European or American. Then press the appropriate button to price the option or to clear existing entries.

HTML FOR OPTION PRICER

To embed this applet in your Web page, use the following HTML:

```
<APPLET CODE=OptionAppBeta.class WIDTH=500 HEIGHT=350>
</APPLET>
```

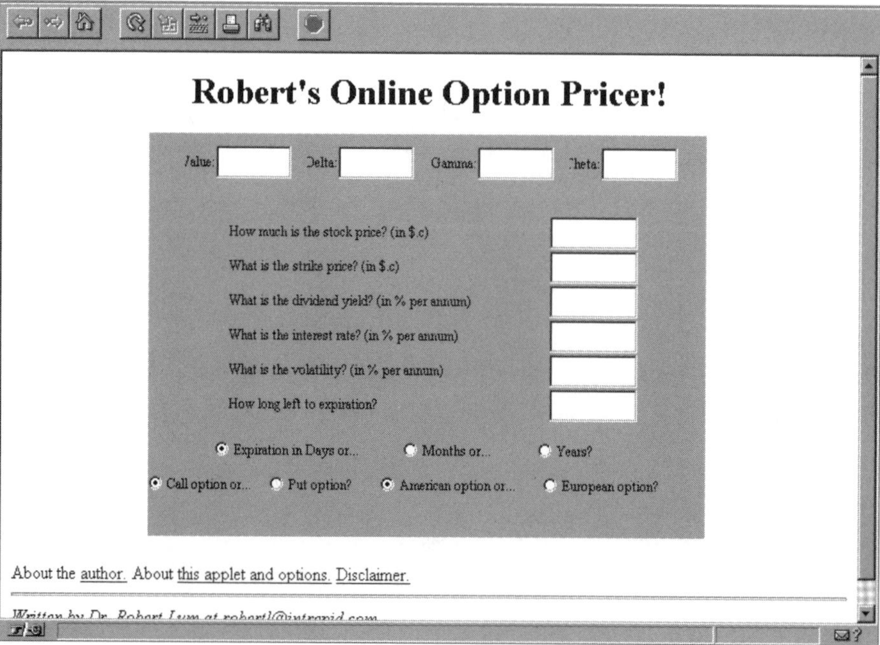

RAINDROPS

Creator: Sea Level Software
E-mail: WebMaster@SealevelSoftware.com

This applet displays various-sized raindrops falling around an image. And if you are patient for a while, you may eventually hear some gulls. Raindrops, created by Jonathan Locke, was rated one of the top Java applets on the Web by the Java Applet Rating Service in December 1995. Raindrops uses threads and graphics techniques to create flicker-free animation.

HTML FOR RAINDROPS

To embed this applet in your Web page, use the following HTML:

```
<applet code="Sealevel.class" width=500 height=200>
</applet>
```

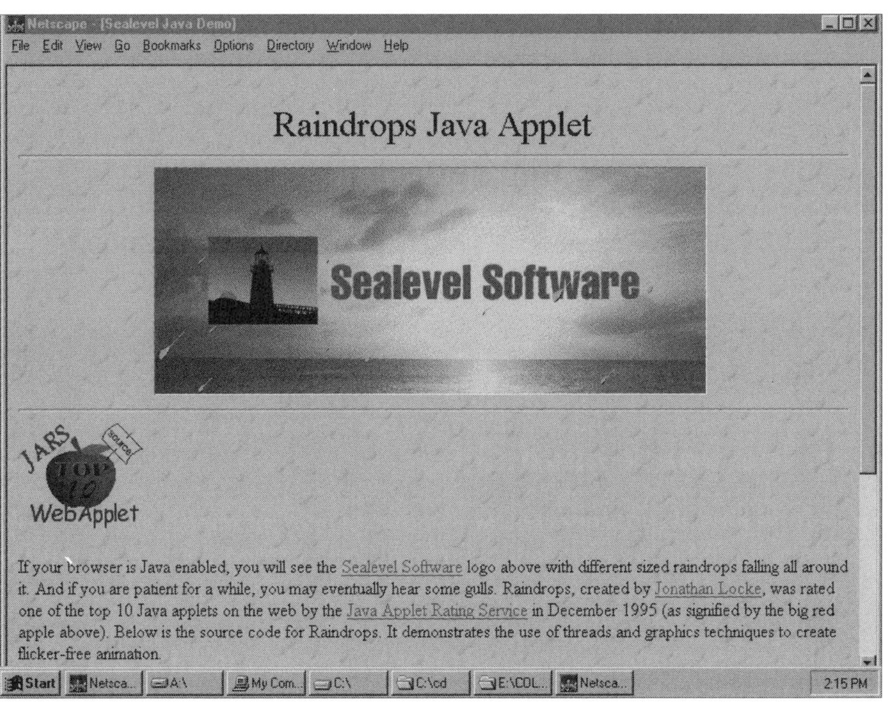

KReversi

Creator: Alessandro Aldo "Kazuma" Garbagnati
E-mail: kazuma@energy.it)
URL: http://www.energy.it/~kazuma/

This applet is a multilanguage version of the Reversi (or Othello) game; the user plays against the computer. You can use a parameter to specify ENGLISH or ITALIAN; any other language can be specified as well, as long as it can be read in as a text file.

KReversi is based on a very simple algorithm that makes the computer the weaker player. The init() part or the program determines which language to display or reads in an external file for any language other than English and Italian. The paint part is simple. It reads an array that contains the board's configuration and repaints it.

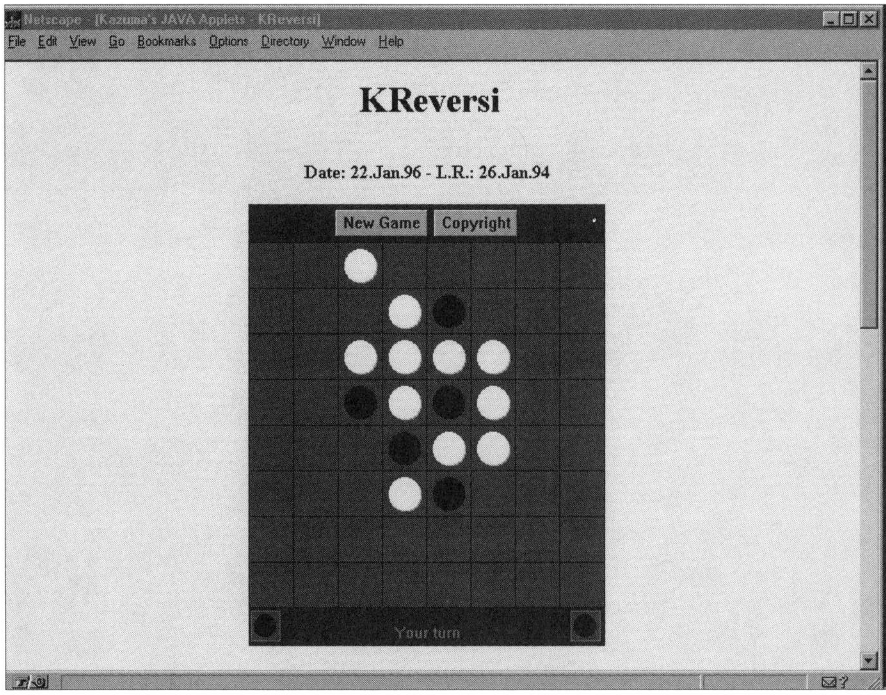

PARAMETERS OF KREVERSI

You can use several parameters to modify this applet on your Web page. To change the size of the applet, modify the following parameter:

```
<APPLET CODE="KReversi" WIDTH=321 HEIGHT=387>
```

You can specify the language of the applet by altering the following parameter:

```
<PARAM NAME="language" VALUE="english">
```

You can specify either "english" (which is the default), "italian", or "external". If you specify English or Italian, you don't need to specify an external language file because the languages are in the code. You can use any language for the applet by including the text file called language.txt which is provided in the KReversi subdirectory on the CD.

HTML FOR REVERSI

To embed this applet in your Web page, use the following HTML:

```
<APPLET CODE="KReversi" WIDTH=321 HEIGHT=387>
<PARAM NAME="language" VALUE="english">
</APPLET>
```

RUBIK UNBOUND

Creator: Karl Hörnell
E-mail: karl@tdb.uu.se
This applet is a Java implementation of the classic Rubik's Cube. The user interface is simple and easy to understand. You can move a side of the cube just by clicking on it with your mouse and rotating it. Twist or rotate by pointing and dragging in the appropriate direction. Press the S key to scramble and the R key to restore (as long as the mouse cursor is somewhere in the applet region).

HTML FOR RUBIK UNBOUND

To embed this applet in your Web page, use the following HTML:

```
<applet code="rubik.class" width=120 height=120>
</applet></td>
```

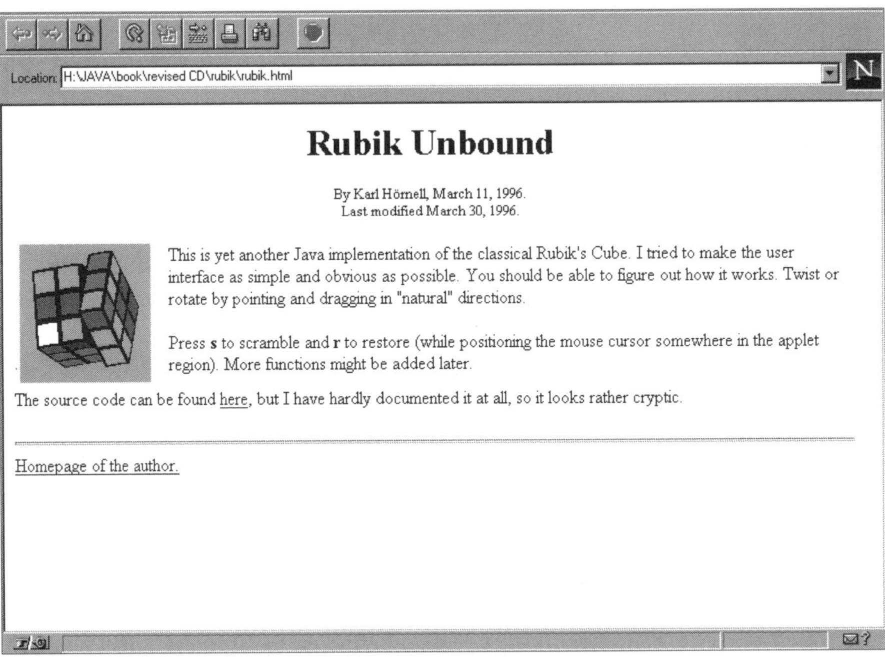

Scrolling Bouncing Text applet

Creator: Man Kam Kwong
E-mail: kwong@mcs.anl.gov

This applet scrolls and bounces any text that you type. It also allows you to change what is displayed in the applet just by clicking on the applet area and using the Control (Crtl) key plus one of the letter options to change the text color, size, style, and font.

To do this, first move the cursor into the applet window. To change the text that is displayed, click and input the new text and press Enter.

To change the color of the text, press Control (Crtl) plus one of the following keys:

a=black

b=blue

c=cyan

g=green

o=orange

r=red

To change the size of the text, press Control (Ctrl) plus *l* for large and *s* for small.

To change the style of the text, press Control (Ctrl) plus one of the following keys:

e=bold

I=italic

n=normal

To change the style of the text, press Control (Ctrl) plus one of the following keys:

t=Times Roman

u=Courier

v=Helvetica

w=Dialog

HTML FOR SCROLLING BOUNCING TEXT

To embed this applet in your Web page, use the following HTML:

```
<applet code="Scroll4.class" width=400 height=120>
</applet>
```

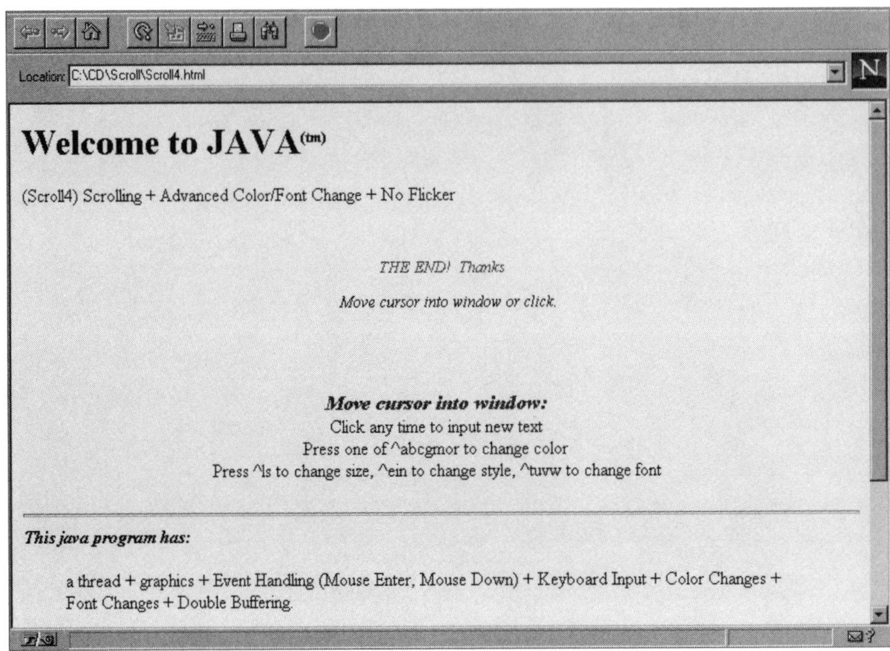

SCROLLING IMAGE

Creator: Man Kam Kwong
E-mail: kwong@mcs.anl.gov
This example shows how an image can be displayed and moved in an applet. The technique of double-buffering is used to reduce flickering. This applet allows the author (in the source code) to choose a time limit for how long the applet will run. The viewer can then click on the applet to initiate the applet again.

HTML FOR SCROLLING IMAGE

To embed this applet in your Web page, use the following HTML:

```
<applet code="ScrollIm.class" width=500 height=200>
</applet>
```

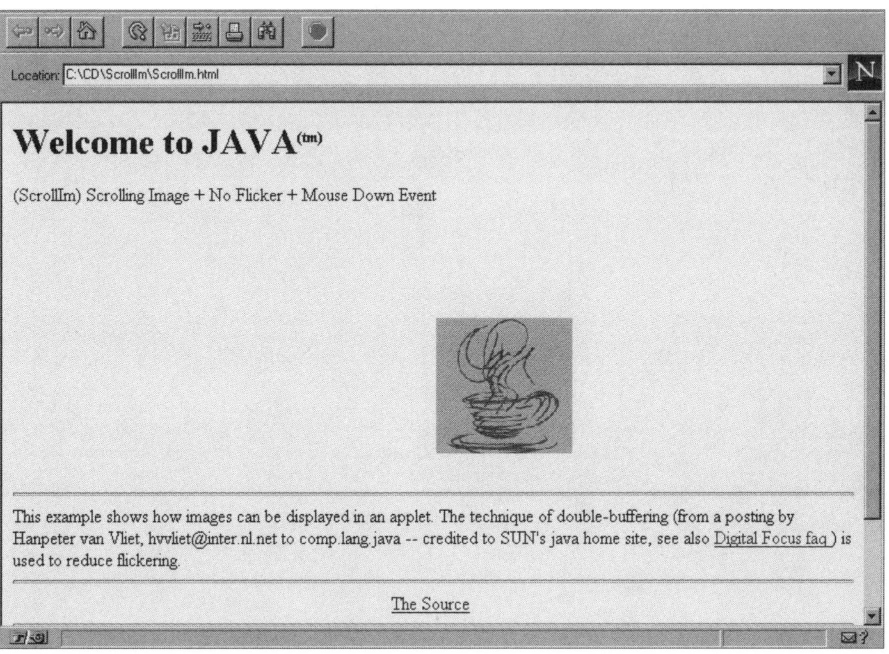

JAVA SOLITAIRE

Creator: Karl Hörnell
E-mail: karl@tdb.uu.se

Java Solitaire (also known as Chinese Checkters) uses some very basic Java to create a great interactive game. The object is to remove as many marbles as possible from the board. The only legal moves are horizontal or vertical jumps of one marble over another, in which the marble lands on an empty hole on the other side of the jumped marble. The marble that was jumped will be removed from the board. To jump a marble, just drag a marble over another marble that has an empty hole on the other side of it.

HTML FOR SOLITAIRE

To embed this applet in your Web page, use the following HTML:

```
<applet code="solitaire.class" width=280 height=190>
</applet>
```

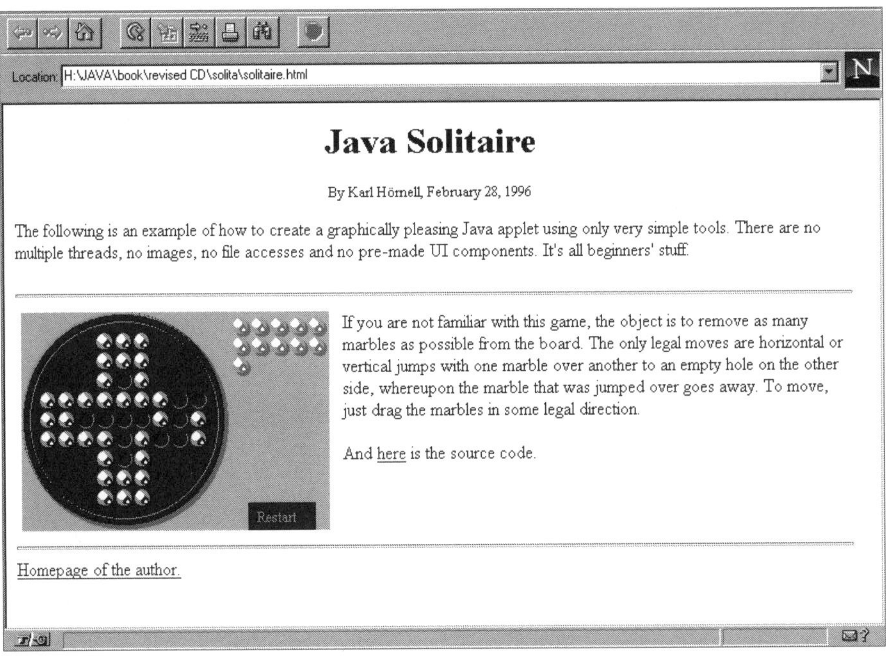

THE JAVA STARFIELD

Creator: Michael Alexander Ewert
E-mail: ewert@morganmedia.com
This applet will display a star field on your Web page.

PARAMETERS

You can use the following parameters to modify this applet:

Parameter Description	Tag
Specify the size of the starfield	`<applet code="stars.class" width=400 height=100>`
Specify the number of stars	`<param name=numstars value="30">`

HTML FOR STARFIELD

To embed this applet on your Web page, use the following HTML:

```
<applet code="stars.class" width=400 height=100>
<param name=numstars value="30">
</applet>
```

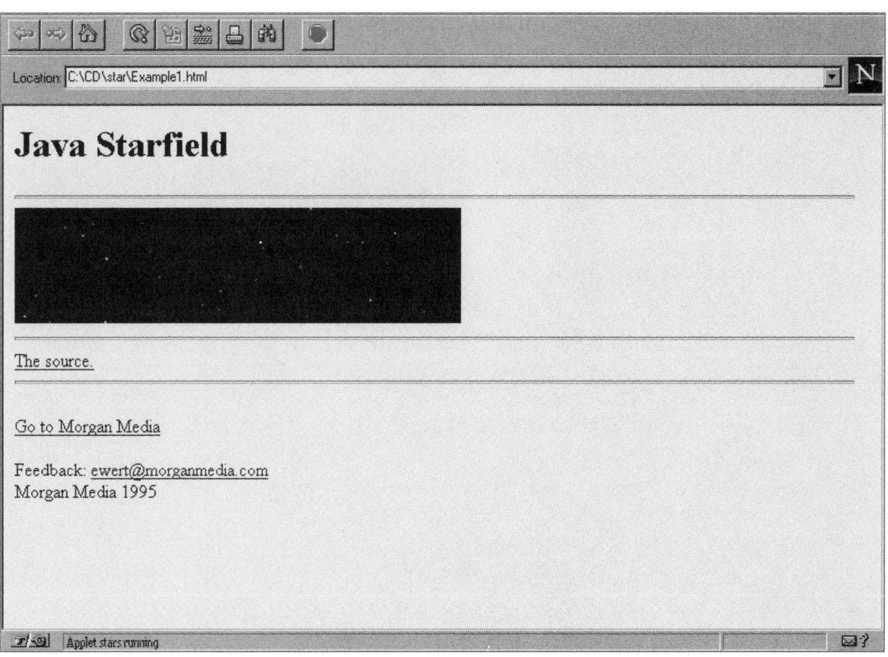

IMAGEZIPPER

Creator: Ted Young
E-mail: Ted@indigocom.com

This applet displays an arbitrary number of images next to one another and then scrolls the images to the left, much like a ticker tape or a zipper. By clicking on one of the images that is scrolling by, the user is taken to the associated URL. An optional image is tiled on the background.

The key to this applet is the standard flicker-prevention, which is achieved by the creation of an offscreen image that is drawn by the normal paint routine; only when it's complete is the offscreen image drawn on the "real" screen. The trick is to figure out which image was clicked, since the images can be different widths; this is handled by mouseUp. Then we just take the URL and use the showDocument() method to take the user to the appropriate link.

PARAMETERS

Use the following parameters to modify this applet on your Web page:

Parameter Function	Tag
Specify the size of the zipper	<applet code=ImageZipper.class width=400 height=78>
Specify the background color of the applet area	<param name=backgroundcolor value="#F0F0F0">
Specify the number of scrolling images	<param name=imagecount value=4
Specify an image	<param name=image1 value="indigo.gif">
Specify the associated URL for an image (the order of the URL must match the order in which the images appear)	<param name=url1 value="http://www.indigocom.com/">
Specify the number of milliseconds between each movement of the images in the ticker	<param name=delay value=100>
Specify the number of pixels to scroll the image each time it is redrawn	<param name=step value=3>

HTML FOR IMAGEZIPPER

To embed this applet in your Web page, use the following HTML:

```
<applet code=ImageZipper.class width=400 height=78>
<param name=backgroundcolor value="#F0F0F0">
<param name=imagecount value=4>
<param name=image1 value="indigo.gif">
<param name=image2 value="duke.gif">
<param name=image3 value="wsolp.gif">
<param name=image4 value="gotham.gif">
<param name=url1 value="http://www.indigocom.com/">
<param name=url2 value="http://www.indigocom.com/training">
<param name=url3 value="http://www.wsolp.com/">
<param name=url4 value="http://www.gothamweb.com/">
<param name=delay value=100>
<param name=step value=3>
</applet>
```

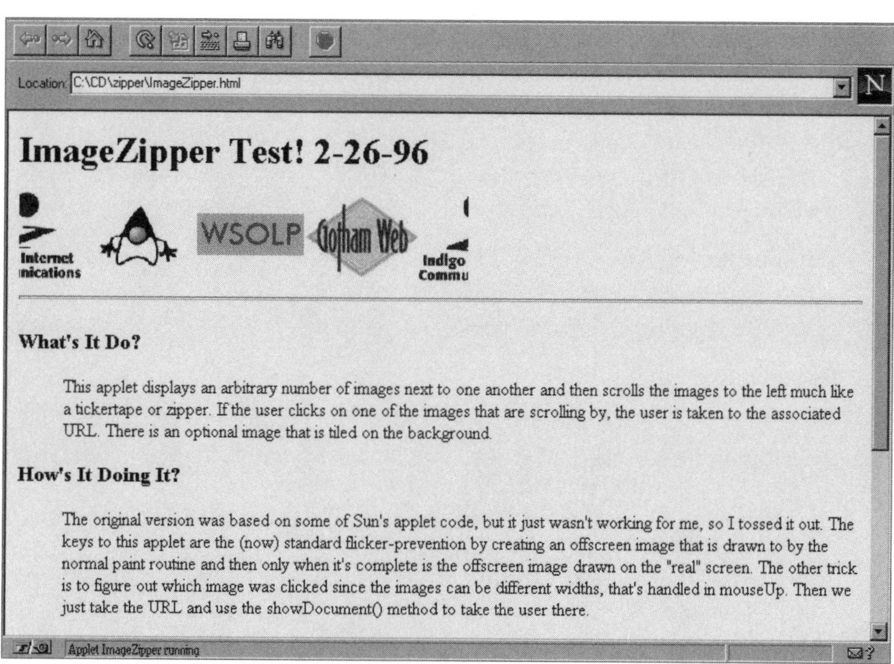

JDK DEMO APPLETS

The following applets appear in the Java Development Kit in the demo subdirectory. Many of the applets were written by the originators of the Java language and provide a useful guide through the fundamentals of Java. Many of these applets can be customized and then placed directly on a Web page.

ANIMATOR

Creator: Herb Jellinek, Sun Microsystems
The Animator demo applet that comes with the Java Development Kit (JDK 1.0) is the same one that we have explained in Chapter 3. The animator displays a series of images and plays sounds associated with each image as it is displayed on the screen.

Parameters of the Animator Applet Here are the parameters of the animator applet:

Parameter Description	Tag
The name of the directory with all the gif files, which can be displayed as part of the animation. The files are named t1.gif, t2.gif, and so on.	<param name=imagesource value="images/Duke">
The counter for the last image. This tells us how many images there are in total. *T10.gif* is the last image.	<param name=endimage value=10>
The directory where the audio files reside.	<param name=soundsource value="audio">
Determines the soundtrack to play continuously through the animation.	<param name=soundtrack value=spacemusic.au>
Determines the sounds that correspond to the images in the animation. There are as many sounds as there are images.	<param name=sounds value="1.au|2.au|3.au|4.au|5.au |6.au|7.au|8.au|9.au|0.au">
Determines the amount of time (measured in milliseconds) that each image stays on the screen.	<param name=pause value=200>

HTML for Animator Applet To embed this applet in your Web page, use the following HTML:

```
<title>The Animator Applet</title>
<hr>

<applet code=Animator.class width=200 height=200>
<param name=imagesource value="images/Duke">
<param name=endimage value=10>
<param name=soundsource value="audio">
<param name=soundtrack value=spacemusic.au>
<param name=sounds
value="1.au|2.au|3.au|4.au|5.au|6.au|7.au|8.au|9.au|0.au">
<param name=pause value=200>
</applet>
```

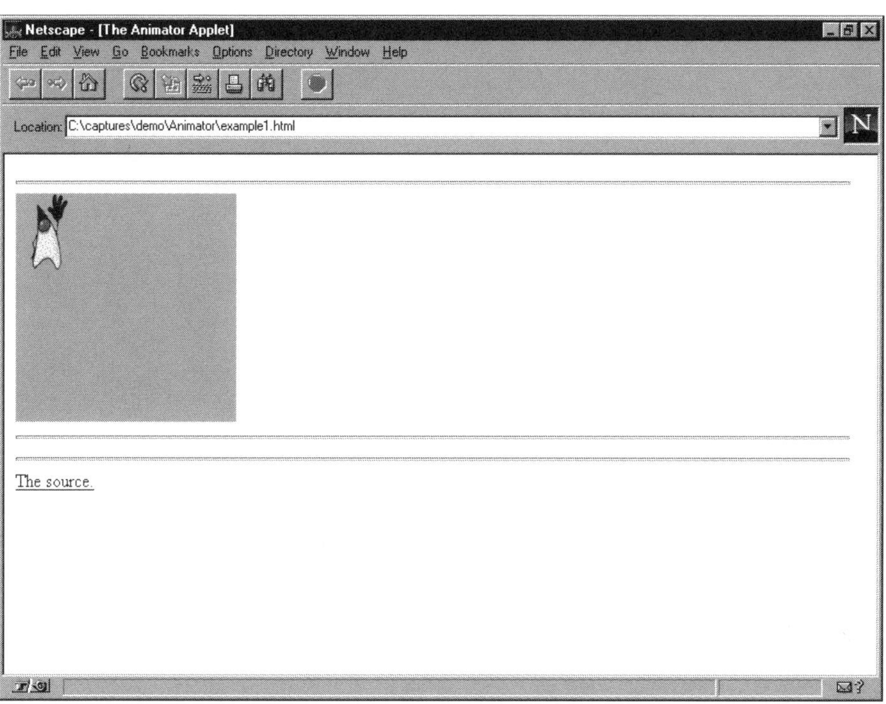

ARCTEST

Creator: Sami Shaio, Sun Microsystems

ArcTest is an interactive test of the Graphics.drawArc and Graphics.fillArc routines. You enter the start and finish angle of the arc and you can then choose to either draw the arc or fill the region specified by the start and finish angles. This is a good applet to start from when you want to build a pie chart or a similar graphic.

Parameters The ArcTest applet does not read in any parameters from the HTML file.

HTML for ArcTest Applet To embed this applet in your Web page, use the following HTML:

```
<applet code=ArcTest.class width=400 height=400>
</applet>
```

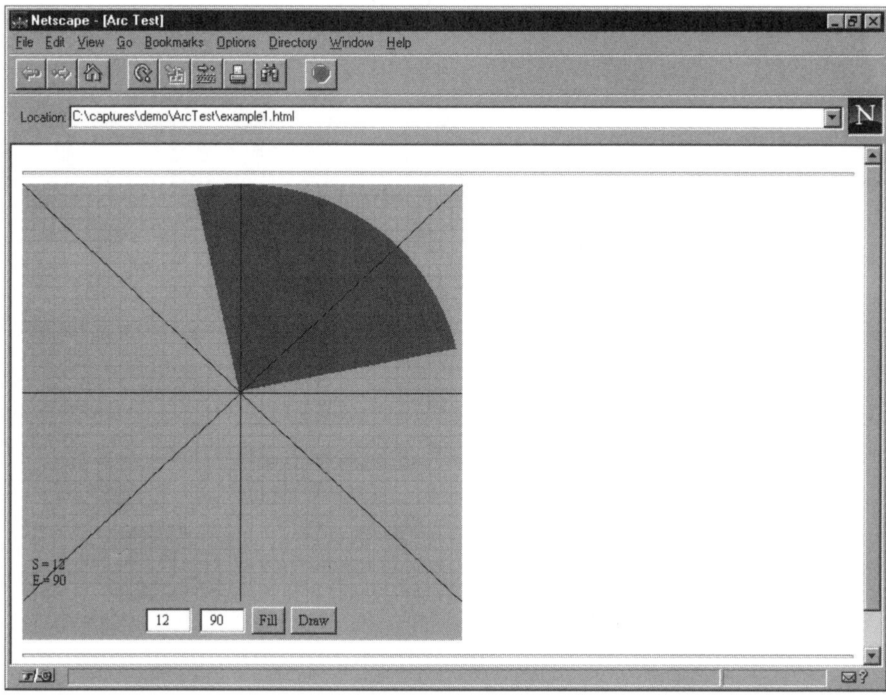

BARCHART

Creator: Sami Shaio, Sun Microsystems

This applet draws a bar chart. The colors, labels, and patters for each bar are customizable from the HTML file. This applet makes extensive use of the drawing functions in the Graphics class. The 3-D effect on the screen is achieved by using a black bar for every column and then placing a solid or striped bar at an offset from the black bar.

Parameters To customize this applet on your Web page, modify the following parameters:

Parameter Description	Tag
Number of columns	`<param name=columns value="4">`
Factor by which to scale the columns in the bar chart	`<param name=scale value="5">`
Color for column 2 in the bar chart	`<param name=c2_color value="green">`
Label for column 2	`<param name=c2_label value="Q2">`
Pattern for the column 2 bar	`<param name=c2_style value="striped">`
Value (height) for column 2	`<param name=c2 value="30">`
Title	`<param name=title value="Performance">`

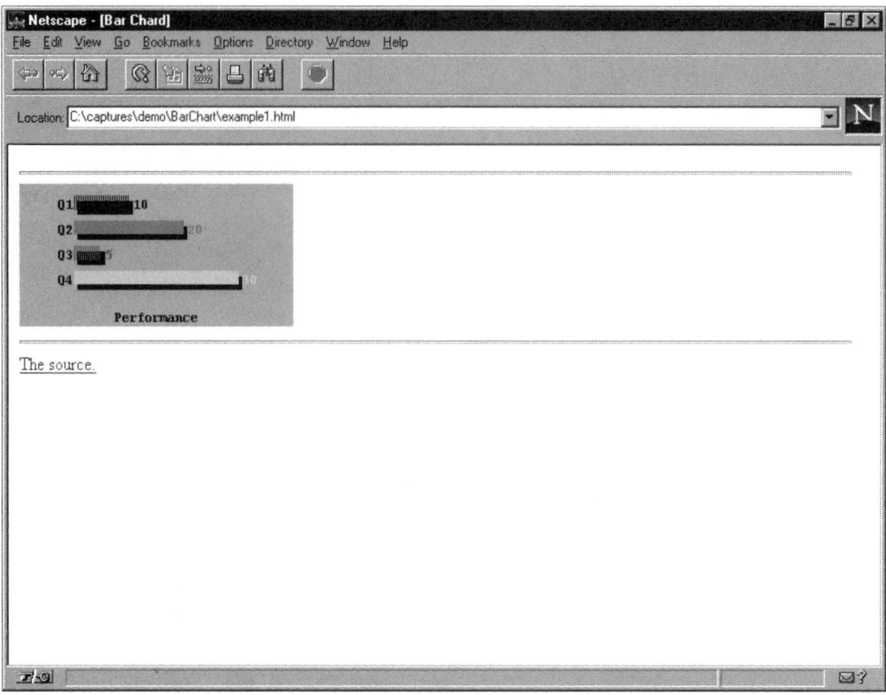

HTML for BarChart To embed this applet on your Web page, use the following HTML:

```
<applet code="Chart.class" width=251 height=125>
<param name=c2_color value="green">
<param name=c2_label value="Q2">
<param name=c1_style value="striped">
<param name=c4 value="30">
<param name=c3 value="5">
<param name=c2 value="20">
<param name=c4_color value="yellow">
<param name=c1 value="10">
<param name=c4_label value="Q4">
<param name=title value="Performance">
<param name=c3_style value="striped">
<param name=columns value="4">
<param name=c1_color value="blue">
<param name=c1_label value="Q1">
<param name=c3_color value="magenta">
<param name=c3_label value="Q3">
<param name=c2_style value="solid">
```

```
<param name=orientation value="horizontal">
<param name=c4_style value="solid">
<param name=scale value="5">
</applet>
```

BLINK

Creator: Arthur Van Hoff, Sun Microsystems

This applet displays blinking words at random points on the screen. The words that you want to display can be specified in the *lbl* parameter in the HTML file. Also, you can specify the time period for which each word stays on the screen with the *speed* parameter.

Parameters You can modify this applet on your Web page with the following parameters:

Parameter	Tag
The string that makes up the words that we want to blink at random on the screen.	<param name=lbl value="This is the next best thing to sliced bread! Toast, toast, toast, butter, jam, toast, marmite, toast.">
Determines the time period for which each word stays on the screen.	<param name=speed value="4">

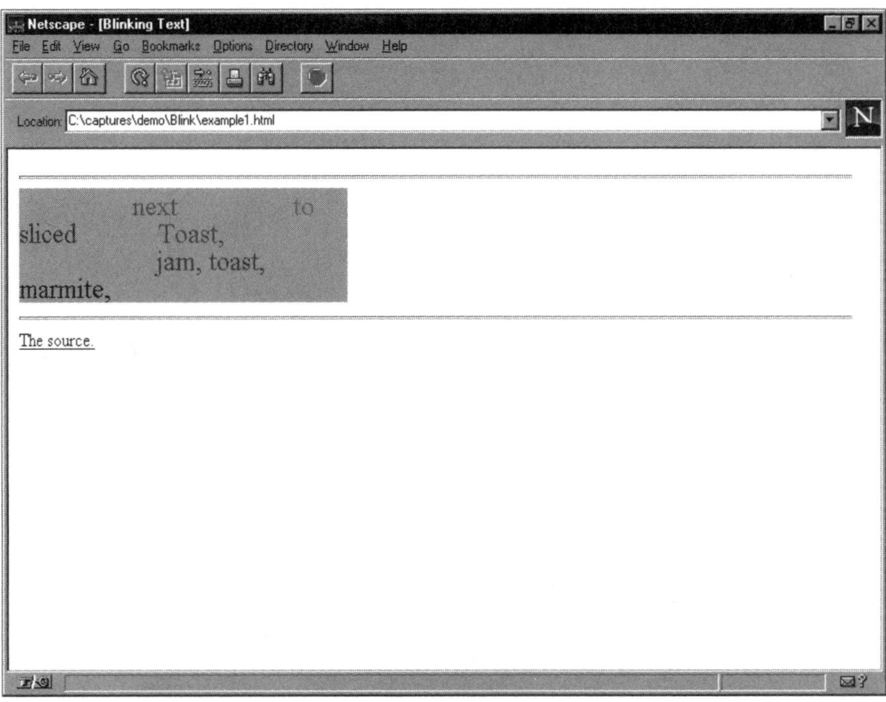

HTML for Blink To embed this applet in your Web page, use the following HTML:

```
<applet code="Blink.class" width=300 height=100>
<param name=lbl value="This is the next best thing to sliced bread!
Toast, toast, toast, butter, jam, toast, marmite, toast.">
<param name=speed value="4">
</applet>
```

BOUNCINGHEADS

Creator: Jonathan Payne, Sun Microsystems

This applet shows parts of an image at random points on the screen. The default image for the applet is the creator's head. The creator has chosen not to make the image a parameter that can be read in from an HTML file. This is easily rectifiable. This is also a good idea if you want to modify this applet with your own images.

Parameters The BouncingHeads applet does not read in any parameters from the HTML file.

HTML for BouncingHeads To embed this applet in your Web page, use the following HTML:

```
<applet code=BounceItem.class width=500 height=300>
</applet>
```

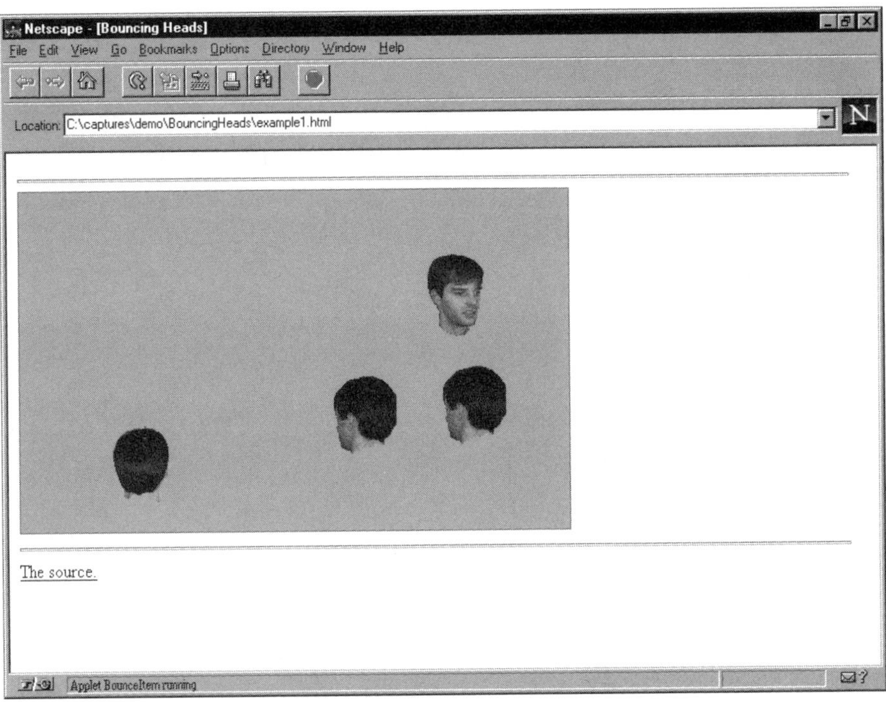

CARDTEST

Creator: Arthur Van Hoff, Sun Microsystems

This applet, which displays various layouts using a CardLayout class, is a good way to learn about layouts in Java. This applet is interactive and the user can choose which CardLayout he or she wants to see. Start with this applet if the layout you want is not too complicated.

Parameters The CardTest applet does not read in any parameters.

HTML for CardTest To embed this applet in your Web page, use the following HTML:

```
<applet code=CardTest.class width=400 height=300>
</applet>
```

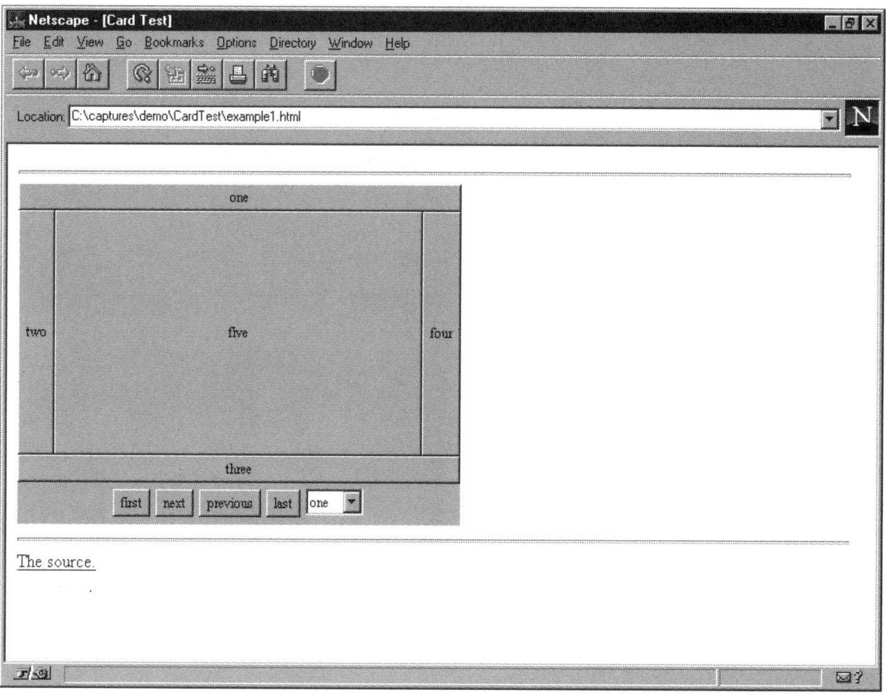

DITHERTEST

Creator: Sun Microsystems

This applet is a good test of the classes in java.Image. The two classes that are tested are ColorModel and ImageMemorySource. This is a good applet if you need different hues or a color spectrum somewhere in your applet and don't know where to start.

Parameters This applet does not read in any parameters from the HTML file.

HTML for DitherTest

```
<applet code=DitherTest.class width=400 height=400>
</applet>
```

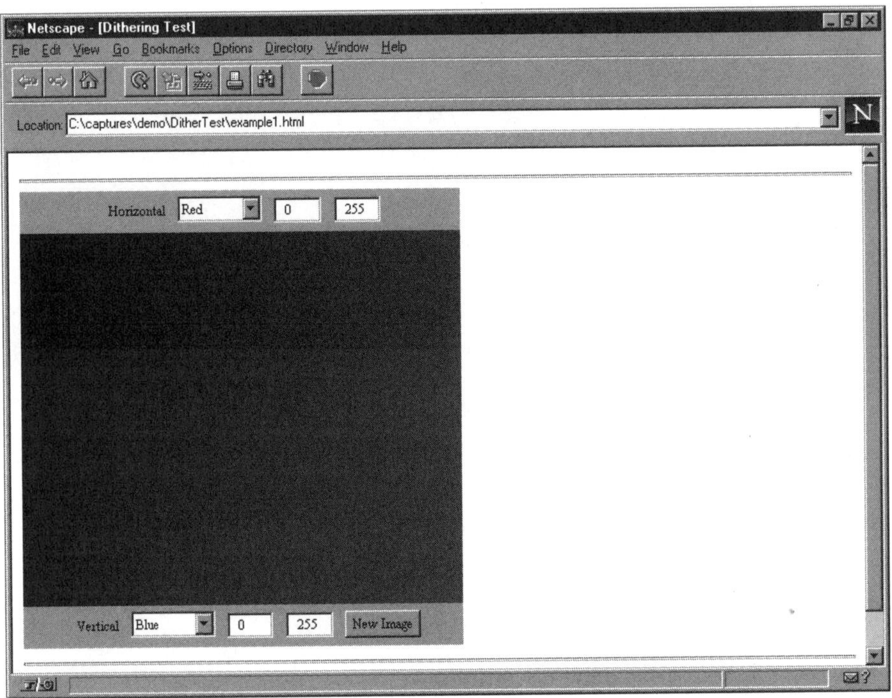

DRAWTEST

Creator: Sami Shaio, Sun Microsystems

DrawTest is an interactive drawing board applet that lets the user draw lines and points in different colors on a canvas. It uses the Java drawing primitives to do its work.

Parameters This applet does not read in any parameters from the HTML file.

HTML for DrawTest To embed this applet in your Web page, use the following HTML:

```
<applet code=DrawTest.class width=400 height=400>
</applet>
```

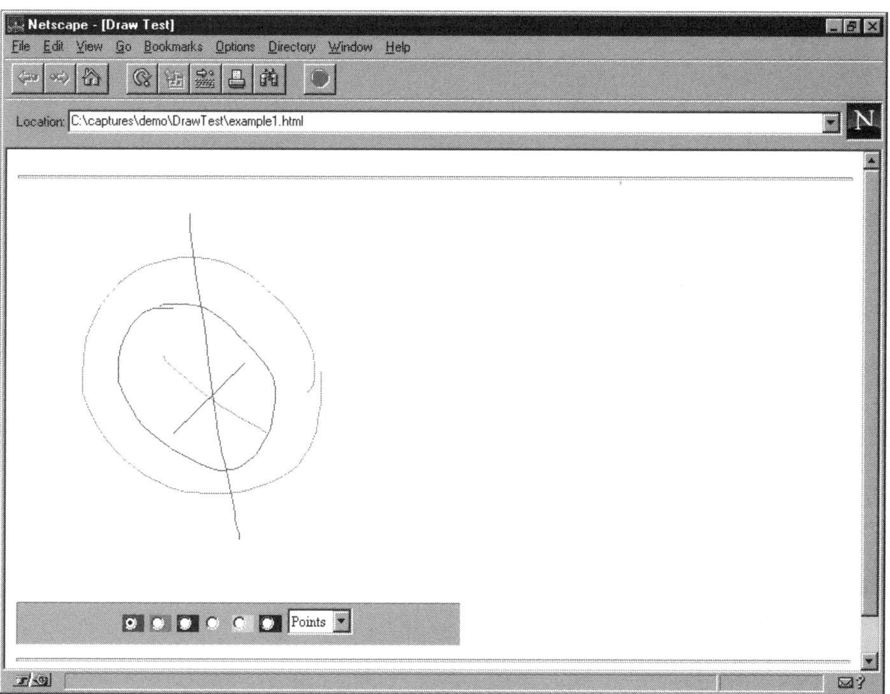

GRAPHICSTEST

Authors: Sami Shaio, Kevin A. Smith; Sun Microsystems

This applet illustrates the use of the Graphics drawing methods, arcs, ovals, polygons, rectangles, and rounded rectangles. This applet also uses a card layout, so that each drawing is done on a successive "card" like HyperCard.

Parameters This applet does not read in any parameters from the HTML file.

HTML for GraphicsTest To embed this applet in your Web page, use the following HTML:

```
<applet code=GraphicsTest.class width=400 height=400>
</applet>
```

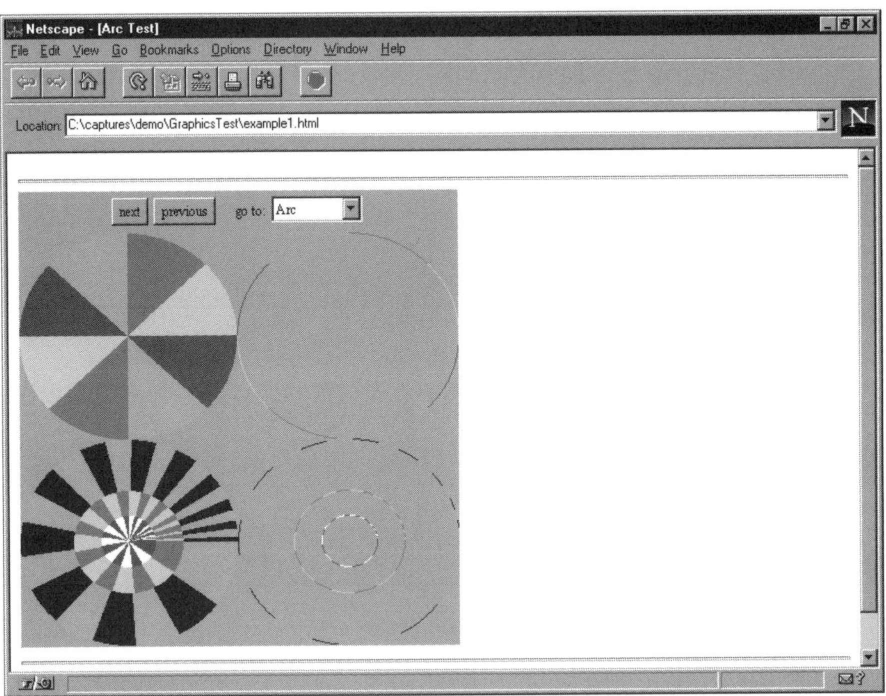

GRAPHLAYOUT

Creator: Sun Microsystems

The GraphLayout applet illustrates node theory. The applet dynamically attempts to display the graph using a heuristic approach, slowly optimizing the tension between each node until the graph drifts into stasis. Nodes repel each other to an optimal value that you can define.

Parameters The GraphLayout applet has two parameters that you can modify:

Description Parameter	Tag
The node which is designated at the center of the layout. This node is depicted by a red box.	<param name=center value="joe">
The edges of the graph, depicted as a comma separated list. Edged have values that specify their connecting pairs, <from>-<to>, and an optional desired length of the edge <from>-<to>/<length>.	<param name=edges value="joe-food,joe-dog,joe-tea,joe-cat,joe-table,table-plate/50,plate-food/30,food-mouse/100,food-dog/100,mouse-cat/150,table-cup/30,cup-tea/30,dog-cat/80,cup-spoon/50,plate-fork,dog-flea1,dog-flea2,flea1-flea2/20,plate-knive">

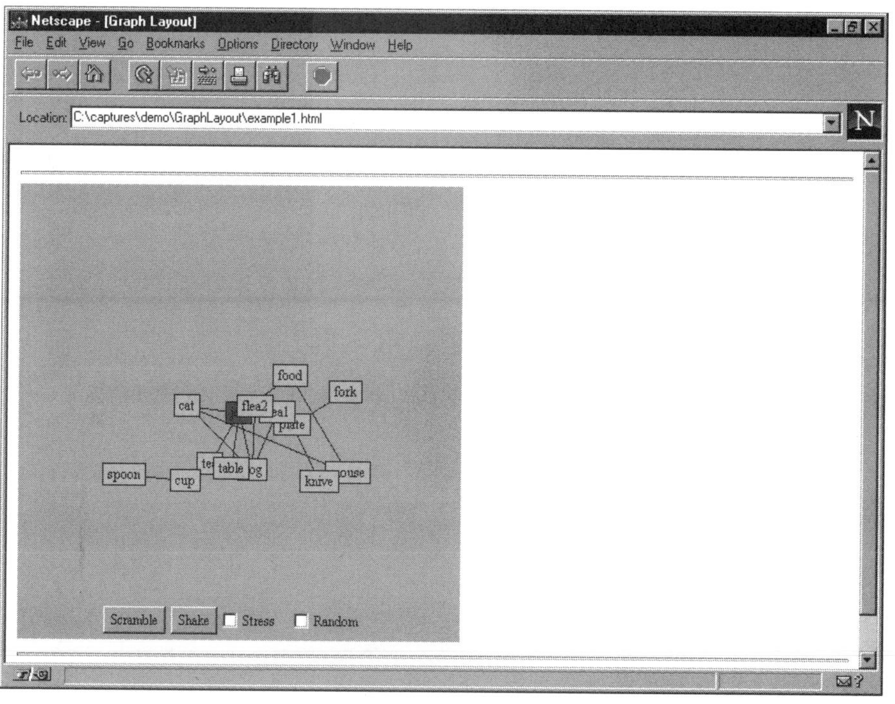

HTML for GraphLayout To embed this applet in your Web page, use the following HTML:

```
<applet code="Graph.class" width=400 height=400>
<param name=edges value="joe-food,joe-dog,joe-tea,joe-cat,joe-table,
table-plate/50,plate-food/30,food-mouse/100,food-dog/100,mouse-cat/150,
table-cup/30,cup-tea/30,dog-cat/80,cup-spoon/50,plate-fork,dog-flea1,
dog-flea2,flea1-flea2/20,plate-knive">
<param name=center value="joe">
</applet>
```

IMAGEMAP

Creator: Jim Graham, Sun Microsystems

This applet allows you to define areas of an graphics image that have particular actions when the mouse passes over that area. The areas can also "highlight" to indicate that there is an action. For example, the demo draws a picture of the author, Jim Graham, and when the mouses passes over the area of the image that is his mouth, his mouth is highlighted and the applet plays an audio that says "Hi."

Parameters Use the following parameters to modify this applet on your Web page:

Parameter	Function
highlight	Either the string "brighter" or "darker" followed by a number that represents the percentage of brighter or darker.
img	The name of the image (gif) file to use
area<num>	A numbered area that defines, in the value string, the name of the area, x and y location of the area relative to the upper left corner, the width and height of the area, and some action: fetch another URL, play an audio, or display a message string.

HTML for ImageMap To embed this applet in your Web page, use the following HTML:

```
<applet code=ImageMap.class width=522 height=486>
<param name=img value="images/jim.graham.gif">
<param name=highlight value="brighter30">
<param name=area1 value="SoundArea,260,180,120,60,audio/hi.au">
<param name=area2 value="NameArea,260,180,120,60,Hi!">
<param name=area3 value="HighlightArea,260,180,120,60">
<param name=area4 value="NameArea,265,125,45,20,That is my right eye">
<param name=area5 value="HighlightArea,265,125,45,20">
<param name=area6 value="NameArea,335,130,45,20,That is my left eye">
<param name=area7 value="HighlightArea,335,130,45,20">
<param name=area8
value="HrefButtonArea,200,7,210,300,../../../people/flar/">
<param name=area9
value="RoundHrefButtonArea,60,0,100,120,example2.html">
<param name=area10 value="SoundArea,425,98,27,27,audio/chirp1.au">
<param name=area11 value="NameArea,425,98,27,27,Chirp!">
```

```
<param name=area12 value="HighlightArea,425,98,27,27">
<param name=area13 value="ClickArea,Ø,Ø,522,486">
</applet>
```

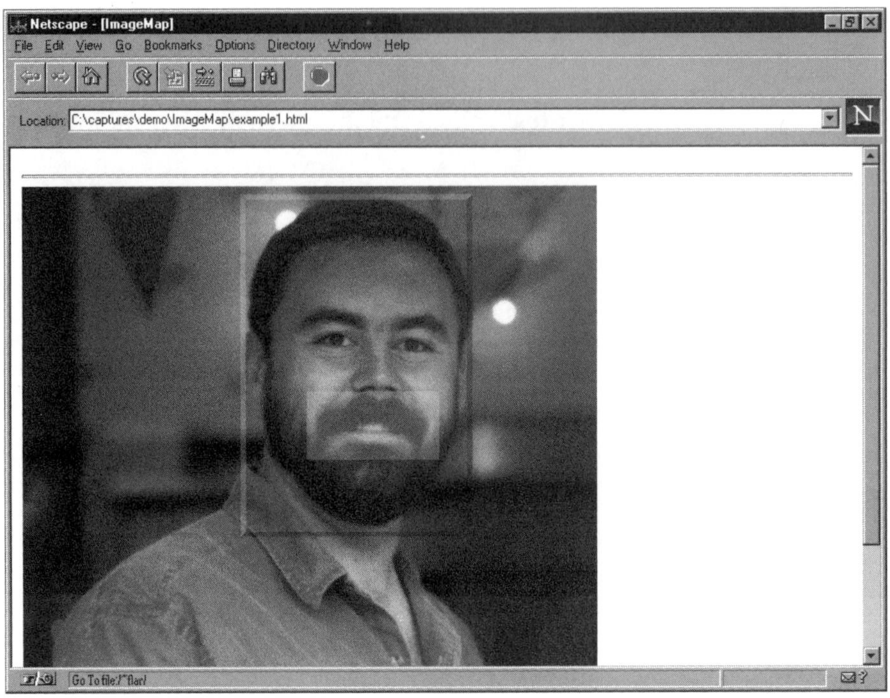

IMAGETEST

Creator: Sun Microsystems

This applet performs various modifications to images at the center of each of the target areas. You can change the color, size, and angle of the images from your keyboard.

Parameters There are no parameters for this applet.

HTML for ImageTest To embed this applet in your Web page, use the following HTML:

```
<applet code=ImageTest.class width=500 height=400>
</applet>
```

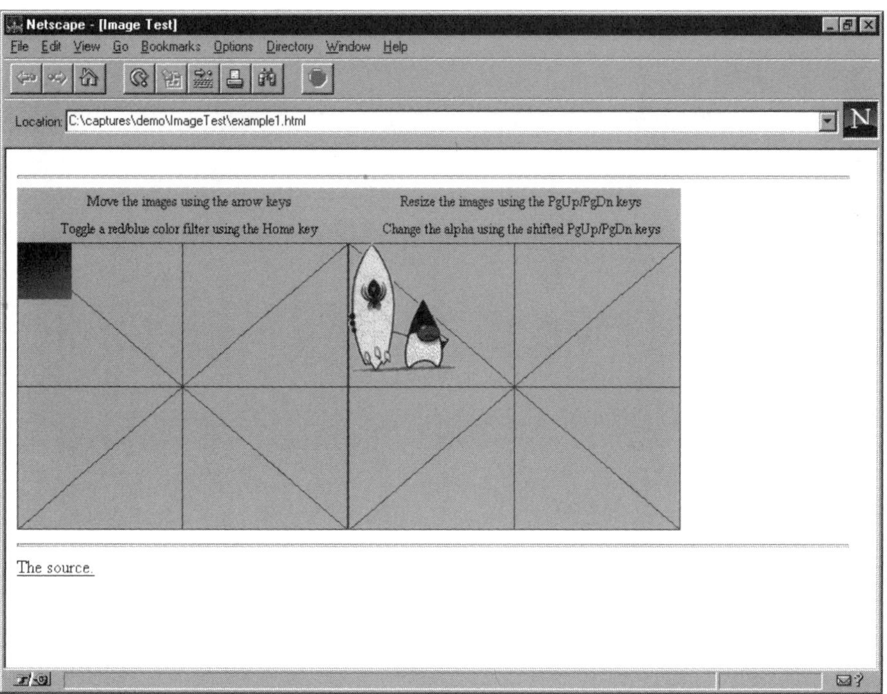

JUMPINGBOX

Creator: Sun Microsystems

JumpingBox is a fun little game applet, where you chase a small box with the mouse and attempt to hit it by clicking the mouse in the box before it jumps away. Different sounds play as the mouse clicks are accumulated. On slower machines this game applet may not be as challenging.

Parameters There are no parameters for this applet.

HTML for JumpingBox To embed this applet in your Web page, use the following HTML:

```
<applet code=MouseTrack.class width=300 height=300>
</applet>
```

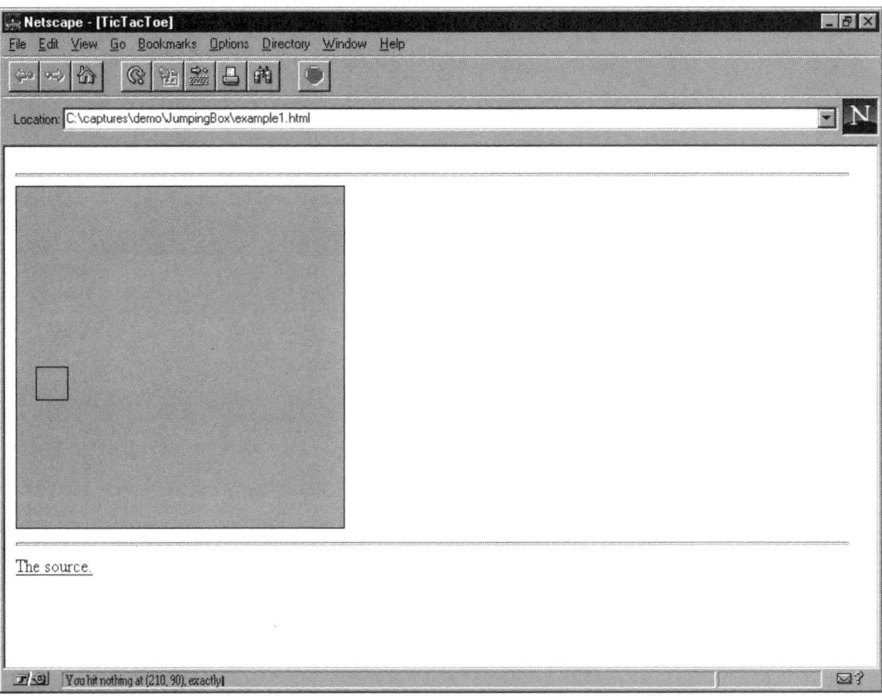

MOLECULEVIEWER

Creator: James Gosling, Sun Microsystems

This applet will draw a chemical compound model based upon a file that contains information about the compound in .xyz formatted files. These files describe the chemical compound from basic chemical elements like carbon, hydrogen, oxygen, and so on. Once drawn, the compound may be rotated in 3-D space just by grabbing it with the mouse and dragging it to the view you wish. More information about .xyz files can be found at http://chem.leeds.ac.uk/Project/MIME.html.

Parameters You can use the model parameter to change the name of the file that contains the .xyz model of the compound.

HTML for MoleculeViewer To modify this applet on your Web page, use the following HTML:

```
<applet code=XYZApp.class width=300 height=300>
<param name=model value=models/HyaluronicAcid.xyz>
</applet>
```

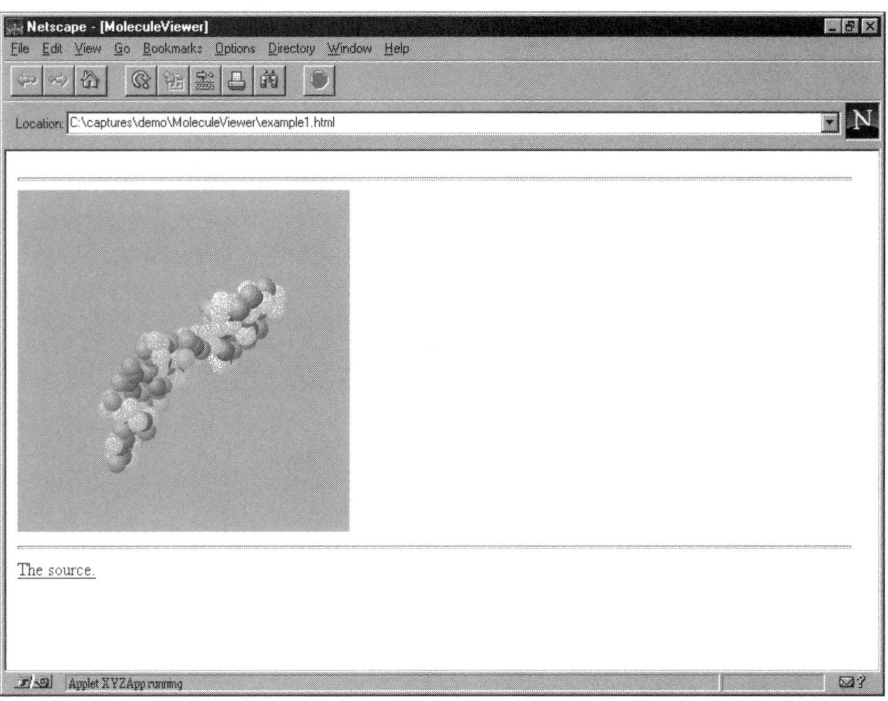

NERVOUSTEXT

Creator: Daniel Wyszynski, Center for Applied Large-Scale Computing (CALC)

The NervousText demo illustrates how Java may be used to spice up a static Web page. Text is passed to the applet in a parameter tag, and the letters are successively drawn and redrawn at different positions relative to each other, so that they appear to be "bouncing" nervously.

Parameters Nervous text takes a single parameter, "text," that can be set to any text string that you want to animate.

HTML for NervousText To embed this applet in your Web page, use the following HTML:

```
<applet code="NervousText.class" width=200 height=50>
<param name=text value="HotJava-Beta">
</applet>
```

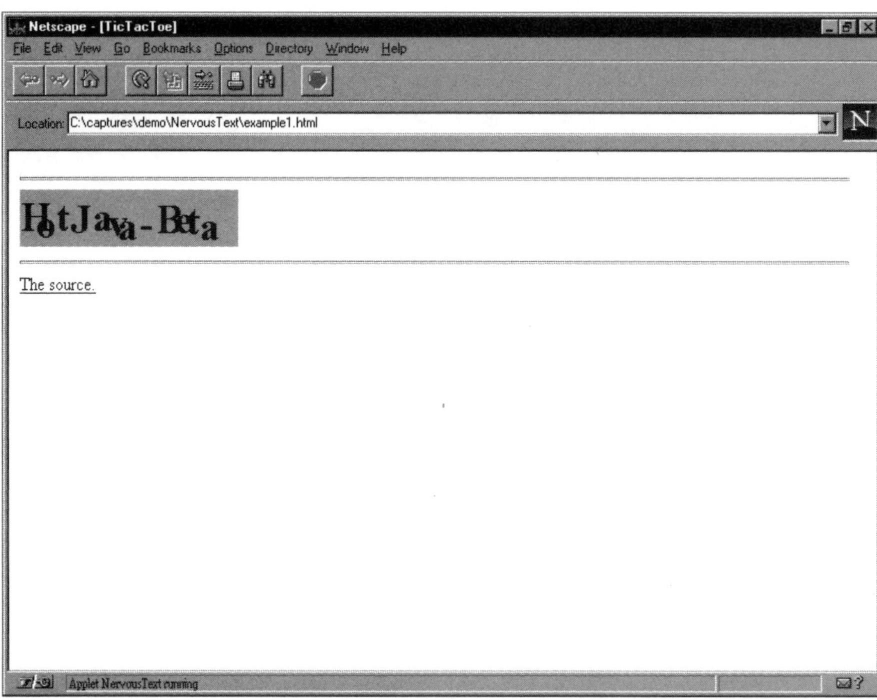

SCROLLING IMAGES

Creator: Arthur Van Hoff, Sun Microsystems

This is the original scrolling image applet, which allows images to be scrolled across the page. You can customize the number of images, the speed of the scrolling, and the direction by just using the parameter tags.

Parameters You can use the following parameter tags to modify this applet on your Web page:

Parameter Description	Tag
The number of times each image is scrolled per second	`<param name=speed value="4">`
The location (URL) of the images to be scrolled. (The images are called by the names of T1.gif, and so on.)	`<param name=img value="images/team">`
The number of pixels and direction that the images are scrolled (to move an image to the right use the numbers 1 through 10, to move it left use –1 through –10)	`<param name=dir value="4">`
The total number of images to be scrolled	`<param name=nimgs value="15">`

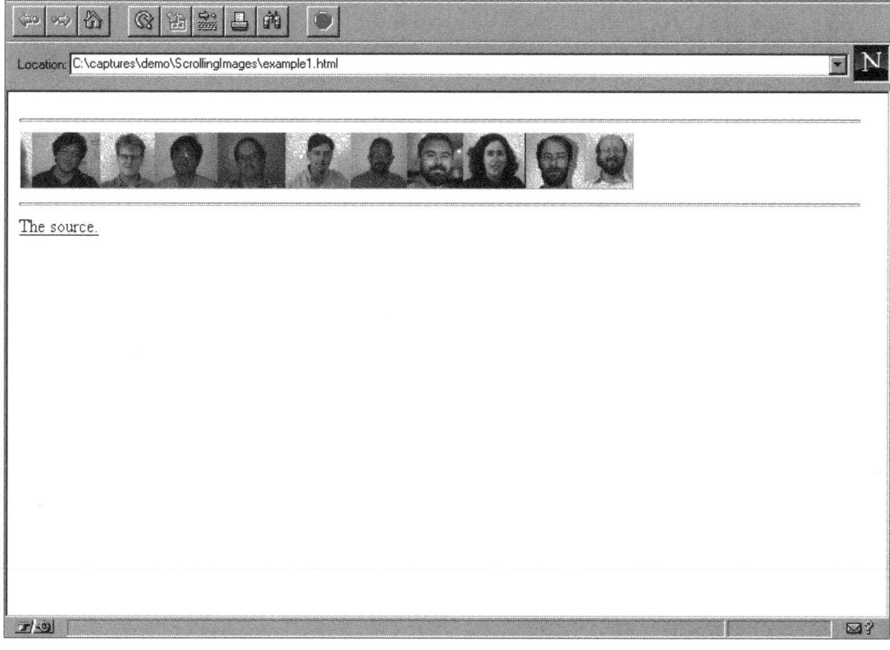

HTML for Scrolling Images To embed this applet in your Web page, use the following HTML:

```
<applet code="ImageTape.class" width=550 height=50>
<param name=speed value="4">
<param name=img value="images/team">
<param name=dir value="4">
<param name=nimgs value="15">
</applet>
```

THE SPREADSHEET APPLET

Creator: Sami Shaio, Sun Microsystems

This is a spreadsheet that can be customized to have varying number of rows and columns. You can also add your own title and starting numbers that will appear when the applet begins.

Parameters Use the following parameters to modify this applet on your Web page:

Parameter Description	Tag
The title of the spreadsheet	<param name=title value="Example">
The number of rows in the spreadsheet	<param name=rows value="4">
the number of columns in the spreadsheet	<param name=cols value="3">
The value of a cell: Values of a cell can either be a label (preceded by the letter l in the parameter) a value (preceded by the letter v in the parameter), or a formula (preceded by the letter f in the parameter). You may add (+), subtract (–), multiply (*), and divide (/).	<param name=c3 value="fC1+C2">

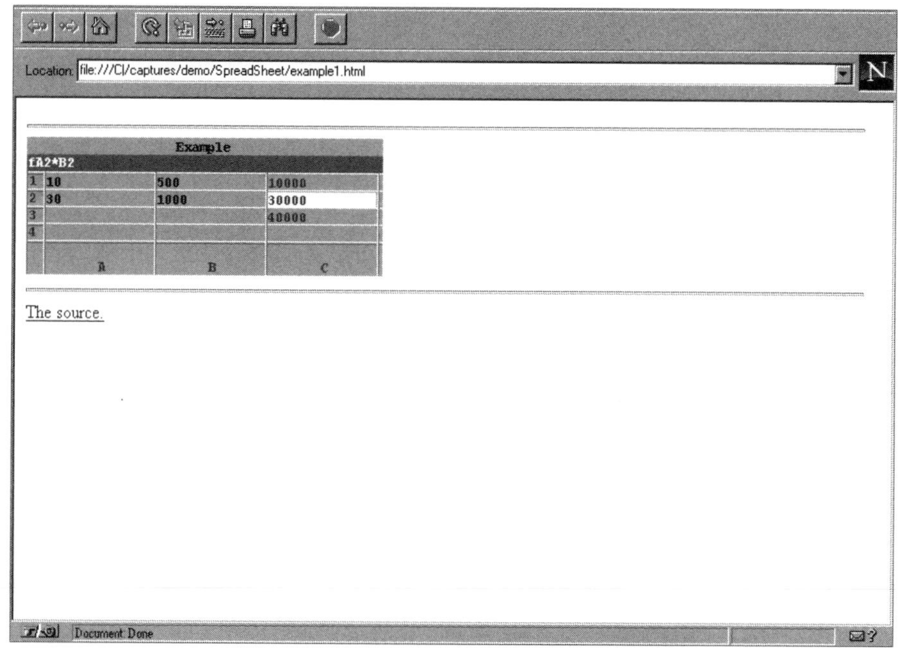

The above parameter indicates that in cell c3, use a formula ("f") and add cell C1 and C2 together. Formulas are computed from left corner downward, which may cause a problem if there is a cell reference that is to the right of below of a cell.

HTML for Spreadsheet To embed this applet in your Web page, use the following HTML:

```
<applet code="SpreadSheet.class" width=320 height=120>
<param name=rows value="4">
<param name=c3 value="fC1+C2">
<param name=c2 value="fA2*B2">
<param name=c1 value="fA1*B2">
<param name=title value="Example">
<param name=b2 value="v1000">
<param name=b1 value="v500">
<param name=cols value="3">
<param name=a2 value="v30">
<param name=a1 value="v10">
</applet>
```

TIC TAC TOE

Creator: Arthur Van Hoff, Sun Microsystems

Here is a "Javatized" Tic Tac Toe. Begin the game by clicking on the box where you want to place your X. After the game is over, click again on the board to start a new game.

Parameters There are no parameters for this applet.

HTML for Tic Tac Toe To embed this applet on your Web page, use the following HTML:

```
<applet code=TicTacToe.class width=120 height=120>
</applet>
```

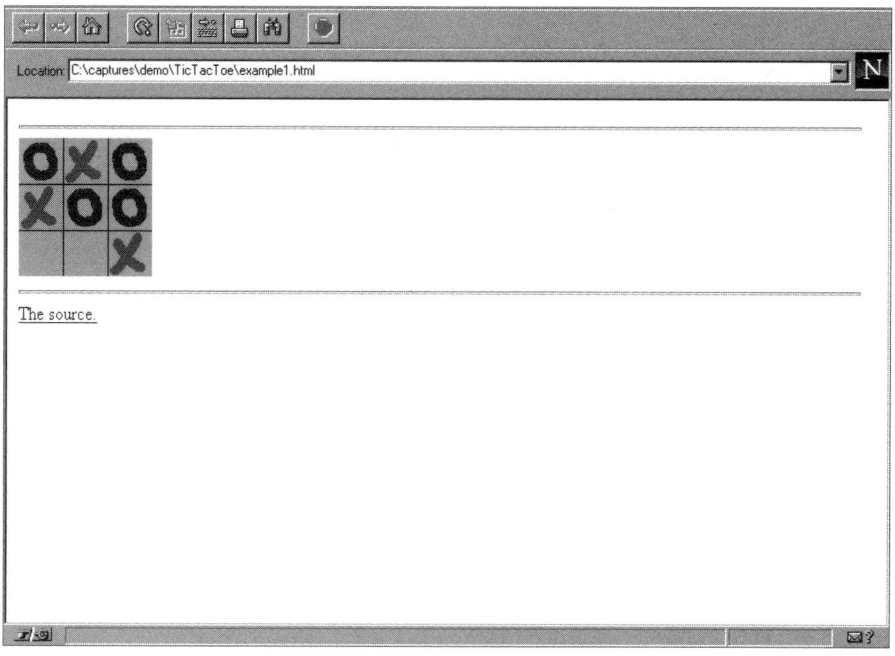

TUMBLING DUKE

Creator: Arthur van Hoff, Sun Microsystems

Tumbling Duke is a simple animation applet that can be customized with im ages of your own. It moves the images from right to left, frame by frame, which creates the illusion of a smooth animation.

Parameters To modify this applet on your Web page, use the following parameters:

Parameter Description	Tag
The widest image, in pixels, of your animation	`<param name=maxwidth value="120">`
The total number of images in the animation	`<param name=nimgs value="16">`
The distance between the last frame of the animation and the first frame	`<param name=offset value="-57">`
The directory (or URL) of the images in the animation (images are named in sequential order, beginning with T1.gif)	`<param name=img value="images/tumble">`

HTML for Tumbling Duke To embed this applet in your Web page, use the following HTML:

```
<applet code="TumbleItem.class" width=600 height=95>
<param name=maxwidth value="120">
<param name=nimgs value="16">
<param name=offset value="-57">
<param name=img value="images/tumble">
</applet>
```

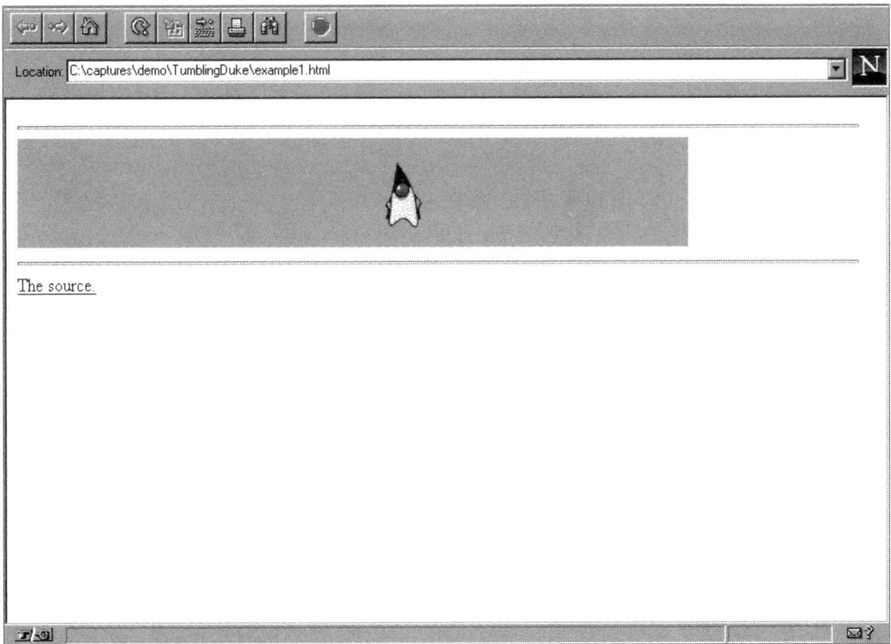
Location: C:\captures\demo\TumblingDuke\example1.html
The source.

UNDER CONSTRUCTION

Creator: Bob Weisblat, Sun Microsystems

This animation applet allows displays Duke with a jackhammer. The animation uses a strip of four images in a single gif file, which is then played. The image moves from left to right.

Parameters There are no parameters for this applet.

HTML for Under Construction To embed this applet in your Web page, use the following HTML:

```
<applet code="JackhammerDuke.class" width=300 height=100>
</applet>
```

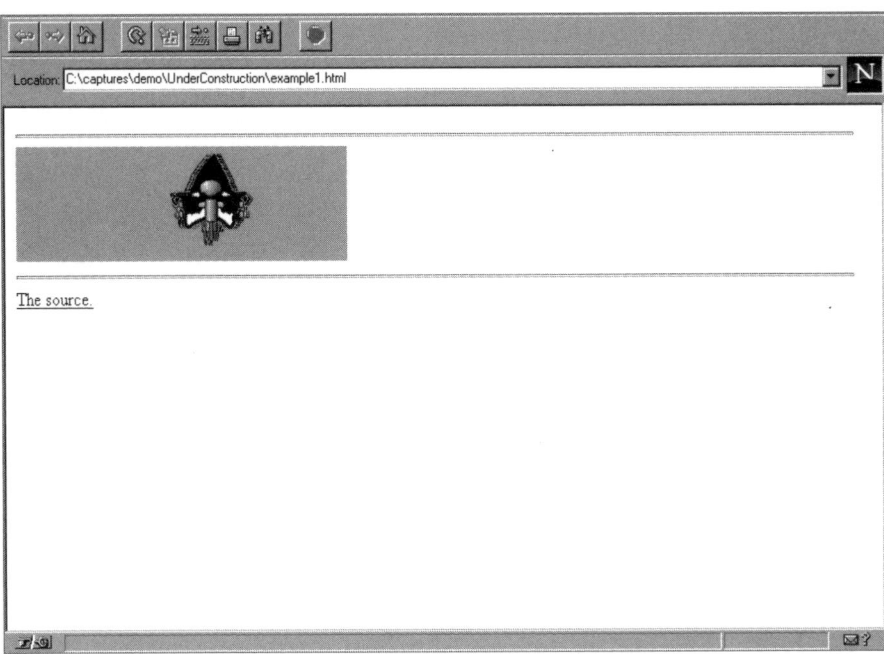

WIRE FRAME APPLET

Creator: James Gosling, Sun Microsystems

This applet allows you to display a 3-D object and renders the object immediately. The applet allows you to specify an object using the Wavefront .obj format, which asks you the define an object by coordinates on the X,Y, and Z axes as well as what edges the objects contain.

Parameters To change the pathname (or URL) for the file that contains the object's coordinates, use the following tag:

```
<param name=model value=models/cube.obj>
```

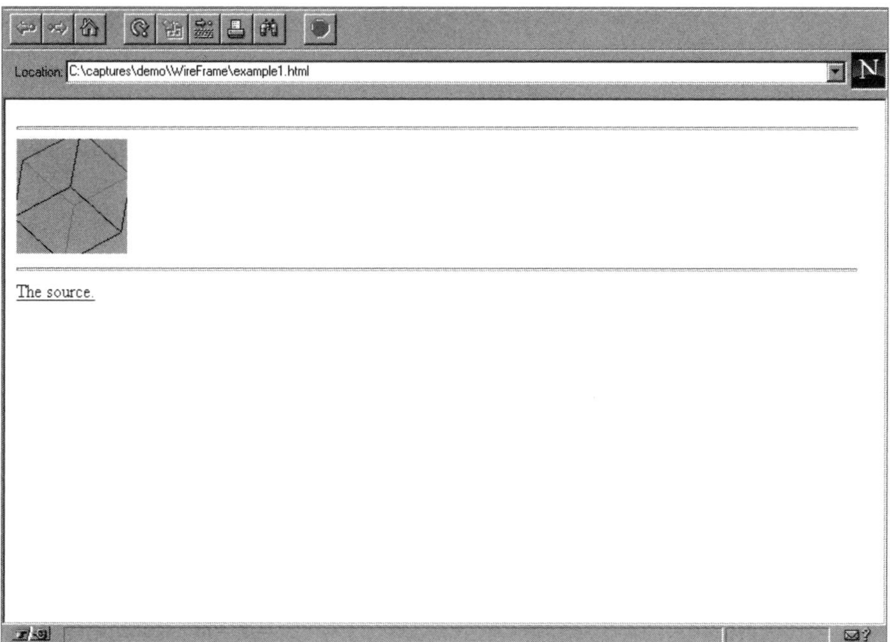

Here is a simple .obj file for the cube that is displayed in the example:

```
v 0 0 0
v 1 0 0
v 1 1 0
v 0 1 0
v 0 0 1
v 1 0 1
v 1 1 1
v 0 1 1
f 1 2 3 4
```

```
f 5 6 7 8
l 1 5
l 2 6
l 3 7
l 4 8
```

The lines that begin with a *v* represent the coordinates of the object, as would appear on the X,Y, and Z axis. The lines that begin with an *f* define the edges of the object. The lines that begin with an *l* define a set of edges.

> **NOTE** To find out more about the Wavefront format, see http://www.pov-ray.org/pov-cdrom/cd/text/formats/obj/index.html

HTML for Wire Frame Applet To embed this applet on your HTML page, use the following HTML:

```
<applet code=ThreeD.class width=100 height=100>
<param name=model value=models/cube.obj>
</applet>
```

DIMENSION X APPLETS

DISSOLVE

Creator: Dimension X
E-mail: info@dimensionx.com
This unique applet allows you to specify an image that will then dissolve into the defined area. You may begin with an initial image that can be either partially covered or wholly covered as the dissolved image appears. The dissolve effect is created by drawing small portions of the image over the Background-Image (the initial image). The size of those small dissolve areas are controlled by the settings BlockWidth and BlockHeight, which are measured in pixels.

Parameters You can use the following parameters for the Dissolve applet:

Parameter Description	Tag
The image of the picture that dissolves over the initial background	`<param name=image value="lr-logo-01.jpg">`

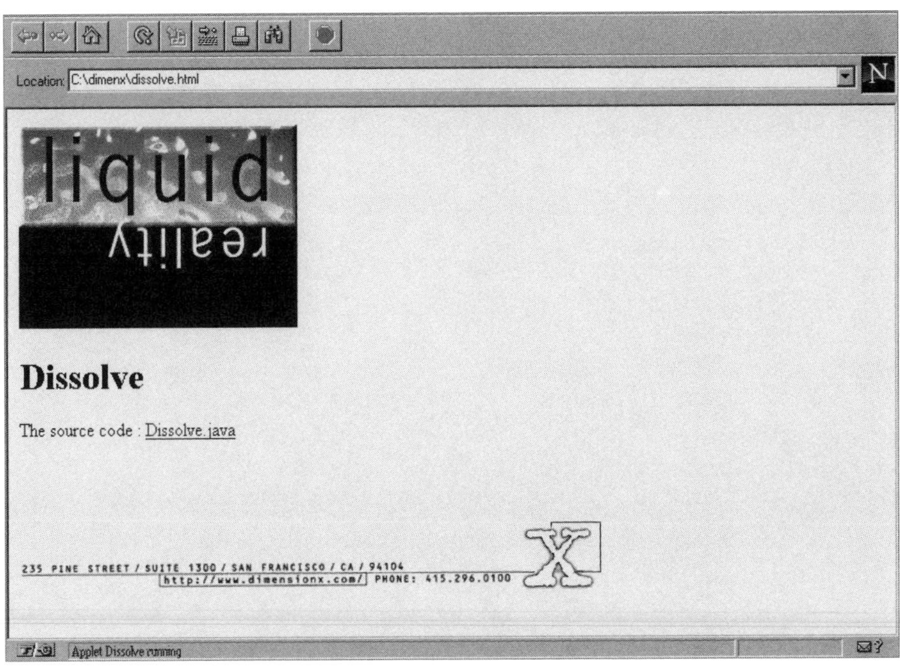

Parameter Description	Tag
The intial image to be displayed	`<param name=BackgroundImage value="lr-logo-03.jpg">`
The width in pixels of an individual dissolve chunk	`<param name=BlockWidth value=4>`
The height in pixels of an individual dissolve chunk	`<param name=BlockHeight value=2>`

HTML for Dissolve To embed this applet on your Web page:

```
<applet code="Dissolve.class" width=247 height=174>
<param name=image value="lr-logo-01.jpg">
<param name=BackgroundImage value="lr-logo-03.jpg">
<param name=BlockWidth value=4>
<param name=BlockHeight value=2>
<IMG WIDTH=247 HEIGHT=174 SRC="lr-logo-01.gif"
     ALT="[liquid reality]" ALIGN=LEFT HSPACE=8><BR>
[If you had java the above would show a digital dissolve]
</APPLET>
```

IMAGE CHUNKS

Creator: DimensionX

E-mail: info@dimensionx.com

This applet allows you to specify an image, which then is broken into small pieces to be reassembled in the applet window. The image effect is created by dividing the image into a number of "chunks" and sliding them in from the sides in a random pattern to slowly form the final image.

Parameters You can use these parameters for the Image Chunks applet:

Parameter Description	Tag
The image you want to be assemble	<param name=image value="hwood6.gif">
The number of pieces to divide the image into horizontally	<param name=xdivisions value=10>
The number of pieces to divide the image into vertically	<param name=ydivisions value=4>
Time (in seconds) for an individual piece to slide from the edge to its final location	<param name=traveltime value="1.0">

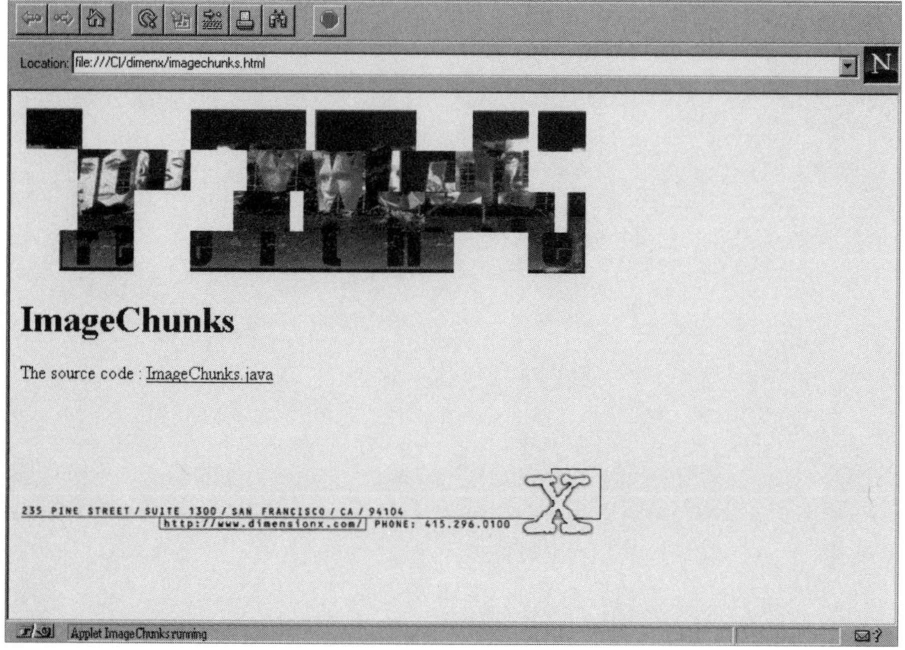

Parameter Description	Tag
Time (in seconds)to allocate to build the entire image from all of the pieces	<param name=totaltime value="3.0">

HTML for Image Chunks To embed this applet on your Web page:

```
<applet code="ImageChunks.class" width=500 height=140>
<param name=image value="hwood6.gif">
<param name=xdivisions value=10>
<param name=ydivisions value=4>
<param name=traveltime value="1.0">
<param name=totaltime value="3.0">
<IMG WIDTH=500 HEIGHT=140 SRC="hwood6.gif" ALT="[HOLLYWOOD]">
[If you had java the above image would have been built from small
squares.]
</applet>
```

Appendix A: Java Resources

If you're interested in learning more about Java or Java-related events, the resources listed here are a great place to start.

Java URLs

http://java.sun.com/
http://www.javasoft.com/
Sun Corporation's Java site. Includes extensive documentation, downloadable development kits, links to other resources, as well as press releases.

http://www.gamelan.com/
An extensive sollection of Java applets

http://www.JARS.com
http://www.surinam.net/java/java.html
A Java applet rating site. Submit your applet for rating and find a large list of rated applets, as well as links to other Java resources.

http://lightyear.ncsa.uiuc.edu/~srp/java/java.html
Contains links to some other Java sites.

http://porthos.phoenixat.com/~warreng/WWWBoard/wwwboard.html
Java Message Exchange. Post your Java-related messages and read other peoples' messages.

http://playground.sun.com/pub/prasadw/javaperf/
A Java performance benchmark site.

http://www.3cat.com/java_os2/javaos2.html
An unofficial OS/2 Java site. Contains links to other resources.

http://cafe.symantec.com/
Symantic Corporation's Java Site. Also contains links to other Java sites.

http://www.digitalfocus.com/digitalfocus/faq/
Java developer site that contains links to other resources, a job bank, as well as a how-to section.

http://www.sun.com/sunworldonline/
Sun Corporation's online magazine includes links to Java-related material.

http://www.netscape.com/comprod/products/naviga-
tor/version_2.0/java_applets/index.html
Netscape's Java applet site with demos and links to other resources.

http://www.inch.com/~nyjava/
The New York interactive Web/Java study group site. Has information about upcoming events and presentations.

http://www.rssi.com/info/java-info.html
Links to other Java resources.

http://www.borland.com/Product/java/java.html
Borland International's Java Site includes downloadable software, press releases, and links.

http://www.acm.org/~ops/java.html
W3VL/Java, a guide to information about the Java language, associated events, reference materials and resources for users and developers.

http://rendezvous.com/java/hierarchy/index.html
Contains Java class hierarchy diagrams.

http://www.pennant.com/java/
http://www.pennant.com/cgi-bin/HNews/get/java.html
A Java WWW forum primarily for discussion of programming issues for the Java language.

http://sunsite.unc.edu/javafaq/
The Java FAQ List. Advanced Java Questions asked and answered. Now fully JDK compatible.

http://www-net.com/java/faq/
Contains a link of Java FAQ archives, including French and Japaneese languages.

http://www.javasoft.com/sfaq
Sun Corporation's Java Security FAQ.

http://www.webcity.co.jp/info/andoh/java/javafaq.html
Japanese language Java FAQ.

http://www.city-net.com/~krom/java-faq.html
FAQ for comp.lang.java.

http://www.online-magazine.com//index.html
http://www.online-magazine.com/javarama.htm
Online Magazine's introduction to Java.

http://www.rpi.edu/~decemj/works/java/info.html
This is a list of online information sources about the Java programming language, the browser HotJava, and related technologies.

http://www.hamline.edu/personal/matjohns/webdev/java/
Contains links to Java-related resources.

http://weber.u.washington.edu/~jgurney/java/
The Java Boutique is a resource for users that would like to add Java applets to their own Web sites. It currently houses more than 100 working beta-API

applets, along with instructions for downloading and including them in other Web pages.

http://www.yahoo.com/Computers_and_Internet/Languages/Java/
Yahoo's listing of Java-related sites.

http://www.ivas-as.attistel.co.uk/java/vc-java.htm
This page has been put together from various contributions to the comp.lang.java newsgroup on the use of Microsoft Visual C++ as a Java IDE.

http://mars.blackstar.com/
Blackstar Publishing Company's site includes their downloadable public Java compiler.

http://www.natural.com/
The creators of a Mac-based Java development tool.

http://www.roguewave.com/
Design applets with RogueWave's visual Java development tool called JFactory.

Newsgroups

news.comp.lang.java
The Java newsgroup.

alt.www.hotjava
HotJava-related newsgroup.

Mailing Lists

http://www.javasoft.com/mail.html
Sun Corporation's mailing list.

http://www.io.org/~mentor/DigitalEspresso.html (condensed)
Digital Espresso, a weekly summary in Web form of the traffic appearing in the Java mailing lists and newsgroups.

Sites Listing Java Books and Newsletters

http://www.javaworld.com/
An online magazine about Java.

http://lightyear.ncsa.uiuc.edu/~srp/java/javabooks.html
Lists current books and newsletters on Java.

http://www.digitalfocus.com/digitalfocus/faq/books.html
Books and newsletters on Java.

http://jollyroger.com/java.html
Lists Java books

http://www.rpi.edu/~decemj/works/java/bib.html
Online Java bibliography.

http://ugweb.cs.ualberta.ca/~nelson/java/JavaTutorial.html
Contains tutorials on Java.

http://javasoft.com/tutorial/index.html
Sun Corporation's Java tutorial page.

http://users.aol.com/thingtone/workshop/index.htm
Thingtone's Java Workshop is a collection of Java programs and annotated source code examples written to help the experienced programmer become productive.

Events

http://www.rpi.edu/~decemj/works/tour.html
World-wide listing of Java events.

http://www.c2.org/~andreww/javascript/
JavaScript site.

Java Newletters

The Java Report
Sigs Publications

71 West 23rd St., 3rd Fl.
New York, NY 10010
212-242-7447
subscriptions@sigs.com
800-361-1279
http://www.sigs.com

Developer's Java Journal
Sys-Con Publications
46 Holly St.
Jersey City, NJ 07305
914-735-3922
Java@JavaDevelopersJournal.com

Appendix B: How to Use the CD-ROM

This CD contains Sun's Java Development Kit, as well as all of the applets discussed in the book. It also contains a great list of resources to get you started exploring java information around the Internet.

The CD is broken into three parts:

- The Applets
- The Java Development Kit
- The Resource List
- Liquid Motion—the animator tool from Dimension X

How to use the CD-ROM

This CD-ROM has been created in HTML and should be used on a Windows 95 or Windows NT system, or a Macintosh using a 68030 (or greater), or Power PC microprocessor running System 7.5, with a browser capable of viewing Java applets.

At the time this CD was produced the only browser capable of reading Java applets was Netscape Navigator (2.0 or greater) for the PC. No final Macintosh version was available. However, the Java Development Kit (JDK) by Sun Microsystems included on this CD-ROM, does have the ability to read Java applets from HTML documents. System requirements for the JDK are the same as above.

NOTE: This CD will *not* run on Windows 3.*x* systems.

TO RUN THE CD WITH WINDOWS 95/NT

1. Place the CD-ROM in your CD-ROM drive.
2. Launch your Java-enabled Web browser.
3. From your Web browser, select Open File from the File menu. Select your CD-ROM drive (usually D), then select the file called welcome.htm.

NOTE: We have found some incompatibilities with NT systems while testing this CD. Should you have any problems running this CD on your NT system, please contact Technical Support at (317) 581-3833.

TO RUN THE CD ON A MACINTOSH

4. Place the CD-ROM in your CD-ROM drive.
5. Launch your Java-enabled Web browser.
6. From your Web browser, select Open File from the File menu. Choose your CD-ROM drive and open welcome.htm.

NOTE: At the time this CD was created, only beta versions of Java-enabled browsers were available for the Macintosh platform. During testing we found that some functions of these browsers were unstable.

To access the applets on the CD

1. Launch a Java-enabled Web browser.
2. Choose the Open Local File option on your browser and select the file "welcome.htm" from the CD. Most likely your CD will be on drive D. You will see the three main sections of the CD.
3. Click on "Java Applets" to display a list of the applets.

To access the Java™ developers (JDK) kit for Windows 95 and NT

We have provided a copy of the most recent JDK on the CD. We urge you to check for updates, which are available to the public at http://www.javasoft.com/JDK-1.0/installation-win32-x86.html. Parts of the following pages were taken from the online instructions that appear in Appendix C as well as online at the above URL.

The Java Development kit provides you with the tools you need to write your own Java applets. The JDK comes with two documents. The Copyright file has copyright and license information about the JDK. The Readme file has information you'll need to use the JDK.

As a self-extracting archive file, the 1.0.1 release is just under 4.4MB. Uncompressed and unpacked, it will take up just under 6.5MB. Documentation is not included in this archive file; it may be found on the URL list above.

The installing and configuring process can be broken down into the following steps:

1 Move the JDK to your hard drive by copying the JDK into a temporary file.
2 Remove any previous JDK files. There should not be any copies of previous versions of the Java Developers Kit on your computer.
3 Unpack the archive file. (See below.)
4 Update environment variables. (See below.)

If you experience trouble along the way, check the Troubleshooting section at the end of this document.

If you have stored any additional Java source code files (files you have written or files you have received from someone else) in a directory under the main JDK Java directory, you should move those files to a new directory before deleting the previous version of the JDK. You can delete the entire Java directory tree using the following command:

```
deltree /Y C:\java
```

To unpack

After removing the previous version of the JDK, execute the new self-extracting archive to unpack the JDK files. You should unpack the file in the root directory of C drive to create a directory called C:\java. If you want the JDK in some other directory, unpack the archive file in that directory. Unpacking the archive will create a Java parent directory and all of the necessary subdirectories for this release.

Unpacking the archive will also create src.zip and lib/classes.zip. DO NOT UNZIP THE CLASSES.ZIP FILE. If you want to review the source for some of the JDK class libraries, you may unzip the src.zip file. However, you must use an unzip program that maintains long file names to unzip src.zip. One such unzip utility program is UnZip 5.12. One good place to find UnZip is http://www.shareware.com.

To update environment variables

After unpacking, you should add the java\bin directory to your path statement (path is equal to C:\java\bin;). The easiest way to accomplish this is to edit the AUTOEXEC.BAT file and make the change to the path statement there. If there are other statements in your path already, be sure you don't delete them.

If you have previously set the CLASSPATH environment variable, you may need to update it. You must replace the old CLASSPATH entries that pointed to the java\classes directory to point to java\lib\classes.zip. Again, the easiest way to accomplish this is to edit the AUTOEXEC.BAT file and make the change to the CLASSPATH environment variable there (class path is equal to C:\java\liv\classes.zip;). See the Troubleshooting section later in this appendix for more information.

After completing these changes to AUTOEXEC.BAT, save the file and reboot, so that the changes take effect.

If you are using Windows NT you can also make these environment variable changes in the Control Panel. Start Control Panel, select System, then edit the environment variables.

Start using the JDK

Your computer system should now be configured and ready to use the Java Development Kit. Please see Appendix C for information on using some of the tools in the JDK. The online documentation for the tools is available at http://www.javasoft.com/doc.html and http://www.javasoft.com/JDK-1.0/index.html.

You can start the AppletViewer by doing the following:

1. Change to the directory containing an applet HTML file by typing, for example, **cd c:\java\demo\TicTacToe**.
2. Run the AppletViewer on the applet file by typing **appletviewer example1.html**.

Please read the Known Bugs page for additional information. Known bugs can be found at http://www.javasoft.com/java.sun.com/JDK-1.0/knownbugs.html.

TROUBLESHOOTING

There is very good online help available at http://www.javasoft.com/java.sun.com/JDK-1.0/installation-win32-x86.html#Troubleshooting.

If you see one of the following error messages

```
net.socketException: errno = 10047
```

or

```
Unsupported version of Windows Socket API
```

check which TCP/IP drivers you have installed. The AppletViewer only supports the Microsoft TCP/IP drivers included with Windows 95. If you are using third-party drivers (for example, Trumpet Winsock), you'll need to change over to the native Microsoft TCP/IP drivers if you want to load applets over the network.

If the Applet Viewer does not load applets, then you might try the following:

1. Type **set HOMEDRIVE=c:**, type: **set HOMEPATH=**, and restart the Applet Viewer (in the same DOS box).
2. Type: **set HOME=c:** and restart the Applet Viewer (in the same DOS box).

If neither of these work, try typing the following command:

```
java -verbose sun.applet.AppletViewer
```

The above command will list the classes that are being loaded. From this output, you can determine which class the AppletViewer is trying to load and where it's trying to load it from. Check to make sure that the class exists and is not corrupted in some way.

If you are getting the fatal error message: Exception in thread NULL when running Java, javac, or AppetViewer, you should check your CLASSPATH environment variable. It may list the "classes" directory from an older JDK release. You can either unset the CLASSPATH variable, or set it to include only the latest version of the JDK class library. (Remember, it was set in the autoexec.bat file previously when you installed the JDK.) For example:

```
type: set CLASSPATH=.;C:\java\lib\classes.zip
```

This will make sure that you are using the correct classes for the JDK 1.0.1 release.

If you are unable to close the AppletViewer copyright window (Windows 95 only), try the following:

In Microsoft Windows 95, the launch bar may partially cover the AppletViewer copyright notice window Accept and Reject buttons. If this happens, you can move the Windows 95 launch bar to the side of the desktop to allow access to the copyright window Accept and Reject buttons.

TO ACCESS THE JDK FOR MACINTOSH COMPUTERS

The JDK requires a Macintosh using a 68030 (or greater) or PowerPC microprocessor running System 7.5 with 8MB of real memory and 7MB of hard disk space. The JDK is fully compatible with virtual memory and most third-party extensions.

As a compressed installer, the 1.0 BETA release is just under 2.5MB. After installation on your hard drive it will take up just over 6MB.

The steps you will follow to install the Macintosh version of the JDK on your Macintosh are

1 Move the JDK for the Macintosh from the CD to a temporary folder on your hard drive.

2 Unpack the Files.

3 Install the JDK.

Additional information about installation and downloading updates is available in Appendix C.

In order to make the release easier to use on the Macintosh, there is a slightly different folder hierarchy than for the other JDK releases. For example, a "bin" folder doesn't make much sense on the Mac, so we moved the executable applications to the top level folder. Naturally, the content remains the same.

The JDK file we have provided for you is a self-extracting archive.

INSTALLING THE RELEASE

After you have copied the self-extracting archive from the CD to your computer, you run the installer program, which will create a folder on your Macintosh called "JDK-beta1-mac" (unless you changed the name). Installation is now complete.

Please see Appendix C for documentation on some of the Java Development Tools. Online documentation can be found at http://www.javasoft.com/doc.html and http://www.javasoft.com/JDK-1.0/index.html.

You can run the AppletViewer by doing the following:

1 Open the folder Sample Applets.

2 Open the folder WireFrame.

3 Drop the file example1.html on the application AppletViewer.

Using the resource guide

We have provided an extensive resource guide for you to find and explore numerous online resources which are all available via your Web browser. To access the resource list and the online resources:

1. Establish an online connection through your Internet Service provider.
2. Open your web browser.
3. Open the local file on the CD called "welcome.html". Most likely your CD drive will be drive D.
4. Click on "Java Resources."
5. Click on any of the resources listed on the page to take you to that resource online.

Liquid Motion helps you create Java applets in no time

Liquid Motion is the simplest and most progressive tool for incorporating 2-D Java animation applets into a Web page. While Java remains a high-level programming language, Liquid Motion gives artists and designers a drag-and-drop interface for easy creation, editing, and sequencing of animation. Liquid Motion features include audio sequencing, motion path control, content management, and simple behavior functionality, and will be extensible to include plug-in libraries for sound, images, and behaviors.

Liquid Motion takes advantage of all the features of the Java language, (platform independence, object orientation, and multithreading), the most talked about Internet technology this year! Dimension X (the company that developed Liquid Motion) is proud to introduce the first product of its kind, and the first in a series of tools to bring advanced technology to the masses and liven up the Web!

To find out how to install and use Liquid Motion, see the README file inside the Liquid Motion directory on the CD. More information about Liquid Motion can be found at http://www.dimensionx.com/index.html.

Appendix C: Java Documentation and Syntax Quick Reference

This appendix includes a variety of additional information about the JDK, which is included with this CD. This information can also be found at the Sun Microsystems Web site. (Documentation copyright © 1996 Sun Microsystems, Inc.)

appletviewer — The Java Applet Viewer

The **appletviewer** command allows you to run applets outside of the context of a World-Wide Web browser.

SYNOPSIS

```
appletviewer [ options ] urls ...
```

DESCRIPTION

The **appletviewer** command connects to the document(s) or resource(s) designated by urls and displays each applet referenced by that document in its own window. Note: if the document(s) referred to by urls does not reference any applets with the *APPLET* tag, **appletviewer** does nothing.

OPTIONS

-debug

Starts the applet viewer in the Java debugger - **jdb** - thus allowing you to debug the applets in the document.

JAVAC - THE JAVA COMPILER

javac compiles Java programs.

SYNOPSIS

```
javac [ options ] filename.java ...
javac_g [ options ] filename.java ...
```

DESCRIPTION

The javac command compiles Java source code into Java bytecodes. You then use the Java interpreter—the **java** command—to interprete the Java bytecodes.

Java source code must be contained in files whose file names end with the *.java* extension. For every class defined in the source files passed to **javac**, the compiler stores the resulting bytecodes in a file named *classname.class*. The compiler places the resulting .class files in the same directory as the corresponding *.java* file (unless you specify the *-d* option).

When you define your own classes you need to specify their location. Use CLASSPATH to do this. CLASSPATH consists of a semi-colon separated list of directories that specifies the path. If the source files passed to **javac** reference a class not defined in any of the other files passed to **javac** then **javac** searches for the referenced class using the class path. For example:

```
.;C:\users\dac\classes
```

Note that the system always appends the location of the system classes onto the end of the class path unless you use the *-classpath* option to specify a path.

javac_g is a non-optimized version of **javac** suitable for use with debuggers like **jdb**.

OPTIONS

-classpath path

Specifies the path **javac** uses to look up classes. Overrides the default or the CLASSPATH environment variable if it is set. Directories are separated by semi-colons. Thus the general format for *path* is:

```
.;<your_path>
```

For example:

```
.;C:\users\dac\classes;C:\tools\java\classes
```

-d directory

Specifies the root directory of the class hierarchy. Thus doing:

```
javac -d <my_dir> MyProgram.java
```

causes the .class files for the classes in the MyProgram.java source file to be saved in the directory *my_dir*.

-g
Enables generation of debugging tables. Debugging tables contain information about line numbers and local variables—information used by Java debugging tools. By default, only line numbers are generated, unless optimization (*-O*) is turned on.

-nowarn
Turns off warnings. If used the compiler does not print out any warnings.

-O
Optimizes compiled code by inlining static, final and private methods. Note that your classes may get larger in size.

-verbose
Causes the compiler and linker to print out messages about what source files are being compiled and what class files are being loaded.

ENVIRONMENT VARIABLES

CLASSPATH
Used to provide the system a path to user-defined classes. Directories are separated by semi-colons, for example,

```
.;C:\users\dac\classes;C:\tools\java\classes
```

JDB - THE JAVA DEBUGGER

jdb helps you find and fix bugs in Java language programs.

SYNOPSIS

```
jdb [ options ]
```

DESCRIPTION

The Java Debugger, **jdb**, is a dbx-like command-line debugger for Java classes. It uses the Java Debugger API to provide inspection and debugging of a local or remote Java interpreter.

Starting a jdb Session
Like dbx, there are two ways **jdb** can be used for debugging. The most frequently used way is to have **jdb** start the Java interpreter with the class to be debugged. This is done by substituting the command **jdb** for **java** in the command line. For example, to start HotJava under **jdb**, you use the following:

```
C:\> jdb browser.hotjava
```

or

```
C:\> jdb -classpath %INSTALL_DIR%\classes -ms4m browser.hotjava
```

When started this way, **jdb** invokes a second Java interpreter with any specified parameters, loads the specified class, and stops before executing that class's first instruction.

The second way to use **jdb** is by attaching it to a Java interpreter that is already running. For security reasons, Java interpreters can only be debugged if they have been started with the *-debug* option. When started with the *-debug* option, the Java interpreter prints out a password for **jdb's** use.

To attach **jdb** to a running Java interpreter (once the session password is known), invoke it as follows:

```
C:\> jdb -host <hostname> -password <password>
```

Basic jdb Commands

The following is a list of the basic **jdb** commands. The Java debugger supports other commands which you can list using **jdb**'s help command.

NOTE: To browse local (stack) variables, the class must have been compiled with the -g option.

help, or ?

The most important **jdb** command, help displays the list of recognized commands with a brief description.

print

Browses Java objects. The print command calls the object's toString() method, so it will be formatted differently depending on its class.

Classes are specified by either their object ID or by name. If a class is already loaded, a substring can be used, such as Thread for java.lang.Thread. If a class isn't loaded, its full name must be specified, and the class will be loaded as a side effect. This is needed to set breakpoints in referenced classes before an applet runs.

print supports Java expressions, such as print MyClass.clsVar. Method invocation will not be supported in the 1.0 release, however, as the compiler needs to be enhanced first.

dump

Dumps an object's instance variables. Objects are specified by their object ID (a hexadecimal integer).

Classes are specified by either their object ID or by name. If a class is already loaded, a substring can be used, such as Thread for java.lang.Thread. If a class isn't loaded, its full name must be specified, and the class will be loaded as a side effect. This is needed to set breakpoints in referenced classes before an applet runs.

The dump command supports Java expressions such as dump 0x12345678.myCache[3].foo. Method invocation will *not* be supported in the 1.0 release, however, as the compiler needs to be enhanced first.

threads

Lists the current threads. This lists all threads in the default threadgroup, which is normally the first non-system group. (The threadgroups command lists all threadgroups.) Threads are referenced by their object ID, or if they are in the default thread group, with the form t@<index>, such as t@3.

where

Dumps the stack of either a specified thread, or the current thread (which is set with the thread command). If that thread is suspended (either because it's at a breakpoint or via the suspend command), local (stack) and instance variables can be browsed with the print and dump commands. The up and down commands select which stack frame is current.

Breakpoints

Breakpoints are set in **jdb** in classes, such as "stop at MyClass:45". The source file line number must be specified, or the name of the method (the breakpoint will then be set at the first instruction of that method). The clear command removes breakpoints using a similar syntax, while the cont command continues execution.

Single-stepping is not currently implemented, but is hoped to be available for version 1.0.

Exceptions

When an exception occurs for which there isn't a catch statement anywhere up a Java program's stack, the Java runtime normally dumps an exception trace and exits. When running under **jdb**, however, that exception is treated as a non-recoverable breakpoint, and **jdb** stops at the offending instruction. If that class was compiled with the *-g* option, instance and local variables can be printed to determine the cause of the exception.

Specific exceptions may be optionally debugged with the catch command, for example: "catch FileNotFoundException" or "catch mypackage.BigTrouble-Exception. The Java debugging facility keeps a list of these exceptions, and when one is thrown, it is treated as if a breakpoint was set on the instruction which caused the exception. The ignore command removes exception classes from this list.

NOTE: The ignore command does not cause the Java interpreter to ignore specific exceptions, only the debugger.

OPTIONS

When you use **jdb** in place of the Java interpreter on the command line **jdb** accepts the same options as the java command.

When you use jdb to attach to a running Java interpreter session, jdb accepts these options:

-host <hostname>
Sets the name of the host machine on which the interpreter session to attach to is running.

-password <password>
"Logs in" to the active interpreter session. This is the password printed by the Java interpreter prints out when invoked with the *-debug* option.

ENVIRONMENT VARIABLES

CLASSPATH
Used to provide the system a path to user-defined classes. Directories are separated by semi-colons, for example,

```
.;C:\users\dac\classes;C:\tools\java\classes
```

Using the JDK on a Macintosh

We have provided a copy of the JDK on the CD that is provided with the book. These instructions are the ones provided by Sun Microsystems on their Web site, where the JDK and updates are publically available. That page may be reached by the URL http://www.javasoft.com/JDK-1.0/Mac-Beta1/index.html.

Java(tm) Developer's Kit (JDK) 1.0, Beta 1 Release—Macintosh

Welcome to the Beta release of the Java Development Kit for Macintosh. The JDK is used specifically to allow people to write Java applets for use in a Java aware browser using the 1.0 Java Applet API. You can not build standalone applications with this release of the JDK.

The JDK incorporates the Java virtual machine, along with the AWT (Abstract Window Toolkit), and networking packages. It also incorporates an applet viewer for viewing applets outside of a web browser.

In order to make the release easier to use on the Macintosh, we have used a slightly different folder hierarchy than for the other JDK releases. For example, a "bin" folder doesn't make much sense on the Mac, so we moved the executable applications to the top level folder. Naturally, the content remains the same.

The JDK requires a Macintosh using a 68030 (or greater) or PowerPC microprocessor running System 7.5 with 8 megabytes of real memory and 7 megabytes of hard disk space. The JDK is fully compatible with virtual memory and most third party extensions.

You may also want to review the known bugs for this release.

DOWNLOADING INSTRUCTIONS, APPLE MACINTOSH

The Java(tm) Developers Kit (JDK) lets you write applets that conform to the frozen applet (1.0) API for the Java Programming Language. This is the first public release of the JDK for Macintosh.

The JDK comes with two documents. The COPYRIGHT file has copyright and license information about the JDK. The README file has information about the JDK, including:

- Why we made the JDK
- What packages comprise the final applet API
- How to get in touch with us

It also has information on using the Applet Viewer and the format of the APPLET tag.

HOW TO DOWNLOAD THE RELEASE

The 1.0 BETA Macintosh release supports System 7.5 running on Power Macintoshes and Macintoshes with at least a 68030 processor.

As a compressed installer, the 1.0 BETA release is just under 2.5 Meg. After installation on your hard drive it will take up just over 6 Meg.

The simplest way to download the release is to click on one of the following links. (Note: The ftp.javasoft.com server at Sun is frequently swamped with requests. Using a mirror site near you may be faster.)

MacBinary (*.bin) format

ftp://ftp.javasoft.com/pub/JDK-beta1-mac.sea.bin (ftp.javasoft.com server at Sun)

ftp://ftp.blackdown.org/pub/Java/pub/mac/JDK-beta1-mac.sea.bin (Mirror site at the Blackdown Organization, USA)

ftp://ftp.dimensionx.com/pub/JDK-beta1-mac.sea.bin (Mirror site at Dimension X)

Macintosh hqx format

ftp://ftp.javasoft.com/pub/JDK-beta1-mac.sea.hqx (ftp.javasoft.com server at Sun)

ftp://ftp.blackdown.org/pub/Java/pub/mac/JDK-beta1-mac.sea.hqx (Mirror site at the Blackdown Organization, USA)

ftp://ftp.dimensionx.com/pub/JDK-beta1-mac.sea.hqx (Mirror site at Dimension X)

This will automatically download a compressed file with the JDK installer to your machine.

If you prefer, you can download the release via anonymous ftp from one of the following sites:

ftp.javasoft.com (198.70.96.253) in pub/JDK-beta1-mac.sea.bin

ftp.blackdown.org in pub/Java/pub/mac/JDK-beta1-mac.sea.bin

ftp.dimensionx.com in pub/JDK-beta1-mac.sea.bin

Or you can use Fetch or Anarchie to download the files and de-compress them at the same time.

UNPACKING THE DOWNLOADED FILE

If you used FTP to download the Macintosh JDK, you must first decompress the file. Use Stuffit to decompress the MacBinary format file, use DeHQX or BinHex4 to decompress the hqx format.

INSTALLING THE RELEASE

After downloading, you can run the installer program which will create a folder on your Macintosh called "JDK-beta1-mac" (unless you changed the name). Installation is now complete.

You can run the Applet Viewer by doing the following:

1. Open the folder **Sample Applets**
2. Open the folder **WireFrame**
3. Drop the file **example1.html** on the application **Applet Viewer**

Last Updated: 14 Feb 1996

Java Developers Kit

We have provided a copy of the JDK on the CD that is provided with the book. These instructions are the ones provided by Sun Microsystems on their Web site where the JDK and updates are publically available. That page may be reached by the URL http://www.javasoft.com/JDK-1.0/installation-win32-x86.html

Version 1.0.1

DOWNLOADING INSTRUCTIONS, MICROSOFT WINDOWS NT (INTEL) AND WINDOWS 95

Java(tm) Developer's Kit (JDK) 1.0.1 Release

The Java(tm) Developers Kit (JDK) lets you write applets that conform to the new, frozen applet API for the Java Programming Language. There have been only two changes since the 1.0 release—these changes are described in Changes Since the Last Release.

The JDK comes with two documents. The COPYRIGHT file has copyright and license information about the JDK. The README file has information about the JDK, including:

- why we made the JDK,
- what packages comprise the final applet API, and
- how to get in touch with us.

HOW TO DOWNLOAD THE 1.0.1 RELEASE

The 1.0.1 Windows release supports only Microsoft Windows NT/Intel and Windows 95.

As a self-extracting archive file, the 1.0.1 release is just under 4.4 MB. Uncompressed and unpacked it will take up just under 6.5 MB. Documentation is not included in this archive file; it may be found under Java Developers Kit.

The downloading, installing, and configuring process can be broken down into the following steps:

1. Download the archive file
2. Remove Previous JDK
3. Unpack the archive file
4. Update environment variables

If you experience trouble along the way, check the Troubleshooting section at the end of this document or our general Java/HotJava FAQ.

Step 1: Download

The simplest way to download the release is to click on one of the following links. (Note: The java.sun.com server at Sun is frequently swamped with requests. Using a mirror site near you may be faster.)

ftp://ftp.javasoft.com/pub/JDK-1_0_1-win32-x86.exe (ftp.javasoft.com server at Sun)

ftp://www.blackdown.org/pub/Java/pub/JDK-1_0_1-win32-x86.exe (Mirror site at the Blackdown Organization, USA)

This will automatically download a self extracting archive file to your machine which you can execute to unpack.

If you prefer, you can download the release via anonymous ftp from one of the following sites:

ftp.javasoft.com in pub/JDK-1_0_1-win32-x86.exe
www.blackdown.org in pub/Java/pub/JDK-1_0_1-win32-x86.exe

Don't forget to put ftp in binary mode before downloading!

```
$ ftp ftp.javasoft.com
    Name (ftp.javasoft.com): anonymous
    331 Guest login ok, send your complete e-mail address as password.
    Password: user@machine
        << informational messages <<
    ftp> binary
    200 Type set to I.
    ftp> cd pub
        << more informational messages <<
    250 CWD command successful.
    ftp> get JDK-1_0_1-win32-x86.exe
    200 PORT command successful.
    150 Opening BINARY mode data connection for JDK-1_0_1-win32-x86.exe
(4391137 bytes).
    226 Transfer complete.
    local: JDK-1_0_1-win32-x86.exe remote: JDK-1_0_1-win32-x86.exe
    4391137 bytes received in 1.4e+02 seconds (30 Kbytes/s)
    ftp> quit
```

Before proceeding further, check that you have downloaded the full, uncorrupted file. As shown just above, the size of the file should be 4,391,137 bytes.

Step 2: Remove previous versions of JDK

There should not be any copies of previous versions of the Java Developers Kit on your computer.

If you have stored any additional Java source code files (files you have written or files you have received from someone else) in a directory under the main JDK Java directory, you should move those files to a new directory before deleting previous version of the JDK. You can delete the entire Java directory tree using the following command:

```
deltree /Y C:\java
```

Step 3: Unpack

After removing the previous version of the JDK, execute the new self-extracting archive to unpack the JDK files. You should unpack the file in the root directory of C drive to create C:\java. If you want the JDK in some other directory, unpack the archive file in that directory. Unpacking the archive will create a java parent directory and all of the necessary sub-directories for this release.

Unpacking the archive will also create **src.zip** and **lib/classes.zip**. DO NOT UNZIP THE CLASSES.ZIP FILE. If you want to review the source for some of the JDK class libraries, you may unzip the src.zip file. However, you must use an unzip program that maintains long file names to unzip src.zip. One such unzip utility program is UnZip 5.12 which can be found at UUNet FTP Site. Look for the file unz512xN.exe or a later version.

Step 4: Update environment variables

After unpacking, you should add the java\bin directory onto the Path. The easiest way to accomplish this is to edit the AUTOEXEC.BAT file and make the change to the path statement there.

If you have set the CLASSPATH environment variable you may need to update it. You must replace CLASSPATH entries that pointed to the java\classes directory to point to java\lib\classes.zip. Again, the easiest way to accomplish this is to edit the AUTOEXEC.BAT file and make the change to the CLASSPATH environment variable there. See the Troubleshooting section below for more information.

After completing these changes to AUTOEXEC.BAT, save the file and reboot, so that the changes take effect.

If you are using Windows NT you can also make these environment variable changes in the Control Panel. Start Control Panel, select System, then edit the environment variables.

Start Using the JDK

Your computer system should now be configured and ready to use the Java Development Kit.

You can start the Applet Viewer by doing the following:

1. cd to a directory containing an html file:

   ```
   cd java\demo\TicTacToe
   ```

2 Run the appletviewer on the html file:

```
appletviewer example1.html
```

Please read the Known Bugs page for additional information.

TROUBLESHOOTING

If you see the following error message

```
net.socketException: errno = 10047
```

OR

```
Unsupported version of Windows Socket API
```

check which TCP/IP drivers you have installed. The Applet Viewer only supports the Microsoft TCP/IP drivers included with Windows 95. If you are using third-party drivers (e.g., Trumpet Winsock), you'll need to change over to the native Microsoft TCP/IP drivers if you want to load applets over the network.

If the Applet Viewer does not load applets then you might try the following:

1 set HOMEDRIVE=c:
set HOMEPATH=\
and restart the Applet Viewer (in the same DOS box)

2 set HOME=c:\
and restart the Applet Viewer (in the same DOS box)

If none of these work, try:

```
java -verbose sun.applet.AppletViewer
```

This lists the classes that are being loaded. From this output, you can determine which class the Applet Viewer is trying to load and where it's trying to load it from. Check to make sure that the class exists and is not corrupted in some way.

- Error Message: Exception in thread NULL

If you are getting the fatal error message: Exception in thread NULL, when running java, javac, or appetviewer, you should check your CLASSPATH environment variable. It may list the the 'classes' directory from an older JDK release. You can either unset the CLASSPATH variable, or set it to include only the latest version of the JDK class library. For example:

```
> set CLASSPATH=.;C:\java\lib\classes.zip
```

This will make sure that you are using the correct classes for the JDK 1.0.1 release.

- Cannot close Applet Viewer copyright window (Windows 95 only)

In Microsoft Windows 95, the launch bar may partially cover the Applet Viewer copyright notice window Accept and Reject buttons. If this happens, you can move the Windows 95 launch bar to the side of the desktop to allow access to the copyright window Accept and Reject buttons.

Last Updated: 08 Apr 1996

JAVA API DOCUMENTATION

Java interfaces and classes are grouped into packages. The following Package Index lists all available packages, from which you can access interfaces and classes.

JAVA PACKAGES

java.lang Package that contains essential Java classes, including numerics, strings, objects, compiler, runtime, security and threads. Unlike other packages, java.lang is automatically imported into every Java program.

java.util Package containing miscellaneous utility classes, including generic data structures, settable bits class, time, date, string manipulation, random number generation, system properties, notification, and enumeration of data structures.

java.io Package that provides a set of input and output streams to read and write data to files, strings, and other sources.

java.net Package for network support, including URLs, TCP sockets, UDP sockets, IP addresses and a binary-to-text converter.

java.applet Package that enables construction of applets. It also provides information about an applet's parent document, about other applets in that document, and enables an applet to play audio.

java.awt Package that provides user interface features such as windows, dialog boxes, buttons, checkboxes, lists, menus, scrollbars and text fields. (Abstract Window Toolkit)

java.awt.image Package for managing image data, such as the setting the color model, cropping, color filtering, setting pixel values and grabbing snapshots.

java.awt.peer Package that connects AWT components to their platform-specific implementation (such as Motif widgets or Microsoft Windows controls).

OTHER PACKAGES

sun.tools.debug Package to support Java debugging and object inspection tools.

This page last modified 2/22/96. (No deeper pages in Java API documentation modified.)

Java Syntax Quick Reference

This is a reference to commonly used Java syntax that can be used by novice and experienced Java programmers. (This is not part of Sun's Java documentation.)

PACKAGE AND IMPORT STATEMENTS

```
package package_name;
```

If you have a package statement, it must be the first statement in your Java program file. You should not need to create a package for your Java programs if all you're writing are small Java applets. The package statement denotes your current program as part of a bigger collection of programs. Once you have a package statement in your program, it must be placed properly in the default CLASSPATH that the Java interpreter checks to find classes.

```
import package.class;
import package.*;
```

The purpose of the import declarations is to lessen the amount of typing required when accessing a class that is not in the current package. If you have imported the class itself, you can refer to it by its name. If you have only imported the package, you have to specify the package name and the class name. For example:

```
import java.applet.Applet;
```

Once you have the above statement in your program, you can refer to the init() method as init(). If you do not have the above statement, you will have to refer to it as Java.applet.Applet.init().

CLASS DECLARATIONS

```
public class class_name {
}
```

A public class is one that you want other people to access: Remember there should be only public class per Java file.

```
private class class_name {
}
```

A private class is one that you do not want other people to access.

```
final class class_name {
}
```

The final class is one that you do not want anyone else to subclass.

```
synchronized class class_name {
}
```

A synchronized class is one that you do not want two processes to access at the same time.

```
abstract class class_name {
}
```

An abstract class is one that you are not implementing but merely defining. You expect a subclass to actually implement this class. You cannot declare an object of this class. You must subclass this class and then create an object of the subclass type.

METHOD DECLARATIONS

```
final void method_name() {
}
```

This method cannot be overridden by a method in a subclass.

```
synchronized void method_name() {
}
```

This method can only be accessed by one routine at a time.

```
static void method_name() {
}
```

This is a class method. Only one copy is allowed for each class. An object of the class does not need to exist for this method to be called.

```
abstract void method_name();
```

There is no implementation provided for this method. The implementation will be provided by a subclass of the class in which this method resides.

VARIABLE DECLARATIONS

final int: This variable is a constant and cannot be assigned another value after this one.

volatile int: This variable changes asynchronously and it should be read every time since it may have changed without notification.

static int: This variable is a class variable. Only one copy of the variable exists. It may be accessed by using the class name or an instance name if an instance of this class exists.

ARRAY DECLARATIONS

```
int int_array[] = new int[10];
int int_array[] = {0,1,2,3,4,5,6,7,8,9};
int int_array[][] = new int[10][10];
```

The first two declarations create one-dimensional arrays. The third declaration creates a two-dimensional array.

To access elements:

```
int i = int_array[0];
sets i = 0.
```

CONTROL STRUCTURES

if - then - else: The if-then-else construct in Java is only to be used for choose between two conditions. For more than two conditions, use the swtich statement explained later in this section.

```
if (condition) {
} else {
}
```

for loop: You can have more than one variable being initialized in the initialization section and more than one variable being changed in the third part of the loop.

```
for (initialize-loop; test-for-end-of-loop; change-loop-control-
variable) {
}
```

Example:

```
for (int i = 0; i < 20; i++) {
System.out.println(i);
}
```

while loop: The while loop executes the statements inside the curly braces if the condition returns true.

```
while (condition) {
}
```

SWITCH STATEMENT

```
switch (value) {
case first-value-to-compare:
    statement(s);
    break;
case second-value-to-compare:
```

```
        statement(s);
        break;
    default:
        statement(s);
        break;
}
```

The default case matches when nothing else does. The break statement prevents the switch from evaluating any further cases after it has already matched one.

Break and Continue Statements

```
break;
```

The break statement shifts control out of nearest control statement or loop.

```
Continue;
```

The continue statement shifts control to the end of the nearest loop.

EXCEPTIONS

```
try {
    statement(s);
}

catch (Exception e) {
    statement(s);
}

finally {
    statement(s);
}
```

The *catch* statement handles exceptions that occur in the try block. The *finally* block cleans up after the try and catch block regardless of how the statements execute.

Index

J

K

L

M

N

O

P

R

S

T

U

V

W

Y

■ END-USER LICENSE AGREEMENT

READ THIS AGREEMENT CAREFULLY BEFORE BUYING THIS BOOK. BY BUYING THE BOOK AND USING THE PROGRAM LISTINGS, CD-ROM, AND PROGRAMS REFERRED TO BELOW, YOU ACCEPT THE TERMS OF THIS AGREEMENT.

The program listings included in this book and the programs included on the CD-ROM contained in the package on the opposite page ("CD-ROM") are proprietary products of Macmillan Computer Publishing USA and/or third party suppliers ("Suppliers"). The program listings and programs are hereinafter collectively referred to as the "Programs." Macmillan Computer Publishing USA and the Suppliers retain ownership of the CD-ROM and copyright to the Programs, as their respective interests may appear. The Programs and the copy of the CD-ROM provided are licensed (not sold) to you under the conditions set forth herein.

License. You may use the CD-ROM on any compatible computer, provided that the CD-ROM is used on only one computer and by one user at a time.

Restrictions. You may not commercially distribute the CD-ROM or the Programs or otherwise reproduce, publish, or distribute or otherwise use the CD-ROM or the Programs in any manner that may infringe any copyright or other proprietary right of Macmillan Computer Publishing USA, the Suppliers, or any other party or assign, sublicense, or otherwise transfer the CD-ROM or this agreement to any other party unless such party agrees to accept the terms and conditions of this agreement. This license and your right to use the CD-ROM and the Programs automatically terminates if you fail to comply with any provision of this agreement.

U.S. GOVERNMENT RESTRICTED RIGHTS. The CD-ROM and the programs are provided with **RESTRICTED RIGHTS**. Use, duplication, or disclosure by the Government is subject to restrictions as set forth in subparagraph (c)(1)(ii) of the Rights in Technical Data and Computer Software Clause at DFARS (48 CFR 252.277-7013). The Proprietor of the compilation of the Programs and the CD-ROM is Macmillan Computer Publishing USA, 5903 Christie Avenue, Emeryville, CA 94608.

Limited Warranty. Macmillan Computer Publishing USA warrants the physical CD-ROM to be free of defects in materials and workmanship under normal use for a period of 30 days from the purchase date. If Macmillan Computer Publishing USA receives written notification within the warranty period of defects in materials or workmanship in the physical CD-ROM, and such notification is determined by Macmillan Computer Publishing USA to be correct, Macmillan Computer Publishing USA will, at its option, replace the defective CD-ROM or refund a prorata portion of the purchase price of the book. **THESE ARE YOUR SOLE REMEDIES FOR ANY BREACH OF WARRANTY**.

EXCEPT AS SPECIFICALLY PROVIDED ABOVE, THE CD-ROM AND THE PROGRAMS ARE PROVIDED "AS IS" WITHOUT ANY WARRANTY OF ANY KIND. NEITHER MACMILLAN COMPUTER PUBLISHING USA NOR THE SUPPLIERS MAKE ANY WARRANTY OF ANY KIND AS TO THE ACCURACY OR COMPLETENESS OF THE CD-ROM OR THE PROGRAMS OR THE RESULTS TO BE OBTAINED FROM USING THE CD-ROM OR THE PROGRAMS AND NEITHER MACMILLAN COMPUTER PUBLISHING USA NOR THE SUPPLIERS SHALL BE RESPONSIBLE FOR ANY CLAIMS ATTRIBUTABLE TO ERRORS, OMISSIONS, OR OTHER INACCURACIES IN THE CD-ROM OR THE PROGRAMS. THE ENTIRE RISK AS TO THE RESULTS AND PERFORMANCE OF THE CD-ROM AND THE PROGRAMS IS ASSUMED BY THE USER. FURTHER, NEITHER MACMILLAN COMPUTER PUBLISHING USA NOR THE SUPPLIERS MAKE ANY REPRESENTATIONS OR WARRANTIES, EITHER EXPRESS OR IMPLIED, WITH RESPECT TO THE CD-ROM OR THE PROGRAMS, INCLUDING BUT NOT LIMITED TO, THE QUALITY, PERFORMANCE, MERCHANTABILITY, OR FITNESS FOR A PARTICULAR PURPOSE OF THE CD-ROM OR THE PROGRAMS. IN NO EVENT SHALL MACMILLAN COMPUTER PUBLISHING USA OR THE SUPPLIERS BE LIABLE FOR DIRECT, INDIRECT, SPECIAL, INCIDENTAL, OR CONSEQUENTIAL DAMAGES ARISING OUT THE USE OF OR INABILITY TO USE THE CD-ROM OR THE PROGRAMS OR FOR ANY LOSS OR DAMAGE OF ANY NATURE CAUSED TO ANY PERSON OR PROPERTY AS A RESULT OF THE USE OF THE CD-ROM OR THE PROGRAMS, EVEN IF MACMILLAN COMPUTER PUBLISHING USA OR THE SUPPLIERS HAVE BEEN SPECIFICALLY ADVISED OF THE POSSIBILITY OF SUCH DAMAGES. NEITHER MACMILLAN COMPUTER PUBLISHING USA NOR THE SUPPLIERS ARE RESPONSIBLE FOR ANY COSTS INCLUDING, BUT NOT LIMITED TO, THOSE INCURRED AS A RESULT OF LOST PROFITS OR REVENUE, LOSS OF USE OF THE CD-ROM OR THE PROGRAMS, LOSS OF DATA, THE COSTS OF RECOVERING SOFTWARE OR DATA, OR THIRD-PARTY CLAIMS. IN NO EVENT WILL MACMILLAN COMPUTER PUBLISHING USA'S OR THE SUPPLIERS' LIABILITY FOR ANY DAMAGES TO YOU OR ANY OTHER PARTY EVER EXCEED THE PRICE OF THIS BOOK. NO SALES PERSON OR OTHER REPRESENTATIVE OF ANY PARTY INVOLVED IN THE DISTRIBUTION OF THE CD-ROM IS AUTHORIZED TO MAKE ANY MODIFICATIONS OR ADDITIONS TO THIS LIMITED WARRANTY.

MACMILLAN COMPUTER PUBLISHING USA'S LICENSOR(S) MAKES NO WARRANTIES, EXPRESS OR IMPLIED, INCLUDING WITHOUT LIMITATION THE IMPLIED WARRANTIES OF MERCHANTABILITY AND FITNESS FOR A PARTICULAR PURPOSE, REGARDING THE SOFTWARE. MACMILLAN COMPUTER PUBLISHING USA'S LICENSOR(S) DOES NOT WARRANT, GUARANTEE OR MAKE ANY REPRESENTATIONS REGARDING THE USE OR THE RESULTS OF THE USE OF THE SOFTWARE IN TERMS OF ITS CORRECTNESS, ACCURACY, RELIABILITY, CURRENTNESS OR OTHERWISE. THE ENTIRE RISK AS TO THE RESULTS AND PERFORMANCE OF THE SOFTWARE IS ASSUMED BY YOU. THE EXCLUSION OF IMPLIED WARRANTIES IS NOT PERMITTED BY SOME JURISDICTIONS. THE ABOVE EXCLUSION MAY NOT APPLY TO YOU.

IN NO EVENT WILL MACMILLAN COMPUTER PUBLISHING USA'S LICENSOR(S), AND THEIR DIRECTORS, OFFICERS, EMPLOYEES OR AGENTS (COLLECTIVELY MACMILLAN COMPUTER PUBLISHING USA'S LICENSOR) BE LIABLE TO YOU FOR ANY CONSEQUENTIAL, INCIDENTAL OR INDIRECT DAMAGES (INCLUDING DAMAGES FOR LOSS OF BUSINESS PROFITS, BUSINESS INTERRUPTION, LOSS OF BUSINESS INFORMATION, AND THE LIKE) ARISING OUT OF THE USE OR INABILITY TO USE THE SOFTWARE EVEN IF MACMILLAN COMPUTER PUBLISHING USA'S LICENSOR HAS BEEN ADVISED OF THE POSSIBILITY OF SUCH DAMAGES. BECAUSE SOME JURISDICTIONS DO NOT ALLOW THE EXCLUSION OR LIMITATION OF LIABILITY FOR CONSEQUENTIAL OR INCIDENTAL DAMAGES, THE ABOVE LIMITATIONS MAY NOT APPLY TO YOU.

Some states do not allow the exclusion or limitation of implied warranties or limitation of liability for incidental or consequential damages, so the above limitation or exclusion may not apply to you.

General. Macmillan Computer Publishing USA and the Suppliers retain all rights not expressly granted. Nothing in this license constitutes a waiver of the rights of Macmillan Computer Publishing USA or the Suppliers under the U.S. Copyright Act or any other Federal or State Law, international treaty, or foreign law.